PHILADELPHIA EAGLES
THE COMPLETE ILLUSTRATED HISTORY

Les Bowen

MVP
BOOKS

First published in 2011 by MVP Books, an imprint of MBI Publishing Company and the Quayside Publishing Group, 400 First Avenue North, Suite 300, Minneapolis, MN 55401 USA

MVP Books titles are also available at discounts in bulk quantity for industrial or sales-promotional use. For details write to Special Sales Manager at Quayside Publishing Group, 400 First Avenue North, Suite 300, Minneapolis, MN 55401 USA.

To find out more about our books, visit us online at www.mvpbooks.com.

Library of Congress Cataloging-in-Publication Data

Bowen, Les.
  Philadelphia Eagles : the complete illustrated history / by Les Bowen.—1st ed.
      p. cm.
  Includes index.
  ISBN 978-0-7603-4035-6 (hardback)
  1. Philadelphia Eagles (Football team)—History. I. Title.
  GV956.P44B67 2011
  796.332'640974811—dc22
                                 2011007906

Editor: Adam Brunner
Design manager: LeAnn Kuhlmann
Series design: John Barnett
Layout: Chris Fayers

Cover and frontmatter photo credits: front cover inset by John Sandhaus/NFL/Getty Images; frontispiece by Drew Hallowell/Getty Images; title page by Hunter Martin/Getty Images; copyright page by Andy Hayt/Sports Illustrated/Getty Images; back cover, from upper left to lower right, by Ronald C. Modra/Sports Imagery/Getty Images; Nate Fine/NFL/Getty Images; Hunter Martin/Getty Images; Jeff Jaynes/AFP/Getty Images; Rob Tringali/SportsChrome/Getty Images; Doug Pensinger/Getty Images; Arthur Rickerby/Diamond Images/Getty Images; Al Bello/Getty Images; Mike Mergen/AP Images

Printed in China

CONTENTS

1 NEVER ON SUNDAY
The 1930s

ED MANSKE

Started in football and basketball at Northwestern. Selected on All-Western Conference team in 1933. Signed to play with Eagles in 1934 but attended Boston College to study law and serve as assistant coach. Marvelous receiver of passes. Sensationally brilliant on offense and defense, aggressive and fearless. 6 feet, 1 inch, 185 pounds. Age 23. Gives promise of developing into best end in league with added experience. Nick-name "Eggs." Home—Nekoosa, Wis.

ED MANSKE
PHILADELPHIA "Eagles"

CLOSE COVER BEFORE STRIKING MATCH

JIM ZYNTELL

MVP Books Collection

ON SUNDAY, NOVEMBER 12, 1933, 17,850 fans assembled for a Philadelphia Eagles home game against the George Halas–coached Chicago Bears. The game ended in a 3–3 tie, but the next morning's *Philadelphia Inquirer* bore the headline "Fans Thrill at First Big Time Sunday Sports Event Since Franklin Flew Kite."

In the twenty-first century, professional sports franchises feel their viability hinges on state-of-the-art stadiums that cost hundreds of millions of dollars. For the fledgling Eagles in their inaugural season of 1933, the key to survival was much less complicated. Since colonial times, so-called blue laws had prohibited certain types of activities from taking place on Sundays. Charging people money to watch men in leather helmets scamper and scuffle around the Baker Bowl at Broad and Lehigh in north Philadelphia was one of those activities.

When former Penn Quaker teammates Bert Bell and Lud Wray took over the bankrupt Frankford Yellow Jackets, paid the $2,500 entry fee to return them to the National Football League, and adopted a new nickname based on the Blue Eagle insignia of President Franklin D. Roosevelt's National Recovery Act, they did so anticipating that in November, voters would grant a sports exception, allowing Sunday football. (The Yellow Jackets had played in the NFL from 1924 to 1931, winning the championship in 1926.)

The citizens did just that, by a 6-to-1 margin, on November 7. The team's home opener, a 25–0 loss to the Portsmouth Spartans, had been held on Wednesday, September 18, and witnessed by no more than 5,000 fans. But, despite the team's

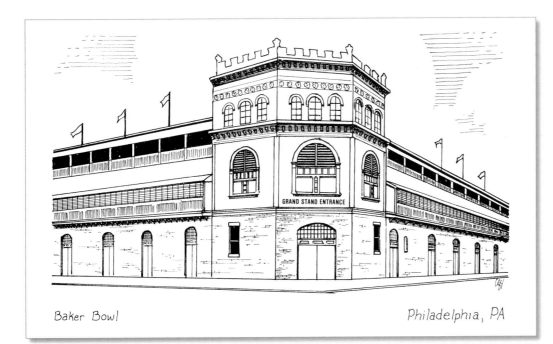

The Baker Bowl, built in 1887, was the Eagles' home for their first three seasons (1933–1935). It was better known as the home of the Phillies for more than 50 years; Babe Ruth made his first postseason appearance there in the 1915 World Series. *MVP Books Collection*

Baker Bowl

Philadelphia, PA

1-3 record as of election day, the picture brightened considerably when the voters went to the polls.

Wray offered the opinion that "Sunday sports means pro football is here to stay." Nearly 80 years later, you'd have to say he was right. For at least half that span, the Eagles have been the focal point of a city that thrives on sports. Today, fans sign up for the Eagles' season-ticket waiting list assuming it will be decades before they have their seats at glittering Lincoln Financial Field.

There was no Baker Bowl waiting list; by 1933, the ballpark that had been built for the Phillies in 1887 was decaying, five years away from being replaced. It was perhaps a tiny bit better than the converted horse-racing track in northeast Philadelphia where the Yellow Jackets had previously played. Accordingly, the Eagles would leave the stadium after the 1935 season.

The 1933 football season was long enough ago that a road game at Green Bay required a grueling three-day bus ride for the new team. Perhaps the travel accommodations contributed to their 35–9 loss, highlighted only by the first score in franchise history, Roger Kirkman's 35-yard pass to Swede Hanson. (Kirkman kicked the extra point as well, and the Eagles' defense recovered an errant snap in Green Bay's end zone for a safety.)

A 1933 game program contains an ad for Esslinger's repeal beer—the repeal in question being that of Prohibition, of course—"with full prewar strength."

Joe Pilconis was an end from Temple who wore four different jersey numbers in his three 1930s seasons with the Birds. Swede Hanson was a former Temple star and South Jersey native who played for the Eagles from 1933 to 1937. *MVP Books Collection*

BERT BELL

The 1939 Eagles, coached by Bert Bell, went 1-9-1, but they did manage to appear in the first-ever televised NFL game against the Brooklyn Dodgers at Ebbetts Field. *AP Images*

DE BENNEVILLE "BERT" BELL, the Eagles' founder and later the NFL commissioner who ushered the league into the modern era, highlighted Philadelphia's paradoxes.

Eagles fans delight in their working-class, row house image. But that isn't the only variety of "true" Philadelphian. The Ivy League campus of Penn, where Bert Bell quarterbacked and coached before founding the Eagles, is every bit as much a part of the city as the cheesesteak emporiums of South Philadelphia that flash neon and grease across the screen every time a sporting event is televised nationally.

Bell was born in Center City and spent his early years around Rittenhouse Square. His father, John Cromwell Bell, served as Pennsylvania attorney general; his brother John later held the same position. Young Bert exemplified a type common in the early part of the twentieth century, much rarer today: the gentleman sportsman. He played quarterback and defense for the Penn Quakers, appearing in the 1917 Rose Bowl, while also handling the kicking and punting chores. Bell interrupted his education to serve with classmates and friends in World War I at Base Hospital Unit No. 20 in France, where he came under artillery fire before leaving the front with dysentery.

One chronicler of that first year, an *Inquirer* reporter named Jerry Cohen, forecast success in a paragraph that careened wildly across the page: "The Quaker City is ripe for such pro football," Cohen wrote, "and once let the nation recover its prosperity, there is gold in them thar teams, stranger, for the bloke who can buck through tough times and stick by the ship."

The Eagles' origins were humble in just about every conceivable way. Bell, Wray, and their partners had to agree to pay off a percentage of some debts to other teams left when the Yellow Jackets folded. They welcomed all of 40 players to their first training camp, at Atlantic City's Bader Field, and they weren't exactly promising untold riches to the attendees.

Bell coached at Penn and Temple and managed the Ritz-Carlton and St. James hotels in Philadelphia, owned by his family, before birthing the Eagles. But mostly, he partied and gambled.

As Robert S. Lyons describes in his authoritative biography, *On Any Given Sunday*, Bell's father grew tired of bailing out his over-30, playboy son. He offered Bert $100,000 to agree to an arranged marriage with a young woman from a prominent family on Philadelphia's Main Line. Bert agreed, but traveled to the racetrack in Saratoga the next day and lost every penny of the $100,000. He returned home, admitted what he had done, and declared he would not be marrying "that broad." Bert Bell never saw another dime from his father.

At that point, Bell wouldn't have seemed a likely candidate to found a pro football franchise much less run a league. But he fell in love with and married Broadway and Ziegfield Follies star Frances Upton, and Bell settled down a bit as a married man. Upton ultimately made him give up drinking, a move that presumably curtailed some of the other activities that went along with it. She also pushed him toward what would become his life's work.

Upton had traveled a lot as a famous performer and had gotten to know some pro athletes. "She had seen the Decatur Staleys play out in Chicago, and the Canton Bulldogs in Ohio, and the New York Giants at the Polo Grounds," their son, Upton Bell, said in *Philadelphia* magazine. "She'd go with Bert to those Penn games and she'd say, 'This can't compare to the pros. They've got people like Jim Thorpe and Red Grange and Bronko Nagurski. You think this is good? You ought to see THEM play! Please get with it, Bert: the pros THROW the football. The running game? Forget about it!'" (Current Eagles fans may wonder if Frances Upton's ghost ever paid a visit to pass-happy coach Andy Reid.)

With $2,500 provided by his wife, Bell partnered with former Penn teammate Lud Wray to buy the defunct Frankford Yellow Jackets, bringing them into the NFL as the Eagles in 1933. A few years later, Bell came up with the idea of the player draft, which the league adopted. But the franchise still hadn't seen a winning season when Bell, 10-44-2 as the Eagles' coach, executed a series of maneuvers with Steelers owner Art Rooney that resulted in Bell's selling the Eagles and ending up part owner of the Steelers.

In 1946, Bell succeeded Elmer Layden as NFL commissioner, on the condition that the league offices be moved from Chicago to Philadelphia. He took over a league in crisis. A handful of teams were financially weak, and the All-America Football Conference began to emerge as a competitor, with deeper pockets in some instances. The new league folded after four seasons of a player bidding war, and teams from San Francisco, Baltimore, and Cleveland were absorbed by the NFL.

Though Bell had been a legendary gambler—he supposedly lost his flashy roadster during his college days when he unwisely bet it on his ability to lead Penn past Dartmouth—he was very vocal and active in his opposition to any NFL taint from gambling. In 1946, he banned the Giants' Frank Filchock and Merle Hapes indefinitely because they failed to report a bribe attempt. Bell pushed for national and state legislation to outlaw offering bribes to athletes, wherever the NFL did business.

Bell negotiated the early TV contracts and sold the owners on the idea of revenue-sharing—the key to making good on his famous "on any given Sunday" catchphrase. He authored the idea of sudden death for the championship game, setting the table for the historic Colts-Giants title game of 1958 that catapulted the NFL toward the prominence it enjoys today.

Bell died on October 12, 1959, at Penn's Franklin Field, where he had starred in college. The commissioner was watching the Eagles host the Steelers, the two teams he had served in ownership roles. He collapsed with just under two minutes left to play, as Tommy McDonald scored a touchdown for the Eagles.

After an interim period, Bell was succeeded by Pete Rozelle, the Rams general manager whom Bell had talked out of quitting during a time of ownership confusion and upheaval in Los Angeles.

"I think he knew what he was creating," Bell's daughter Jane told the *Philadelphia Inquirer*. "I think he sensed just how big pro football would become."

GETTING STARTED

The Eagles' archives contain a letter written by Wray, their first coach, to a prospective player, Stan Sokolis of Wildwood, New Jersey. The letter asked players to bring their own equipment for practice, explaining that "the club only supplies the equipment used in league games."

"Be sure to be in the best physical condition, for we are going to make a real thing of the club this year here in Philadelphia," Wray writes. "We are paying linemen only $90 per game but will raise the ante in your case to $110. This shows that we are very anxious to have you with us."

That first edition of the Eagles finished 3-5-1, wearing blue-and-yellow uniforms that mimicked the official

THE ALABAMA PITTS SAGA

BY 1935, the novelty of playing on Sunday had worn off and Bell and Wray were looking for a new gate attraction. They found one, at least briefly, in Edwin "Alabama" Pitts, a halfback and defensive back. Pitts emerged as a storied athlete, in both baseball and football, while serving a prison sentence in Sing Sing for robbing a grocery store. His attempts to be allowed to sign a pro baseball contract after his release became a nationwide issue, ultimately settled by commissioner Kenesaw Mountain Landis. Landis ruled for Pitts, who signed with Albany, New York, of the International League, but he proved to be a terrible outfielder who was often injured, so he was soon available to give pro football a try.

The Eagles gave Pitts a reported $1,500 to spend a season in the NFL—and to garner a little publicity for a team that hadn't had much success on the field. In that regard, Pitts paid off instantly, explaining to reporters when he arrived in Philadelphia that his baseball failure could be traced to having been forced to play at night. "You see, where I was, we didn't get out much at night," Pitts said. "If anybody did, it wasn't to play ball."

As for his football career, it came and went without much fanfare at all. Pitts played in just three games for the Eagles in 1935, catching just two passes for 21 yards. Pitts ultimately would return to baseball, again without notable success. He had settled down and was playing semipro baseball in Valdese, North Carolina, when he was stabbed to death in a dance hall in June 1941.

Alabama Pitts was a talented, raw athlete whose claim to fame was having served a prison sentence. He attempted to play pro baseball after his release, and he was an Eagle for three games in 1935, a much shorter stretch than he'd served in Sing Sing for robbing a grocery store. *MVP Books Collection*

city flag (which reflected that the city was first settled by Swedes).

The 1934 season ended with the team at 4-7; the Birds lost five of their first six before winning three of the last five. Every victory was a shutout, but then, so were three of the losses. The Eagles scored all of 27 points in their seven defeats. Fans were considerably less than enthralled.

The opener that year was at Green Bay. End Joe Pilconis later recalled that they boarded a bus on Wednesday, beginning a journey that allowed for only two stops a day. The players slept on the bus, he said.

"We blew a tire the first day. We put on the spare and kept going. Then we blew out the spare," Pilconis said. "We couldn't patch it, so we filled it with rocks, weeds, and anything else we could find. It wasn't great, but at least it kept the tire on the rim. That's how we rode the last 200 miles to Green Bay." Swede Hanson broke free for an 82-yard touchdown run in the third quarter, but that was all the Eagles' offense could muster as they fell to the Packers, 19–6.

The 1934 season was not without notable achievements, however. Their 64–0 drubbing of the Cincinnati

Jay Berwanger, then a halfback for the University of Chicago, struck this pose in 1934. A year later he became the first winner of the Downtown Athletic Club Award, which was renamed the Heisman Trophy in 1936. The trophy bears his resemblance to this day, but that's the extent of the impact Berwanger would have on the football world. The Eagles drafted Berwanger with the top pick of the inaugural NFL draft, in 1936, but they couldn't sign him. He never played a snap in the NFL. *AP Images*

180 Aerial View of Municipal Stadium and Navy Yard, Philadelphia, Pa.

Municipal Stadium, site of the 1926 Jack Dempsey–Gene Tunney fight, was the Eagles' home from 1936 to 1939 and for four seasons in the 1940s and 1950s. It seated more than 100,000 people, but the NFL didn't command that kind of following at the time.
Lake County Museum/ Getty Images

Reds at the Baker Bowl still stands as the biggest regular-season blowout in NFL history. The Eagles entered the game 1-5, the Reds 0-7. The Reds' players found out on game day that their franchise was being disbanded, which may have contributed to the lopsided outcome. Hanson, a former Temple star and South Jersey native, scored three touchdowns while rushing for 170 yards.

MORE STRUGGLES

Despite the attention attracted by the presence of Alabama Pitts, a former baseball player coming off a stint in Sing Sing for robbery, 1935 wasn't a great year for the Eagles: they went 2-9 in their last season at the Baker Bowl. However, 1936 would be a season of change, in some ways. The Eagles found a new home at Municipal Stadium, Bell decided he'd try his hand at coaching, and the NFL adopted his idea of an entry draft for college players. Bell, who also became the sole owner with a $4,000 bid, drafted the winner of the first Heisman Trophy, Jay Berwanger of Northwestern, but failed to sign him. On the field, it was more of the same for Bell's Eagles, as the team went 1-11, followed by a 2-8-1 mark in 1937.

The NFL of the 1930s was a truly distant ancestor to the game we know and love today. A 1934 roster for a game against the Boston Redskins lists guard Joe Kresky as the beefiest Eagle, at 6 feet, 220 pounds. Kresky would have to try to make it as a running back or safety if he showed up at that size in 2011.

But not everything was different. Think showboating is an ESPN-age phenomenon? A cartoon from the game program for an August 25, 1937, Eagles game against the Eastern College All-Stars shows a player running away from a defender, balancing the ball on the tip of one finger. "It gratifies his sense of the dramatic," a bystander explains.

Locker room humor might not have changed all that much, either. The same program lists Eagles end Forrest McPherson as "Forrest 'Aimee' McPherson," a reference to a popular female evangelist of the time.

The program also delineates differences between college and pro rules, one of which being that in the NFL, "substitutes may talk with teammates immediately upon entering the game."

The next month, rosters for a September 19 exhibition clash with the Wilmington Clippers show Wilmington

A swing and a miss for Eagles defensive back Woody Dow, trying to bring down Giants runner Tuffy Leemans, who scored on the play in a 1938 game at the Polo Grounds. *New York Daily News/Getty Images*

Hall of Fame end Bill Hewitt snags a pass in the first televised NFL game, October 22, 1939, at Ebbetts Field against the Brooklyn Dodgers. Hewitt and the Eagles lost, 23–14. *Pro Football Hall of Fame/AP Images*

TCU's Davey O'Brien was the Eagles' first-round draft pick, fourth overall, in 1939. He is shown here with Eagles owner Bert Bell. O'Brien, a quarterback, led the NFL in passing yards as a rookie but retired after two seasons to join the FBI. *AP Images*

A LITTLE HOPE, QUICKLY DASHED

In 1939, the Eagles drafted quarterback Davey O'Brien, Texas Christian's 5-foot-7, 170-pound Heisman Trophy winner, touted in an introductory newspaper story as "one of the greatest forward passers ever developed. Also a hard runner, blocker, and better than average punter." O'Brien, reportedly given $12,000 a year and a percentage of the gate receipts, set a league passing mark with 1,324 yards, but he couldn't keep the team from going 1-9-1.

On October 22, the Eagles' game at Brooklyn was the first televised NFL game, although it reached only about 1,000 sets, all of them in Brooklyn.

A game program from that season underscores yet another huge difference between the early NFL and today. With players' photos are their "offseason occupations," which included "school teacher," "coal salesman," "manufacturer of gloves in partnership with a brother," "minor league baseball catcher," "rancher," and "laborer in milling company," among others. Three players opted for the listing "oil field worker."

Fullback Chuck Newton, the program notes, "made the trip from Alaska, where he was employed in a fish cannery, to join the Eagles."

The Eagles failed to build a competitive team around O'Brien, who recorded their first 300-yard passing game, and after the 1940 season he quit the game to become an FBI agent. Eagles fans wouldn't witness a winning season until their franchise combined with the Pittsburgh Steelers, in 1943, to form the "Steagles," who went 5-4-1 under head coach Greasy Neale.

fielding a 5-foot-11, 192-pound guard named Vince Lombardi, who could not prevent a 14–6 Eagles victory. But even the acquisition of future Hall of Fame end Bill Hewitt couldn't keep the 1937 Birds from going 2-8-1.

In 1938, the Eagles improved to 5-6, a franchise record for victories at the time. They were no match for Halas's Bears, though; a contemporary newspaper account of the 28–6 October 2 home loss concludes that "from the opening charge, when they whirled the kickoff almost back to midfield, there was no doubt which 11 roosts on top of the pay-for-play circuit."

The final game of that season was a 21–7 victory at Detroit that knocked the Lions out of what would have been a first-place tie with the Packers. "So confident was the Detroit management that tickets already had been printed for the prospective playoff with Green Bay next Sunday," a Philadelphia newspaper account said.

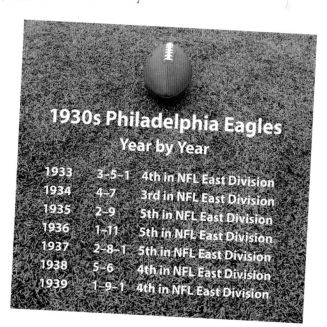

1930s Philadelphia Eagles
Year by Year

Year	Record	Standing
1933	3-5-1	4th in NFL East Division
1934	4-7	3rd in NFL East Division
1935	2-9	5th in NFL East Division
1936	1-11	5th in NFL East Division
1937	2-8-1	5th in NFL East Division
1938	5-6	4th in NFL East Division
1939	1-9-1	4th in NFL East Division

2 POSTWAR POWER
The 1940s

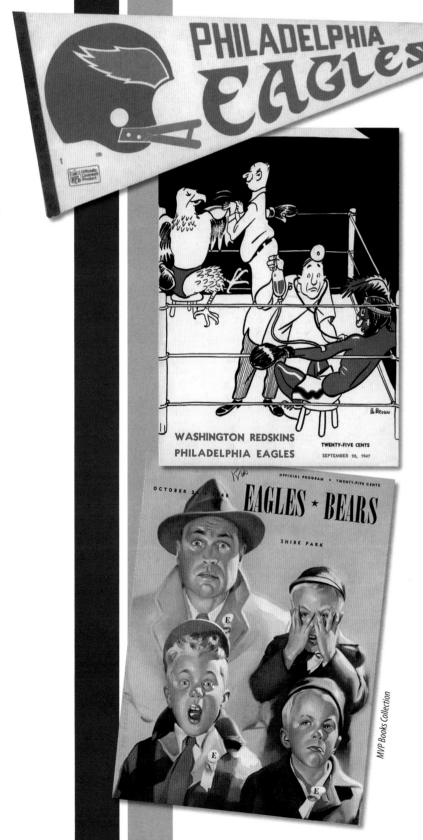

WASHINGTON REDSKINS
PHILADELPHIA EAGLES
TWENTY-FIVE CENTS
SEPTEMBER 28, 1947

OCTOBER 24, 48   OFFICIAL PROGRAM • TWENTY-FIVE CENTS
EAGLES ★ BEARS
SHIBE PARK

MVP Books Collection

THE 1940S ENDED UP being the decade that really made the Eagles—the years that built the foundation of the place they now occupy at the heart of Philadelphia sports—but it didn't start out that way.

The Birds, having settled into their new home at Shibe Park, lost their first nine games of the decade, managed to eke out a 7–0 win over the Steelers, then closed their 1940 season with a loss to the Redskins for a 1-10 record under Bert Bell. They actually managed more first downs than their opponents, 122–115, but their yards didn't translate into points and they were outscored 211–111. They generated just 15 touchdowns, with Don Looney and Dick Riffle scoring 5 apiece.

After that debacle, capped by the retirement of budding star Davey O'Brien, Bell stepped aside for Earl "Greasy" Neale, a change that would take a while to resonate but one that would end up making the Eagles champions. Bell also sold the team and became part owner of the Steelers, another change that would have hard-to-foresee consequences.

ENTER THE STEAGLES

Neale's first two years produced no discernible benefits. You have to wonder if a twenty-first-century coach could go 2-8-1 and then 2-9, and still be around for a third try. But the 1940s were different from today in many ways, one of them being something called World War II. Going into Neale's third season, with so many able-bodied men wearing a different sort of green uniform, the Eagles could muster only 16 players under contract. Still, they were better off than the Pittsburgh Steelers, who had all of six. A few years earlier, the talks that ended with Bell selling the Eagles and buying into the Steelers had also included a discussion of merging the teams and calling the "new" team the Pennsylvania Keystoners. These talks

Exterior and interior views of Shibe Park, which was also known as "Connie Mack Stadium" for a time.

With rosters depleted due to World War II, the Philadelphia Eagles and Pittsburgh Steelers joined forces in 1943. Unofficially known as the "Steagles," the combined team posted a better record (5-4-1) than the Eagles ever had by themselves. *Temple University Libraries, Urban Archives, Philadelphia, PA*

The Eagles took on the Redskins at Griffith Stadium in the nation's capital on December 7, 1941. The 20–14 final score, an Eagles loss, would quickly be forgotten on this day that would live in infamy. *The Washington Post/Getty Images*

led to a combination team for the 1943 season, which fans, at first just in Pittsburgh and then elsewhere, called the "Steagles."

This was never the team's official name. The league, which narrowly voted to approve the merger and tried to ensure the combo team wouldn't be in the playoffs by stipulating the deal would end after the regular season, officially recognized the franchise as the Philadelphia Eagles. The uniforms were Eagles green and white.

Eagles publicity director Al Ennis—later the team's general manager—wrote an explanatory message "to the loyal Pittsburgh fans from the Philadelphia Eagles" in the game program for the first contest: "It is with a definite feeling of pride that we come to Pittsburgh for our first game as part of the Eagles-Steelers, or as you will probably prefer to call the team, the Steelers-Eagles."

Close, Al, but not quite.

Training camp didn't get off to a grand start, with co–head coaches Neale and Walt Kiesling clashing. They ultimately decided Neale would run the offense and Kiesling the defense; Neale started teaching a new concept called the T formation, which seemed to fit his personnel very well. The Steagles went 5-4-1, the first winning season in Eagles history and only the second in the history of the Steelers.

Lineman Al Wistert, a rookie in 1943, later remembered being horribly disappointed, going from a first-class college program at Michigan to such a bedraggled pro environment. Wistert said the team practiced at St. Joseph's University, dressing under the stands in lighting so weak "we couldn't even see to lace our shoes." He said the practice field was a weed-strewn lot behind a gas station. And despite what many accounts say about Kiesling coaching the defense and Neale the offense, the way Wistert—who started both ways—remembers it is that Neale pretty much took over. "Greasy was the type of personality who dominated a situation, and that was just how it was going to be," Wistert said.

Wilbur Moore of the Redskins gets behind the Steagles secondary for a pretty over-the-shoulder catch, but the conglomerate of players from Pittsburgh and Philadelphia pulled out a 27–14 victory, one of five in the unique 1943 season. *Nate Fine/NFL/Getty Images*

GREASY NEALE

THERE'S A STRONG ARGUMENT to be made that Greasy Neale's era as the Eagles' coach was the franchise's finest hour to date.

There would be no argument, really, except that current coach Andy Reid has been able to easily surpass Neale's 66-44-5 record, with the advantages of a 16-game season (vs. the 12 Neale's teams played) and supportive, stable ownership. Neale was fired a year after leading the Eagles to back-to-back NFL championships, which might go down as the all-time most puzzling coaching move in the history of a franchise that has more than a few contenders. So he only stayed 10 years in a job that should have been his for life—and certainly would be, if Neale were to accomplish such a feat coaching the Eagles of today.

Reid has been a much more prolific winner of games than Neale, but he can't claim even one NFL championship, let alone two in succession. Neale's 1948–1949 teams were the most dominant in Eagles' history, week in and week out.

Neale was hamstrung in his early Eagles years by the absolutely terrible roster bequeathed to him by Bert Bell—the hopelessness was enough to drive would-be-QB-savior Davey O'Brien out of football and into an FBI career after just two Eagles seasons—and by World War II, which took away quarterback Tommy Thompson, among others, while forcing Neale to co-coach the "Steagles" in 1943. Once the war started winding down and Neale was able to get some of his own players into key spots, he was amazingly effective. From 1944 through 1950 (the year he was fired for allowing key players to get injured and finishing 6-6), Neale was 54-22-3. His 1949 team outscored opponents by an average margin of 19 points, then won the championship game 14–0 over the host Los Angeles Rams.

Neale, one of pro football's greatest innovators, had a fascinating background. He coached his Parkersburg, West Virginia, high school team while playing on it, which is fairly rare. He also was a baseball standout.

"My first love was baseball, and my consuming ambition was to become a big leaguer," Neale wrote in a 1951 *Collier's* magazine piece. "The football I played as a youngster was merely a fill-in to keep busy until it was warm enough for baseball."

In fact, Neale became a major league outfielder, mostly for the Cincinnati Redlegs, and he led his team in hitting in the 1919 World Series, a victory stained by the infamous "Black Sox" scandal.

A 1947 Eagles game program story says that when reminded of the scandal, Neale "still stoutly maintains that of those games, all but the first one were honestly played, and backs up his argument with minute descriptions of plays that occurred over 20 years ago."

NFL/AP Images

Neale also played pro football for Jim Thorpe's Canton Bulldogs, under the assumed name of "Foster." Neale was coaching at West Virginia Wesleyan at the time, and college administrators apparently found the pro game disreputable.

Neale got his nickname early in childhood, or so he always said. He told a story about a playmate, whom he accused of being dirty. The playmate, not exactly the Dorothy Parker of the West Virginia playgrounds, supposedly answered, "Oh yeah? Well, you're greasy."

Among his inventions was the "naked reverse," a bootleg with a fake handoff he unveiled while coaching Washington and Jefferson, to the consternation of opposing Lafayette and its head coach, Jock Sutherland. Neale also had the first defensive line that shifted, but much like Reid with today's Eagles, his heart was with the offense. Neale supposedly once said he would rather lose a game 100–99 than win it 3–0, the sort of sentiment that would "SportsCenter" a coach right out of the game today.

Neale was coaching as an assistant at Yale when Eagles owner Lex Thompson hired him to take over the Eagles for the 1941 season. The Chicago Bears had just won the NFL title game 73–0 over

Coach Neale had a talented and attentive roster in the late 1940s, led by halfback Steve Van Buren, tackle Al Wistert, and quarterback Tommy Thompson. This quartet led the Eagles to consecutive NFL titles in 1948 and 1949. *AP Images*

the Washington Redskins, and one of the first things Neale did was borrow the Bears' new T formation idea.

"I didn't borrow the Bears' T formation, I stole it," Neale said. "Anything that could score 73 points, I wanted."

Neale started preparing much more elaborately for the college draft than most teams were used to doing. Given that he came up with future Hall of Famers Steve Van Buren, Pete Pihos, and Chuck Bednarik during his tenure, the extra prep must have paid off.

Tommy Thompson, his quarterback for those back-to-back titles, said many years later that "Greasy was the smartest football man I ever met." Bednarik, who later won the 1960 NFL championship under Buck Shaw, presented Neale at his 1969 Hall of Fame induction and declared that Neale "was the best coach I ever played for."

Two-way lineman Al Wistert was at first put off by Neale's profanity and negativity when Wistert joined the team as a rookie in 1943. "He cursed a lot. I wasn't used to that," he said. "I grew up in a household where cursing was not allowed."

Wistert later told author Gordon Forbes, in *Tales from the Eagles' Sidelines*, that he once limped off the field. Neale asked him what was wrong. Wistert replied that he thought he'd broken his leg. "Get back in there 'til you're sure," Neale replied.

But in several interviews, Wistert noted that Neale's approach to the team evolved as the team evolved.

"Once we had the great team, he backed off," Wistert recalled. "He didn't rant and rave like he did in the early years. He'd stop practices after an hour and say, 'Let's go play golf.' He knew when we were ready."

Wistert's thinking on Neale also evolved, he said. "Once I got beyond my own prejudices, I realized he was a fine man. I admired

him very much," Wistert said. "He knew the game exceedingly well, both offense and defense. He had thought it through."

On long train rides, Wistert said, Neale was so close to his players that he would organize card games—often pinochle, his favorite—and would spend hours at a time in the middle of the action, swapping jokes and wagers.

"He liked to play cards," Wistert said. "He was always with the players. He and his wife, Genevieve, had no children; they adopted us as their children."

Neale's demise was hastened when owner Lex Thompson, losing money despite winning it all in 1948, was forced to sell the team. Thompson had known Neale since Thompson was a student at Yale and Neale was a coach; in their relationship, it was clear who really called the shots.

The new team president, James Clark, was a trucking executive used to speaking his mind. Neale gave him little to complain about in 1949, but when Van Buren started to break down and the team sagged in 1950, Clark angrily confronted Neale in the locker room, affronted by a 7–3 loss to the Giants at the Polo Grounds.

Clark later apologized, and the matter seemed forgotten, until February, when Neale, vacationing at Lake Worth, Florida, received a telegram from Clark relieving him of his duties.

"We have had our ins and outs on running the team, but I always knew more about coaching than he did," Neale told the Associated Press, when he announced his firing. He said he had been in Philadelphia the previous week and had heard nothing from Clark, after attending a league meeting with him earlier in Chicago.

Neale never coached again, retired to Florida, and passed away in 1973, just shy of his eighty-second birthday.

Wistert, a star at Michigan, recalled that he literally had no idea what he was getting into when he signed with Philadelphia.

"Everything was first class at Michigan, so [the facilities] were a shock, but the main thing that bothered me was that I had no idea they were combining the Eagles and the Steelers," Wistert said. Birds general manager Harry Thayer had failed to mention that detail, Wistert said. How did Wistert find out? "Eventually I began to realize that some of these guys were Steelers players."

The emphasis clearly was on survival, not glamour.

Running back Jack Hinkle, who led the Steagles in rushing with 571 yards and also intercepted four passes, had signed with the Eagles for the final game of the 1941 season. That was a 20–14 loss at Washington, on a day more widely remembered for the repeated PA announcements asking all servicemen in the crowd of 27,102 to report to their posts. It was Sunday, December 7, 1941.

Hinkle served briefly in the army in 1942 before returning in 1943, discharged because he suffered from ulcers. Most of his teammates (and opponents) had physical issues that kept them from serving; leading receiver Tony Bova (17 catches, 419 yards, five TDs), for example, was blind in one eye and partially blind in the other.

The war not only siphoned off most of the available talent, but it also stigmatized those who remained and played—big, fit guys, who seemed able-bodied to fans, even if they had been rejected by the service.

Management was acutely aware of the marketing problem. Ennis's open letter on behalf of Steelers owners Bell and Art Rooney, and Eagles general manager Harry Thayer and owner Alexis "Lex" Thompson—who was serving in the army and was always referred to in print as "Lieutenant Alexis Thompson" —declared that "the object of the merger was to provide the loyal fans of both cities with a team worthy of their support," a job that was growing increasingly difficult in view of the manpower shortage. But more important in the eyes of those responsible for the team's policies was the job of aiding the general war effort. Ennis wrote, "And so our 'War Council,' Messrs. Bell, Rooney, Thompson and Thayer, decided that every man on the club roster, unless he were prevented from doing so by illness or physical ailment, must work at least 40 hours a week in some essential war industry."

Ennis's letter goes on to detail the war industry jobs undertaken by several players, describing them in heroic terms: "Larry Cabrelli, Eagle end for the past two seasons, works six days a week in the Kellett Aircraft Corporation in Philadelphia. Larry has a draft classification of 4F because of a calcium deposit on his knee."

Despite the winning mark the combined team was able to achieve, the Eagles were eager to get back to a normal setup, and did so the next season. The Steelers found another wartime partner, the Chicago Cardinals.

AT LAST, SOME SUCCESS

Suddenly, in 1944, the Eagles were a good team, all on their own. This had a lot to do with drafting LSU's Steve Van Buren, who averaged a snappy 5.6 yards per carry as a rookie and was runner-up for Rookie of the Year. The team went 7-1-2, but missed the playoffs by a half-game.

The next season, Van Buren led the NFL in rushing, with 832 yards on 143 carries, and scored 15 touchdowns, and the Eagles went 7–3. Quarterback Roy Zimmerman improved dramatically; Zimmerman, originally a wartime replacement for Tommy Thompson, the star Neale had converted to quarterback from tailback, completed 52.8 percent of his passes, after managing just 37.1 percent in 1944 and 34.7 percent for the Steagles in 1943. Zimmerman added value as a defensive back as well, with seven interceptions in 1945.

Zimmerman's success left Neale in a quandary in 1946, with Thompson back and expecting to start. To solve the problem, Neale split the job between them. As is so often the case, however, this solution didn't work very well. Throw in a chest injury that slowed Van Buren, and the result was a 6-5 record that included three losses in a row in November.

For 1947, Neale traded Zimmerman and welcomed Pete Pihos, who would become a Hall of Fame receiver. Pihos had actually been drafted by the Birds in 1945, but he was a little busy just then, serving in Europe under General Patton. Pihos had a great ability to gain yards after the catch, and Neale installed the screen pass in his playbook to take advantage of the Eagles' new weapon.

"We weren't the typical college kids," Pihos said in a 1987 interview for an Eagles game program. "There were a lot of guys like me, just back from the war. I was in the

Halfback Steve Van Buren (No. 15) helped turn the Eagles' fortunes around as soon as he arrived in 1944. The team posted a combined record of 51-17-3 from 1944 to 1949, including three postseason victories that netted two championships. *Nate Fine/NFL/Getty Images*

Though his teammate Steve Van Buren received the lion's share of attention, Bosh Pritchard joined him in the backfield to form one of the most feared one-two punches featured in the mid- to late 1940s. *MVP Books Collection*

Second-year end Pete Pihos (No. 35) made 46 catches for the NFL-champion Eagles in 1948, including this grab against Los Angeles at the L.A. Memorial Coliseum on October 3. Pihos caught two touchdown passes on the day, but the Eagles could only tie the Rams, 28–28. *Vic Stein/NFL/Getty Images*

Steve Van Buren's fourth-quarter lunge into the end zone—which lay somewhere under those mounds of snow—proved to be the only score in Philadelphia's 7–0 win over Chicago for the 1948 NFL championship. *AP Images*

Even the players lent a hand to clear the snowy Shibe Park field before the NFL Championship Game on December 19, 1948. *Tim Culek/NFL/Getty Images*

It was a challenge staying warm on the bench as the snow continued to fall during the Eagles-Cardinals championship battle in 1948. *NFL Photos/AP Images*

STEVE VAN BUREN

THE BIGGEST PROBLEM the Eagles might have had with Steve Van Buren was convincing him to report.

Van Buren spent most of his LSU career blocking for Alvin Dark, who went on to fame as a major league baseball player and manager. According to then–Eagles publicity director Ed Hogan, although the Birds had drafted Van Buren in the first round, he was far from convinced he could help them.

"Shucks, man, you don't want me," Hogan quoted Van Buren as saying, in a November 16, 1947, game program piece Hogan penned. "There's a kid on this team that's got me beat all hollow. Get him. I'm not good enough for your league."

Hogan said it took almost a week for the team's emissary to convince Van Buren to give pro football a try. (Other accounts differ: Van Buren later told a story about taking an Eagles offer that was lower than what he wanted, because he was in the hospital at the time with appendicitis and wasn't sure he'd be able to play as a rookie.) Either way, Van Buren apparently harbored doubts about his suitability for fame, something he never seemed all that thrilled about. Hogan said that even after becoming a top star, Van Buren remained "untouched by the heady wine of success."

Called back by the Eagles in 1994 for a pre-game celebration honoring Van Buren's naming to the NFL's seventy-fifth anniversary team, the Hall of Famer allowed that he was surprised by all the attention; he had "almost forgotten that I ever played football."

Walking out to midfield, Eagles special-teams captain Ken Rose asked Van Buren if he'd ever played there [Veterans Stadium]. Rose said Van Buren, whom he had confused with the late Norm Van Brocklin, smiled and said, "No, I played in the Ice Age."

Around that time, Van Buren acknowledged he had kept few souvenirs of his playing days. Awards and pictures just didn't mean much to him, he said.

Van Buren, 6-foot-1, 210, was ahead of his time as an athlete—a bruising inside runner as big as many of the linemen he confronted, bigger than many of the linebackers and most of the defensive backs. A native of Honduras, he was orphaned at age 10 and then moved to live with his grandparents in New Orleans.

"He weighed about the same as I did, around 215," said Wistert. "Steve just ran through guys, knocked 'em down."

He got off to a slow start after reporting late in 1944 because of appendicitis; even so, Van Buren was runner-up for Rookie of the Year. His potential was clear, as he made all-NFL for the first of six successive times.

Van Buren would lead the NFL in rushing four times and become the first runner to post multiple 1,000-yard seasons.

"He knocked off more helmets than you could count. And when Steve got near the goal line, brother, he could smell the end zone," Wistert recalled.

Van Buren's style helped ensure he would not have a long career, though he was the NFL's all-time leading rusher (5,860 yards) when he was forced to retire after severely breaking a leg in training camp in 1952. Nineteen forty-nine, the only time the Eagles have ever repeated as champions, was Van Buren's last healthy season, that title game (31 carries, 196 yards) his best day. He averaged just 3.19 yards per carry his final two years.

"I used to take maybe six [painkilling injections] each half," Van Buren once told a *Daily News* reporter. "Into the ribs. And the big toe, too. Once you hurt that big toe, it never gets better. . . . The only time [the shots] bothered me was when they hit the bone. The needle would bend and sometimes it would break. I didn't like it. When they hit the bone, it really hurt . . . and anybody would give it to you. Everybody wanted to shoot me with the needle."

After a 1989 fund-raiser held for Van Buren as he recovered from a stroke (suffered as he was driving home in northeast Philadelphia), ex-teammate and fellow Hall of Famer Alex Wojciechowicz said: "More than any other individual, he is responsible for the tradition of Eagles football.

"The Bears have a winning tradition; so do the Giants and 49ers. The Eagles' tradition really started with our [championship] teams and he was the heart and soul of our club. He'll never say that about himself, but it was true. I'll never forget it, and neither will anyone else."

Around that same time, another former teammate and Hall of Famer, Pete Pihos, said he considered Van Buren the best of all time.

"Remember, we were going up against six- and seven-man lines in the 1940s," Pihos said. "When we had third-and-short, everyone knew Steve was getting the ball and he still got the yards. He would keep fighting and dragging [tacklers] along until he made it."

Wistert said, "Steve is a wonderful guy, easy to get along with, good sense of humor. He was modest, but he knew that he had great talent."

Future Hall of Famer Steve Van Buren was a star pitchman for Wheaties in the late 1940s.
MVP Books Collection

Thirty-fifth Infantry. Went in as a private, came out a second lieutenant. Yeah, we saw some heavy fighting. We were in the Battle of the Bulge. I don't like to talk about the war, even now. I just know when I got out, I was happy to be alive."

A game program story from that season notes that every player to score a touchdown got free dinner at the Bookbinder's restaurant on Walnut Street; the whole team dined for free in the event of an Eagles shutout, something that happened three times in the regular season.

"Plenty of dinners at Bookbinder's that year," Wistert recalled. "If we had a shutout at halftime of a game, we'd start talking about it—'Let's go to Bookbinder's!'"

Van Buren became the league's first 1,000-yard rusher in 13 years, and the 8-4 Eagles gained their first playoff victory, 21–0 over the Steelers, before losing the NFL Championship Game to the host Chicago Cardinals, 28–21, on icy turf at Comiskey Park. It was later alleged that the tarp came off a day early, because workers would have been paid overtime for coming in to take it off on a Sunday.

Wistert suggested that the Cards, as the home team, had more equipment on hand and were able to find an appropriate cleat length.

"They could adjust. We could not adjust," he said. "We filed our cleats down to a pinpoint so they would dig into the frozen turf better. The Cardinals got wind of that and told the referee we were using illegal equipment. The referee examined the cleats and wouldn't let us wear them; if we'd stepped on someone, that would have been disastrous."

It's hard to know, so many years later, how much of a home-field advantage the Cardinals had in such conditions, how close the Birds really were to the start of what might have been a championship "threepeat." What is clear is that the Eagles were embarking on what would become the most dominant stretch in their history.

The 1948 season started with a loss, in a rematch of that 1947 title game, at Chicago. Perhaps out of sorts over not avenging that defeat, the Eagles played poorly the next week and tied the Rams, 3–3. But the next two contests, wins over the Giants and Redskins, saw the Eagles outscore the opposition by a combined 90–0. That was the start of an eight-game victory streak that ended only when the divisional title was clinched.

Pihos caught 11 touchdown passes. Van Buren and Bosh Pritchard, the NFL's most lethal one-two rushing punch, combined for 1,462 rushing yards and 14 TDs. The 9-2-1 Eagles outscored their opponents 376–156.

TITLE IN THE SNOW

The note under "weather conditions" on the official play-by-play sheet for the December 19, 1948, NFL Championship Game between the Chicago Cardinals and the Eagles at Shibe Park sums up the situation pretty well: "Heavy snow falling on top of 5 inches on field throughout the game. Lights turned on prior to start. Falling snow and poor light made visibility poor."

In fact, "poor" doesn't quite do it justice; reports indicate all markings on the field were quickly obliterated, not long after an estimated 90 men, including players from both teams, wrestled the snow-laden tarp off the North Philly field, which was primarily the home of the Phillies.

As tends to be the case, the visiting team wanted to play, regardless of conditions; it had traveled from Chicago and didn't want to go home and come back a week later. Greasy Neale was a little more reluctant, given his memories of Eagles sliding around the icy turf in Chicago the previous year.

The defending champions were favored, even on the road; they had just gone 11-1, defeating the Eagles in that season opener. Neale beat the underdog drum hard, and by game day his players were very keen to play the Cards, who had won their last five meetings with the Birds. While team and league officials deliberated the possibility of postponing the game, the Eagles voted to play, which turned out to be the decision the people in charge made, too.

The game started around 2 p.m., 30 minutes later than scheduled. One man who needed the extra time was Van Buren—he'd slept late after seeing the snowfall, figuring the game would be postponed.

Then Van Buren got a phone call, from his coach.

"He said, 'You'd better get there,'" Van Buren recalled in a 1994 interview with the Philadelphia *Daily News*. "I said, 'Greasy, have you looked out the window? There is no way we will play today.' He said, 'Go to the park, for God's sake. It's the championship game.'

"I went, but I was cussing Greasy the whole way."

Then, when the tardy star tried to navigate to Shibe Park from his home in Drexel Hill, Delaware County, west of the city, by bus, trolley, and subway, Van Buren

The Eagles made sure to lock in coach Earle "Greasy" Neale following the championship season of 1948. Here he signs a new three-year contract in February 1949, with Eagles president Jim Clark at his side. *AP Images*

encountered delays. He ended up walking the final stretch, making it to the stadium around 1:30, arriving with the crowd of 28,864, which undoubtedly would have been much larger in better weather. About 37,000 tickets were sold.

"I couldn't believe it when I got there and saw they were going to play," Van Buren said later. "It was snowing so hard, you couldn't see."

Van Buren told the *Daily News* he recalled being able to see the linemen and linebackers in front of him, but not the defensive secondary.

Al Wistert spent his entire nine-year NFL career with Philadelphia as a tackle and guard and was named first-team all-pro four years in a row (1944 to 1947). *AP Images*

Yardage was estimated; there was no measuring for first downs. The Eagles were angry at the offside call negating their 65-yard opening-play touchdown pass from Tommy Thompson to Jack Ferrante; they felt the official was just guessing that Ferrante had crossed the line of scrimmage early.

The Eagles had the better power running game, which came in handy, although Van Buren (26 carries, 98 yards) said he didn't feel the footing was as bad as it had been in the Chicago ice the previous year.

Van Buren might have been in the minority there. The game was scoreless for three quarters, which indicates somebody must have been having a little trouble. Thompson, the NFL's leading passer that season, completed two of seven and was picked off twice.

Finally, right at the end of the third quarter, Philadelphia's own Frank "Bucko" Kilroy, a longtime Patriots executive later in his career, helped force a fumble by Chicago QB Ray Mallouf, and Kilroy recovered at the Cards' 17.

Four plays later, with 13:56 left in the game, Van Buren took a handoff at the 5 and scored. Various reports and the play-by-play indicate he went in standing up. "Van Buren on a big hole at right tackle drives over for touchdown standing up," the sheet says. But in photos, Van Buren ends up lying in the end zone, albeit with no Cards around him. One photo, snapped earlier, shows him lunging forward, more or less diving over the goal line, which was how Van Buren remembered it in later interviews.

However it happened, the Birds were on the board. Chicago never seriously threatened again, and the game ended with the ball in the hands of the Eagles, just two yards from another TD.

Wistert, who helped open the hole for Van Buren's touchdown, recalls "almost a foot" of snow on the field at the time. "It was pretty deep," Wistert said. "It bothered both teams a lot. We managed better than they did."

"After many years of waiting, the Philadelphia Eagles finally have won the National Football League Championship," one newspaper report began. Contemporary fans might take issue with that "many years of waiting," since the franchise right then was ending just its sixteenth season. In 2010, the Eagles celebrated the fiftieth anniversary of their most recent title, the 1960 championship.

"Joyous fans rushed on the field and carried Van Buren off on their shoulders," the newspaper account said. "The hero halfback, who had pounded out 98 yards in 26 tries, pleaded to be let down, but it was not until the rooters had almost reached the runway to the dressing quarters that he was permitted to walk, and even then, the crowd made it almost impossible for him to get into the room."

Van Buren got there, though. In famous photos he is at the center of the crowded locker room celebrants, alongside Neale, whose suit is protected by an overcoat that appears to be spattered with beer or champagne.

LET'S DO IT AGAIN

The Eagles have won back-to-back titles only once in their history. The 1949 team was even more dominant than the previous season's version, outscoring opponents by an average margin of 19 points per game and fielding four future Hall of Famers: Pihos, Van Buren, and lineman Alex Wojciechowicz were joined by rookie linebacker and center Chuck Bednarik, who would become perhaps the greatest Eagle of all time. (Neale, the coach, also made it to Canton, of course.)

Oddly enough, Lex Thompson sold the team in the wake of the 1948 championship, having missed the title game while hospitalized with appendicitis (he had to settle for listening to the radio broadcast instead). A poorly timed health crisis wasn't Thompson's only problem. With the NFL in a bidding war for players against the All-America Football Conference, he lost money during the 1948 season and even had to be bailed out by the league to make payroll the final week.

So Thompson ended up selling the best team in the league to a group of 100 investors for a reported $250,000. Trucking executive James P. Clark organized the group that bought the team, and Clark became the Eagles' new president.

On the field in 1949, there was no such intrigue. With the addition of top draft pick Bednarik, the Birds allowed just 134 points in going 11-1. Other than the Bears, who thumped them 38–21 on October 16, nobody could touch them. Ten of the wins were by double digits. Take away the Bears game and opponents scored a little less than 9 points per game against them.

The 1949 title game was once again defined by field conditions—how many times in NFL history has a

The Eagles made it back-to-back championships with their 14–0 win over the Rams on December 18, 1949. Steve Van Buren, seen here with the ball, gained 196 rushing yards in the muddy conditions at Los Angeles Memorial Coliseum. *Vic Stein/NFL/Getty Images*

Chuck Bednarik grits his teeth as he tackles Giants QB Charlie Conerly in a 1949 game. Bednarik was in the first season of his long and illustrious Eagles career. *MVP Books Collection*

franchise played in three such successive situations? This time, the Eagles faced the Rams on December 18 in Los Angeles, in heavy rains. Once again, there was talk of postponement. An Associated Press story noted: "So bad was the weather that the management of both Eastern and Western winners were willing to postpone the playoff until Christmas. But Commissioner Bell, in his home in Philadelphia, said no."

It wasn't that the players were unwilling to get wet or to slip and slide in the mud. Their championship shares depended upon the paid gate. Forty-five years later, running back Bosh Pritchard told the Philadelphia *Daily News*: "The weather killed us. We figured with the game in the L.A. Coliseum (102,000 capacity), we'd have the biggest live gate in NFL history. We were calculating shares in our heads on the train ride to the coast.

"We figured around $11,000 apiece, which was more than most guys made for the entire season. We were happy as could be, so were our wives. Then we got to L.A. and it was like a monsoon on the day of the game; hardly anybody showed up."

In fact, in what might have been a commentary on the sporting hardiness of the respective Philadelphia and Los Angeles fan bases, 22,245 people showed up to sit through the downpour—6,619 fewer than braved the blizzard at Shibe Park a year earlier.

"One of the guys, I think it was Piggy [Walter] Barnes, had a funny line," Al Wistert told the *Daily News*. "He said, 'It doesn't make any difference to me how much we get. I spent [the money] already.' Knowing our guys, there probably was some truth to that."

In the end, each winning player got $1,096—a lot more money back then than today, but considerably less than Pritchard and his pals had calculated. But in fairness to Bell, in 1949, it would have been hard to postpone such a game for a week. Because of the time required for rail travel back to Philadelphia, the Eagles would have needed to be housed and fed in Los Angeles for seven days, with still no guarantee of a huge Christmas Day gate.

"We really wanted to fill that stadium, but it was not practical for us to postpone it for a week," Wistert said.

The 1949 championship game was Van Buren's finest hour and also his last moment of true greatness before injuries dimmed his brilliance. He carried 31 times in the mud, gaining 196 yards.

"Steve Van Buren ran today the best I ever saw a man run," Neale said after the game. "Maybe Red Grange was better than Van Buren today. Maybe Bronko Nagurski was better. But nobody ever ran like Van Buren did in this mud."

Rams coach Clark Shaughnessy said: "He is the equal of any player I've ever seen."

"I'll never forget the sight of him running the ball that day," recalled Wistert, who said the Rams keyed on Van Buren, to no avail. "The mud was up above his ankles and he just kept going."

Later, it emerged that once when Van Buren was tackled along the L.A. sideline, Rams players yelled that they were going to "kill" him.

Van Buren was unimpressed, he told the *Daily News* in 1994. "The way they were tackling, they couldn't kill anybody."

Later, at a post-game Hollywood party, Van Buren met Roy Rogers, Clark Gable, and Tarzan himself, former Olympic swimmer Johnny Weismuller.

"The thing I remember about Weismuller was he had a drink in each hand," Van Buren said. "I never thought of Tarzan as a two-fisted drinker."

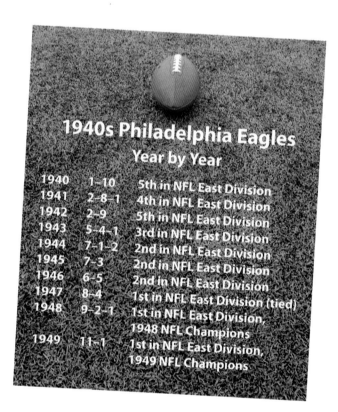

1940s Philadelphia Eagles
Year by Year

Year	Record	Finish
1940	1–10	5th in NFL East Division
1941	2–8–1	4th in NFL East Division
1942	2–9	5th in NFL East Division
1943	5–4–1	3rd in NFL East Division
1944	7–1–2	2nd in NFL East Division
1945	7–3	2nd in NFL East Division
1946	6–5	2nd in NFL East Division
1947	8–4	1st in NFL East Division (tied)
1948	9–2–1	1st in NFL East Division, 1948 NFL Champions
1949	11–1	1st in NFL East Division, 1949 NFL Champions

3 QUICK REVERSAL
The 1950s

PHILADELPHIA EAGLES

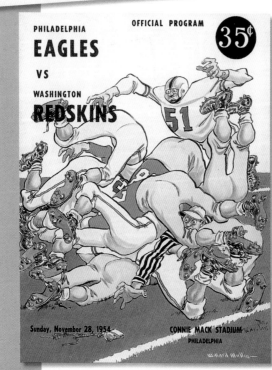

PHILADELPHIA EAGLES VS WASHINGTON REDSKINS

OFFICIAL PROGRAM 35¢

Sunday, November 28, 1954

CONNIE MACK STADIUM
PHILADELPHIA

All MVP Books Collection

THE EAGLES ENTERED 1950 as the NFL's show-case team. As Greasy Neale put it, after two successive NFL titles, "This is the best team ever put together. Who is there to beat us?"

Neale got the answer to that question very quickly, in the 1950 season opener. This was the year the NFL absorbed three teams from the All-America Football Conference, including the Cleveland Browns, who had won the AAFC title in each of the league's four seasons. The NFL decided it would be neat to open up with the AAFC champs visiting the NFL champs, on September 16.

The buildup was extraordinary, and in Philadelphia, much of it carried a condescending tone. Even the fact that the Eagles were going to be missing Steve Van Buren (toe) and Bosh Pritchard (knee) didn't cause a lot of concern among Eagles fans, though their team went from a seven-point favorite to "pick 'em" in the final days before the game.

As the game approached, Frank O'Gara reported in the *Philadelphia Inquirer* that Neale didn't expect to have Van Buren. "But the veteran coach seemed far from disheartened at the prospect. Clyde (Smackover) Scott, who has been running wild in Steve's left half position ever since the latter retired for a foot operation Aug. 21, bids fair to continue his sensational scampering, starting with the 8:45 kickoff."

Scott, who was not then and never would be a runner at Van Buren's level, despite his 1948 Olympic silver medal in the high hurdles, suffered a shoulder separation in the first half against the Browns and didn't return.

The 71,237 fans who flocked to huge but inelegant Municipal Stadium on South Broad Street—the city's major north-south corridor having been turned into a one-way, eight-lane highway for the game—were deeply shocked by the Browns' 35–10 victory, the "Super Bowl III" of the day. (The Eagles played two home games at

Guard Cliff Patton and running back Clyde Scott both played on the 1949 championship team. *MVP Books Collection*

Municipal Stadium in 1950.) Otto Graham began his NFL career by completing 21 of 38 passes for the then unheard-of total of 346 yards and three touchdowns. When receivers Dante Lavelli (Graham's fellow future Hall of Fame member), Mac Speedie, and Dub Jones weren't shredding the Eagles' secondary, 238-pound Marion Motley was blasting through the line. (Motley was not only bigger than any back the Birds fielded, but he was also the first African American star they'd faced. It would be two more years before integration reached the Eagles.)

"Big Otto kept sending ends Mac Speedie and Dante Lavelli out for buttonhooks and they fooled the Eagles constantly," the *Bulletin* reported. "The creeping slowness that catches up with aging athletes was never more evident as the Eagles, champions of the NFL for the last two years, gradually disintegrated before the great passing attack of the newcomers to their league."

Neale seemed stunned. "I never saw a team with so many guns," he said.

Neale had been widely quoted as proclaiming, at some point during the Browns' AAFC exploits, that the ball was in the air so much, Browns coach Paul Brown should consider coaching basketball. It's hard to pin down exactly when and where Neale actually said this, if he did, but the larger point remains: Neale, the great innovator of the 1940s, was out-innovated by Brown, who ultimately would be recognized as one of the handful of most influential figures in the history of the league. Brown, nearly 17 years younger than Neale, came up with concepts such as playbooks and draw plays. He also brought the face-mask, used here and there in college football, to the pros.

"You could hear a pin drop on the bus afterward," Al Wistert recalled. "We were just humiliated."

In retrospect, the Browns had some serious advantages in the opener. They had known for some time that they'd be making their debut against the 1949 champs; they scouted the Eagles' title game victory over Los Angeles with their matchup in mind. The Eagles had no such warning, and even if they had, Brown had fortified his 1949 team substantially in the draft that dispersed the players from AAFC teams that weren't moving on to the NFL. Who knew that personnel better than Brown? There was no game tape of the new and improved Cleveland squad that joined the NFL.

"We wound up playing an AAFC All-Star team," Bucko Kilroy later told author Shelby Strother, in *NFL Top 40*.

Wistert agreed that Neale was overconfident.

Francis "Bucko" Kilroy was known as an extraordinarily tough two-way lineman. He began his career as a "Steagle" in 1943 and stayed in Philadelphia for his entire career, retiring after the 1955 season. He went on to a career as a coach and administrator, including a stint as general manager of the Patriots during their run to the Super Bowl in 1985. *MVP Books Collection*

CHUCK BEDNARIK

SOMEHOW IT FITS that the guy who symbolized the Eagles for everyone who grew up in the 1950s and 1960s—a big chunk of today's fan base—is not a warm and fuzzy fellow. Has any franchise ever featured a more fittingly cantankerous icon?

Chuck Bednarik has feuded with Eagles management several times over the years, over this or that perceived slight. He was an associate coach, a sort of ambassador from the old days, during the Dick Vermeil Eagles era, but through two more ownership changes, Bednarik and the Eagles were up and down. Most famous was his falling out in 1996, after Bednarik insisted Eagles owner Jeffrey Lurie buy 100 copies of a Bednarik book to give to players. The Eagles replied, correctly, that they weren't allowed to give such gifts to players, but Bednarik, angry over the vast difference between what he made as a two-way star and the salaries paid today, stayed estranged for years. When the Eagles played the Patriots in Super Bowl XXXIX, Bednarik made headlines by declaring he would root against the Eagles.

"I hope the 1960 team remains the last one to win. I hope it stays that way," he said.

Bednarik loves to autograph photos of his legendary hit on Frank Gifford, often expressing pungent thoughts about Gifford, a handsome New Yorker who went on to fame and riches as a broadcaster. His most famous quote is what he said after tackling Green Bay's Jim Taylor on the final play of the 1960 NFL Championship Game. "This f——g game is over!" Bednarik exclaimed.

Whenever a modern player goes both ways, as Deion Sanders did in the 1990s and Troy Brown did in the last decade, reporters ask Bednarik for comment. He makes it clear they are not comparable to him. Bednarik feels modern players are sissies, "overpaid and underplayed." The idea that many defensive linemen and linebackers don't even play all three downs is a frequent topic.

"Deion couldn't tackle my wife, Emma," Bednarik complained.

But Bednarik's bluster should not overshadow what he did as a Hall of Fame player, in getting his No. 60 retired by the Birds.

When the *Sporting News* ranked the NFL's top 100 players of all time in 1999, he was No. 54. He was selected for 8 of the first 11 Pro Bowls and was the league's last full-time two-way player. He was truly an ironman, missing three games in 14 years.

Bednarik, born in Bethlehem, Pennsylvania, to Slovak immigrants, flew 30 missions over Germany in World War II as a waist gunner, then went to the University of Pennsylvania when the war ended. He became a three-time All-American as a two-way center/linebacker and was the first overall pick in the 1949 NFL draft.

He was a marvelous athlete, born to play football.

Eagles teammate Marion Campbell remembered, "I asked him

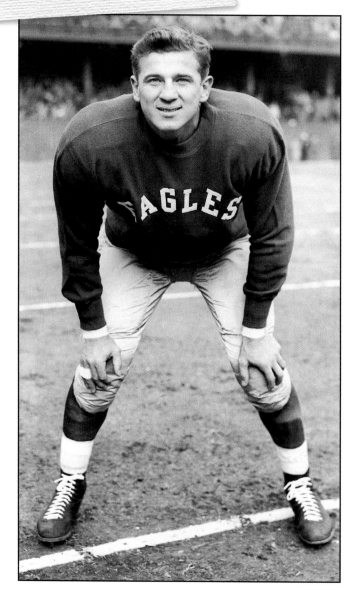

Hall of Famer Chuck Bednarik in 1951 *AP Images*

one time, 'Chuck, what do you key?' He looks at me, 'Key? The ball takes me to the play, that's my key.' His instincts were incredible. He was the most instinctive guy who ever stepped on a field."

George Allen called Bednarik "the best linebacker I ever saw" and ranked him among the greats as a center.

"A linebacker is like an animal," Bednarik told ESPN in a feature called "Last of the 60-Minute Men." "He's like a lion or a tiger and he goes after prey. He wants to eat him, he wants to kick the —— out of him. That's a linebacker."

At the 1960 team's fiftieth anniversary celebration, Bednarik said: "When I played football, I wanted to stay on the field, not like these kids today. The game has changed drastically. In my generation, if you were a good football player, you stayed on the field as long as you could. You never went to the coach and said, 'I'm tired.'"

On their way into that fiftieth anniversary celebration, the team's survivors walked a red carpet. The team mascot, "Swoop," flapped and fluttered around them, and the old players smiled and laughed. Then Bednarik walked the carpet. When Bednarik, 85 years old but still imposing, saw "Swoop," he lowered his head, squared his shoulders, and cocked his arms as if preparing to make a tackle.

"Swoop" nearly laid an egg.

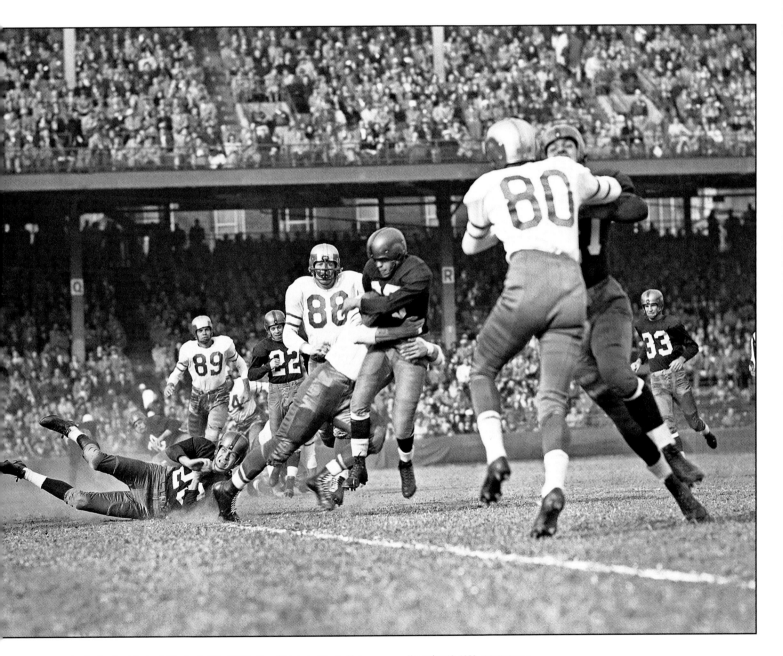

Linebacker Chuck Bednarik lifts the Redskins' Bill Dudley off his feet with a tackle in a game on November 12, 1950. *WCA/AP Images*

"Greasy was so proud of his team, he didn't go scout [the Browns]," Wistert said. "They were so good—he needed every bit of scouting he could get to figure out how to play 'em, but he didn't."

When the teams met again that year, December 3 in Cleveland, the score was a much more respectable 13–7, the Browns again winning. But Brown underscored his one-upmanship by defeating Neale's Eagles despite never passing the ball once the entire game.

NEW ERA

The stark rise to dominance of the Browns, who would play for the NFL title seven times in the 1950s, might have hastened Greasy Neale's departure. Van Buren ran for just 629 yards on 188 carries in 1950, 3.3 yards per carry. The

QB Adrian Burk threw seven touchdown passes in a 1954 game against the Redskins, an NFL record he shares with Sid Luckman, George Blanda, Y. A. Tittle, and Joe Kapp. *MVP Books Collection*

quarterback, Thompson, also was at the end of the line. The team finished the season with four losses in a row, and ultimately, Neale was replaced by Bo McMillin, who coached just two games in 1951 (winning both) before being diagnosed with stomach cancer and resigning. McMillin, 56, had entered the hospital for ulcer surgery.

The Eagles were not prepared to lose their new coach two games into the season. They lost 8 of their final 10 games under emergency replacement Wayne Millner, a 39-year-old first-year assistant. New quarterback Adrian Burk threw 23 interceptions and just 14 touchdowns.

The next season, under Jim Trimble, the Eagles returned to respectability. They signed their first African American players, halfbacks Ralph Goldston and Don Stevens, and went 7-5, even though Trimble took the job under circumstances almost identical to the ones Milner faced. Milner had been given a chance to coach a season from the start, at least, but he became so stressed out, losing 20 pounds during training camp, that he followed his doctor's advice and resigned.

Goldston and Stevens actually were something of a fallback plan. The Eagles' first-round draft pick that year was Drake's Johnny Bright, who was African American as well. But Bright was leery of the NFL and signed to play in Canada instead, where he would go on to become the CFL's all-time leading rusher at the time of his retirement. Bright had encountered vicious prejudice as a college player for Oklahoma State, once suffering a broken jaw after being punched by end Wilbanks Smith in a game against Oklahoma A&M. He thought he might find less racial strife north of the border.

Trimble coached the Birds for four seasons, three of them winning seasons, but he couldn't get them past the dominant Browns.

Trimble's greatest contribution to football came long after he left the Eagles. In 1966, he and a friend developed the one-post, "slingshot" goal post still used today, supplanting the old two-post model.

"MUMBLES" WALSTON AND A FADING POWER

Kicker and tight end Bobby Walston set a franchise scoring record in 1954, with 114 points, even though he managed just four field goals. It would take 30 years for anyone to surpass Walston, who scored 11 touchdowns that season and kicked 36 extra points.

Jim Trimble, the Eagles' head coach for four seasons in the 1950s, made a bigger mark as the inventor of the slingshot goalpost. *MVP Books Collection*

Walston, who played in an era of 12-game seasons, worked pretty hard to set that record, staying in the lineup after suffering a broken jaw against the Steelers, *Daily News* columnist Jack McKinney recalled, after Walston passed away in 1987 at age 58.

"When Walston objected to having his jaw wired shut; the team doctor told him it was the only way to stabilize the injured mandible. But the next day, Bobby got pliers from the equipment manager and removed the wiring himself," McKinney wrote. "On game days, he would then fashion his own makeshift brace out of gauze and tape.
continued on page 42

TOM BROOKSHIER

If you met Tom Brookshier late in his life, or maybe even if you primarily knew him from his stint as the analyst on the NFL's No. 1 TV announcing crew in the 1970s, you might never have guessed what he was like as a player.

Brookshier in retirement was an unassuming figure, genial and relaxed. In the mid-2000s, he did a TV appearance alongside a guy who was then an Eagles player. The player looked at the rumpled, silver-haired fellow in the next seat, who seemed smaller than the 6 feet, 196 listing in faded game programs, and asked, "What did you run the 40 in?" The inference was clear: if this little old dude really played football well enough to get his jersey number (40) retired by the Eagles, he must have been *fast*, or something.

"Four-three," Brookshier said, seeming unfazed by the question.

But it wasn't his speed that made "Brookie" an Eagles legend, really.

"The thing you remembered about him was how he tackled," longtime Eagles executive Jimmy Gallagher told the *Inquirer* after Brookshier passed away at age 78, on January 29, 2010. "He hit you around the thighs, and he went down to your ankles to make sure he took you down. He and Irv Cross were the best tacklers I ever saw."

In the Philadelphia *Daily News*, columnist Bill Conlin memorialized Brookshier: "Tom Brookshier did not invent the art of playing modern cornerback, but he was one of the few men in NFL history able to bring down the great Jim Brown one-on-one. He was not blessed with blazing speed, but he was a cover corner who hit like a linebacker. Brookie was good for a few human pinwheels a game when he launched low and flat and turned a receiver or ballcarrier into an identified flying object."

"He was a tough, intense, and committed player," said Dick Vermeil, former Eagles coach and a Brookshier broadcast partner in the 1980s. "He wanted everybody else around him to be just as dedicated. He loved the Philadelphia Eagles and Andy Reid, but he hated when a guy in the secondary missed a tackle. It would really bother him. He'd say, 'They're getting paid all that money and not hitting anybody.'"

Brookshier made the Pro Bowl twice and was a key figure on the Eagles 1960 NFL championship team, but he gained greater fame after his playing career ended prematurely in 1961, following a gruesome leg fracture suffered against the Bears. (The Eagles, 7-1 when Brookshier went down, couldn't stop anybody after that, giving up 83 points in two season-ending blowout losses.) Brookshier became a TV analyst, and when he was paired with ex–New York Giant Pat Summerall in the 1970s, they became an iconic duo, CBS's top announcing pair until the network brought in John Madden to work with Summerall in 1981.

All-pro corner Tom Brookshier drags down the Cardinals' Ken Hall in a November 15, 1959, game. Brookshier's fame as a broadcaster lasted long after his playing career ended. *Bill Ingraham/AP Images*

Summerall and Brookshier remained close friends, and Summerall later credited Brookshier with saving his life, getting him into alcohol rehab in 1992.

In Philadelphia, Brookshier is also remembered for his role in birthing the caustic, sometimes toxic sports talk radio formula that has dominated the market for a couple of decades—even though Brookshier's on-air style was very different from that of Angelo Cataldi, the morning host whose career Brookshier launched during Brookshier's time as part owner of radio station WIP.

In a 1980 column, the late *Daily News* columnist Jack McKinney, defending Brookshier's TV analysis after a print critic had called it "languid," wrote: "The day after Brookie went down [with the career-ending injury], Tom Swafford, who was then general manager of WCAU Radio, phoned his hospital room and offered him a sportscasting job. His brain still fogged by anesthesia, Brookie accepted.

"He was not just a token talking jock, coasting on his athletic fame while reading scripts written by some anonymous, underpaid grunt in the newsroom. Brookie was bright, knowledgeable, and articulate. . . . [He] had that rare gift of seeming loose as the proverbial goose while, at the same time, being totally together. He also wrote all his own stuff. Brookie was good from the git-go and he did nothing but get better, as his quick transition through Channel 10 sports anchor to the top echelon of CBS Sports will attest."

FLIGHT REPORT

... from the eagles' nest

TO ALL EAGLES' FANS

MEMORANDUM NUMBER THREE FOR 1955

Since our last report to you, preparations for the 1955 season have increased in tempo and, believe it or not, by July 18 the Eagles will be in training at Hershey, Pa. That's the date Head Coach Jim Trimble has set for the advance guard to report at Chocolate Town. From then on action will commence on all fronts and football will be with us again. You will get your first chance to see the 1955 edition of the Eagles at our free OPEN HOUSE PARTY on Sunday, August 7, when an intra-squad game will highlight a day of activity designed to bring you, the fan, closer to the players. Players and coaches will be available to you and your children for photographs, autographs, etc., for one hour prior to the game. Don't forget admission is FREE! Why don't you resolve right now to visit Hershey for the OPEN HOUSE and bring the family along with you. Hershey offers many attractions including an excellent amusement park. We hope to see you there.

Now to get into the question and answer department:

— 1955 SCHEDULE —
PRE-SEASON GAMES

Sat. Aug. 13 8:05° Nite.....Baltimore Colts, Hershey, Pa.
Fri. Aug. 26 8:35° Nite .Chicago Bears, Municipal Stadium, Philadelphia, Pa.

CHAMPIONSHIP GAMES
Home—Connie Mack Stadium

Sat. Sept. 24 7:35° Nite ....New York Giants
Sat. Oct. 1 7:35° Nite... Washington Redskins
Sun. Oct. 30 2:05 .... Pittsburgh Steelers
Sun. Nov. 13 2:05 .... Cleveland Browns
Sun. Nov. 27 2:05 .... Los Angeles Rams
Sun. Dec. 4 2:05 ...... Chicago Cardinals

Times are EST Except ° (EDT)

AWAY

Sun. Oct. 9 .Cleveland Browns, Cleveland, O.
Sat. Oct. 15—Nite .... Pittsburgh Steelers, Pittsburgh, Pa.
Sun. Oct. 23 . Chicago Cardinals, Chicago, Ill.
Sun. Nov. 6 .Washington Redskins, Wash., D. C.
Sun. Nov. 20 . New York Giants, New York City
Sun. Dec. 11 ... Chicago Bears, Chicago, Ill.

Q. WHO'S THE OLDEST PLAYER ON THE TEAM?

A. Well, we don't think there's any doubt about that one. Frank Bucko Kilroy, a young, bouncing 34, is eagerly awaiting his 13th season in professional football and all with the Eagles. Frank is the oldest player on the team in years and the oldest in the league in point of service.

Q. WHAT PLAYERS LIVE IN THIS AREA IN THE OFF-SEASON?

A. Quite a few. Some of them are natives of Greater Philadelphia such as Frank Kilroy, Eddie Bell, Chuck Bednarik, and Jess Richardson. Others from various parts of the country now settled and working in this area are Bobby Thomason, Bob Hudson, Pete Pihos, Tom Scott and Lum Snyder. Norman (Wild Man) Willey lives in nearby Penns Grove, New Jersey.

Q. DOES COACH TRIMBLE PLAN ANYTHING NEW FOR 1955?

A. That one we threw at Coach Jim Trimble. Jim was quick to reply with: "The Eagles of 1955 will be most interesting to watch. We'll be better balanced than in any year since I've been with the Eagles and, with the men to do it, we plan quite a few surprises, innovations, etc. I hope you'll forgive me if I don't tip my hand this early."

Q. WILL THE EAGLES HAVE A RUNNING OFFENSE IN 1955?

A. We also threw that one at the head man. And here's Trimble's answer: "Very definitely," said Trimble. "We'll run the ball much more than we did in 1954."

A year ago we just didn't have the horses to carry the mail. Now we do. We'll have Penn's Eddie Bell and Bibbles Bawel for the defense which will relieve a great runner like Jerry Norton for offense. And don't forget our rookie fullback, Dick Bielski. Dick's the kind who'll get us the tough yardage. Our passing game should be better in 1955 because of the stronger running game. One always helps the other."

Q. WHEN IS THE FIRST PRE-SEASON GAME AT HERSHEY?

A. The new Eagles of 1955 will be unveiled against the Baltimore Colts on Saturday night, August 13, at the Hershey Stadium. Kickoff time is 8:05 P.M. Why not plan to come up and see the Birds fly high?

Q. MAY TICKETS BE PURCHASED ON A BUDGET PLAN?

A. Yes. You may set up any plan convenient to you. Weekly or monthly payments on all types of SEASON TICKETS may be made in person or by mail at the Eagles' Ticket Office. SEASON TICKET PRICES ARE: $25.50, $20.40, $15.30 and $10.20. THESE PRICES INCLUDE A FIFTEEN PER-CENT REDUCTION!

Q. WHAT ARE THE PRICES FOR SINGLE GAMES?

A. There is no increase in ticket prices for our six games at Connie Mack Stadium. They are: $5, $4, $3 and $2.

All MVP Books Collection

The Birds' defense gets good pressure on Giants QB Charlie Conerly during a 1956 game in New York. The Giants won 20–3. *Robert Riger/Getty Images*

NORM VAN BROCKLIN

AT THE MEMORIAL SERVICE for Norm Van Brocklin in May 1983 on his Georgia farm, they played "My Way" on the organ.

That was how the Eagles did it in 1960, when they won their most recent NFL title—Van Brocklin's way. Veterans of that team have long maintained that though head coach Buck Shaw should get his due, it was Van Brocklin's leadership that carried the Birds to an unlikely title.

"Buck Shaw, God bless him, he was the coach," halfback Billy Ray Barnes said at the service, "but Dutch, by God, he was our leader! He was the greatest leader of any quarterback who ever lived. He didn't make us feel like we might win. With Dutch, we felt like we couldn't lose."

Van Brocklin arrived in 1958, in a trade with the Rams; apparently, Shaw made Van Brocklin's acquisition a prerequisite for accepting the floundering franchise's head coaching job. It was a bit of a surprise move in that the Eagles had a well-regarded young quarterback in Sonny Jurgensen. Later, Van Brocklin maintained he hadn't wanted to come to Philadelphia, but there had been a deal, brokered by NFL commissioner and former Eagles owner Bert Bell, that the Dutchman would ascend to head coach when Shaw retired, providing a graceful transition to Jurgensen at quarterback. Bell died suddenly in 1959, watching the Eagles play, and the deal never materialized when Shaw stepped down as planned following the 1960 championship season.

Van Brocklin maintained that cost-conscious management wanted him to somehow become the playing head coach, a concept that even then seemed ridiculously dated. He ended up

AP Images

Continued from page 39
Over the back half of his record-setting season, Walston looked like Lon Chaney Jr. in 'The Mummy's Curse.' His voice was so muffled under all that swathing, his teammates took to calling him 'Mumbles.'"

But other than Chuck Bednarik, who came in as a rookie in 1949 toward the end of the Neale era, the key players from the late 1940s Eagles dynasty were fading out. In 1955 Bucko Kilroy suffered a career-ending knee injury, and Pete Pihos retired at age 32, after leading the league in receiving three years in a row and making six successive Pro Bowls. Retiring amidst such stellar statistics is not likely to happen today, but the once-proud team went 4-7, and back then, a player could actually think about making more money in business than he made playing football, which was Pihos's plan.

Pihos might have known something. The 1956 Eagles went 3-8-1 and finished last. When 1957 produced a 4-8

retiring and taking over coaching duties with the first-year expansion Minnesota Vikings, with bitterness in his heart. It's a wonder, given the Eagles franchise's close-but-not-quite travails since then, that more is not made of the "curse of the Dutchman."

When Van Brocklin died, *Philadelphia Inquirer* columnist Frank Dolson extolled his feistiness, and recalled his departure from the Eagles: "I'll never forget Van Brocklin's farewell appearance at the Philadelphia Sports Writers banquet in January 1961. There were close to 1,000 people at the old Sheraton Hotel that night, and they gave the Dutchman a standing ovation," Dolson wrote. "Finally, when the applause had subsided, Van Brocklin told the crowd that he was going to Minnesota to coach the expansion Vikings because of 'the belief of my former employers that I am incapable of coaching their team. . . . Contrary to some denials, the offer [to coach the Eagles] had been extended to me, and the promises had been expressed. I want to say this very publicly and I want to say it in front of everybody.'"

The title team Van Brocklin led had the next-to-worst rushing attack in the NFL and played from behind almost habitually. They lost their opener 41–24, at home against the Browns, then nearly lost the next week, before squeaking past (27–25) the Dallas Cowboys, an expansion team that would go winless. The only player on the team who finished in pro football's top five in an individual statistical category was safety Don Burroughs, who managed nine interceptions.

But Van Brocklin made champions of them, achieving this alchemy at least partly through bonding that took place on Mondays at Donoghue's, a bar at Sixty-second and Walnut.

In Bob Gordon's 2001 book, *The 1960 Philadelphia Eagles*, lineman Bob Pellegrini recalls that, even after the opening loss, "Dutch kept everyone on an even keel. 'We're still going to win the championship,' he told everyone."

"It was kind of an order [to meet at Donoghue's]," said Marion Campbell, a defensive end in 1960, who was the Birds' head coach when Van Brocklin died, 23 years later. "Everyone knew he should be there. . . . That's the way Norm was. He had a strong personality."

Gordon, who experienced the 1960 title as a 12-year-old fan, acknowledged to a reviewer that he didn't know the real impetus behind the team until he began interviewing players.

"I started out thinking it was gonna be Chuck Bednarik's book," Gordon confessed. "Giant of a man, played 60 minutes, the hit on Frank Gifford, the year he had. And then I started talking to the guys. And they all went back to Van Brocklin, how it was Dutch's team, the Dutchman this, the Dutchman that.

"It manifested itself in those Monday get-togethers at Donoghue's, in giving guys like Pete Retzlaff confidence in himself. I've worked in corporations, and it seems amazing that Van Brocklin had the ability to tick people off, yet not lose their respect. That's the key right there."

In Philadelphia in recent years, fans have debated whether Van Brocklin or Donovan McNabb is the franchise's all-time best quarterback (with minority factions holding out for Ron Jaworski or Randall Cunningham). Statistically, the question is absurd: Van Brocklin only played for the Eagles his final three NFL seasons; McNabb's eleven Eagles campaigns garnered him just about every significant passing record. And even if you include his nine seasons with the Rams, Van Brocklin was a 53.6 percent passer who finished with more interceptions (178) than touchdowns (173). Van Brocklin once threw six interceptions in a 1955 Rams championship loss to the Browns.

But Van Brocklin's case is built on something McNabb never did with the Eagles, in all those stat-filled 11 seasons. The Dutchman won the franchise's most recent title. And he did it in the swashbuckling, profane style Philly fans prefer, a very different demeanor than McNabb projected.

record, it almost seemed the Birds were back to their pre–World War II haplessness. But even though results didn't immediately follow, new talent was trickling in. Hard-tackling corner Tom Brookshier, who had a fine rookie season in 1953 before being inducted into the military, finally finished his Air Force commitment and joined the Eagles for good in 1956. An obscure fullback from South Dakota State named Pete Retzlaff was claimed off waivers from the Lions, and switched to wideout, where he

became a stalwart. Late in his career he switched again, to tight end, and helped pioneer that position's transition to the offensive force it is today.

In 1957, the Eagles drafted a promising rookie quarterback, Sonny Jurgensen, along with a pair of fine rookie backs, Billy Ray Barnes and Clarence Peaks. (Actually, there were three promising rookie runners, but 5-foot-7, 172-pound Tommy McDonald, from Oklahoma, would
continued on page 48

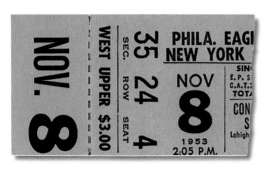

OFFICIAL PROGRAM

35¢

CONNIE MACK
STADIUM
PHILADELPHIA
NOVEMBER 8, 1953

PHILA. EAGLES vs. NEW YORK GIANTS

On November 8, 1953, The Eagles trounced the visiting Giants by a score of 30–7. Quarterback Bobby Thomason shredded the Giants' secondary, throwing two touchdowns apiece to Pete Pihos and Bobby Walston, who also added a field goal and 3 extra points to lead all scorers. *All MVP Books Collection*

Bobby Walston

END – EAGLES

Franklin Field, on the University of Pennsylvania campus, was the Eagles' new home for the 1958 season. It was familiar territory for star linebacker Chuck Bednarik, who was a three-time All American at Penn during his college days.

BUCK SHAW

BUCK SHAW WAS A LINK between the modern NFL and the game's origins, having blocked for George Gipp at Notre Dame, under Knute Rockne in the 1920s, and then having coached men such as Norm Van Brocklin and Marion Campbell, who would lead NFL teams in the 1970s and 1980s.

Rockne was Shaw's inspiration, the coach of the Eagles' 1960 championship team told the *Des Moines Register* upon his induction into the Iowa Sports Hall of Fame in 1970, seven years before he died.

"Thirteen of us graduated in 1922, and all went into coaching," said Shaw, who retired to Menlo Park, California. "This was the start of the Rockne era, and he influenced many more of his players to enter coaching."

Shaw was born on a cattle ranch in Iowa in 1899. He transferred to Notre Dame from Creighton after a flu epidemic ended Creighton's 1918 season prematurely, with the idea of competing for the Irish in track. Rockne soon convinced him to play football, where he was a tackle and kicker, who hit 38 of 39 extra points during his career.

Rockne convinced Shaw to go into coaching, as an assistant at N.C. State, Nevada, and Santa Clara before his former Notre Dame teammate, Santa Clara head coach Maurice "Clipper" Smith (how many guys could say they knew a Clipper and a Gipper?) took the head coaching job at Villanova. Shaw was named Smith's successor, and he immediately led the Broncos to extraordinary success. They were 18-1 his first two seasons and won the Sugar Bowl both years.

Santa Clara dropped football because of World War II in 1942—a prelude to dropping it for good in 1993, which helps explain why Buck Shaw Stadium today is a noted soccer venue—and Shaw stayed on the campus for a few years, working with an Army phys ed program. He then coached a year at Cal while waiting for a promised job running the San Francisco 49ers of the All-America Football Conference.

The 49ers, absorbed into the NFL in 1950, were San Francisco's first pro sports franchise, and Shaw got them off to a fine start, going 71-39-4 through 1954. Shaw spent two years starting up football at the Air Force Academy before old Notre Dame friend Vince McNally prevailed upon him to take over the Eagles.

Problem was, Shaw had already started to edge toward retirement, as part owner of a corrugated box company in Northern California. He wasn't real interested in coming to the Northeast, a region where he'd never lived. Shaw asked McNally to agree to let Shaw go home to California every year when the season was over. This was a complication, and according to the Vince Lombardi biography *When Pride Still Mattered*, it led to the Eagles offering the job

Eagles coach Buck Shaw chats with Packers coach Vince Lombardi before the 1960 NFL title game at Franklin Field. Shaw coached the Birds to a 17–13 victory. *Vernon Biever/NFL/Getty Images*

to Lombardi, then a Giants assistant. Lombardi, the book said, initially agreed but was wooed back by the Giants. McNally went back to Shaw and agreed to the offseasons in California.

A 2-9-1 first season convinced McNally and Shaw that they needed to gut the team, especially the secondary. The team went 7-5 in 1959, and defensive tackle Ed Khayat (who later would coach the Eagles) said the players could sense something special was happening.

"Big turnover in personnel between '58 and '59," Khayat recalled. "We felt we improved tremendously and we had a good chance" coming out of 1959. "We had a great coaching staff."

Shaw, as he neared the end of his career, delegated authority—Van Brocklin more or less ran the offense, and defensive coordinator Jerry Williams, a highly praised innovator, ran the defense.

"Buck kind of turned it over to Van Brocklin. 'What did Norm want to do?' We would be in practice and a storm would come up, or there would be a cloud in the sky, and he would say, 'What do you think, Norm?' He would ask him whether or not he should call practice," backup Sonny Jurgensen recalled at the fiftieth anniversary gathering of the 1960 champs.

Defensive lineman Marion Campbell, who played for Shaw in San Francisco and Philadelphia, recalled him as "just a good, calm person. We had a lot of leaders, and he was the perfect guy to oversee everything."

Continued from page 43

make his true mark after being switched to flanker, in the ninth week of the season.)

Coach Hugh Devore, who had been reluctant to try future Hall of Famer McDonald as a receiver, was fired after going a combined 7-16-1 in 1956 and 1957, to be replaced by Buck Shaw. At age 58, the former 49ers head coach was coaching the Air Force Academy and edging toward retirement when an old friend, Eagles general manager Vince McNally, convinced him to give the pros another try. "If you saw him [Shaw] on the street, you thought he was a banker," Barnes later recalled in an interview with a pro football researchers' newsletter.

The 1958 Eagles also had a new quarterback and a new home field. They acquired veteran Norm Van Brocklin from the Rams in exchange for lineman Buck Lansford, defensive back Jimmy Harris, and a first-round draft choice. Attendance doubled with the move to Penn's Franklin Field, but the Birds still went 2-9-1, losing their final four games by a combined score of 93–38. Fans weren't sure acquiring Van Brocklin, a 32-year-old five-time Pro-Bowler, was such a great move.

Shaw knew he had to make more changes.

"We were on the train coming back from Washington, they had shut us out the last game of the year, and Buck said, 'Take a look around you, boys, because you're not going to see each other. There's going to be one team coming, one team going, and one team playing,'" Brookshier recalled in a 2005 interview with the Eagles' website. "So with that, he started bringing in new players. He got Don Burroughs from the Rams, Bobby Freeman from Cleveland, Jimmy Carr from the Cardinals. That's our secondary [along with Brookshier] on the team that ended up winning it in '60.

"A lot of people thought it was about the third- or fourth-best team [in the NFL in 1960] and I can't think of a better compliment than to not be the best team and win it all. That's the reason Buck Shaw quit. He said, 'I can never duplicate this. If you're the best team and you don't win it, you ought to be ashamed.' But if you're like the third or fourth team and you win the championship, that's special. That is very special."

In 1959, Shaw started to put it together. The Birds finished 7-5, their first winning season since 1954. Van Brocklin, McDonald, and Retzlaff gave the team a solid offensive base.

"Van Brocklin was the catalyst of the whole thing, there ain't no question about that," Barnes said. "If you made a mistake on that field, you sure as heck didn't want to come back to that huddle. The quarterback is like the CEO of any company. He runs the show out there, and the more confidence that he has, the more confidence he's going to instill in everybody else. And he instilled in us that nobody could beat us."

Barnes said Shaw inspired confidence.

"Buck Shaw should have been president of a bank or a big corporation somewhere," Barnes said. "Ran a very good ship. Very gentlemanly, but if he said something, you listened. He was a very good coach."

Still, the success of 1960 would arrive quite suddenly—very much unlike the teams fielded in the 2000s, who posted winning records eight times in ten seasons, went to five conference championship games and a Super Bowl, but never won the whole thing. From 1955 through 1964, the Eagles managed just three winning seasons, but the 1960 Eagles would accomplish a feat no other Birds team has matched since: they won an NFL title.

"You would think that somebody in there, once or twice, they would have won a championship. Goodness gracious," Bednarik told the Philadelphia *Daily News* during the fiftieth anniversary celebration of the 1960 title. "But I tell you what: when I die and go to heaven, I will make sure they win one."

1950s Philadelphia Eagles
Year by Year

Year	Record	Finish
1950	6-6	3rd in NFL American Division
1951	4-8	5th in NFL American Division
1952	7-5	2nd in NFL American Division
1953	7-4-1	2nd in NFL East Division
1954	7-4-1	2nd in NFL East Division
1955	4-7-1	4th in NFL East Division
1956	3-8-1	6th in NFL East Division
1957	4-8-0	5th in NFL East Division
1958	2-9-1	5th in NFL East Division
1959	7-5	2nd in NFL East Division

Pete Retzlaff was a star wideout who later helped redefine the tight end position. He also was president of the NFL Players' Association. *NFL Photos/AP Images*

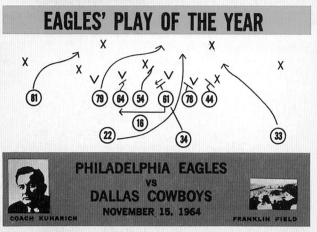

MVP Books Collection

THAT CHAMPIONSHIP SEASON

When 20 surviving members of the Eagles' 1960 NFL Championship team gathered for a fiftieth anniversary celebration at the start of the 2010 season, they were asked repeatedly how they did it. The Green Bay Packers, whom they defeated 17–13 in the December 26 championship game, were a budding dynasty; the major players were in place for the iconic Packers group that would win five titles, including the first two Super Bowls more than half a decade later, at a point when the Eagles would be back in their familiar scrambling, scrapping mode.

Just about every ex-Eagle at the reunion basked in the fact that, as McDonald noted with his customary enthusiasm, "They were supposed to win. We won!"

"We surprised 'em," running back Tim Brown recalled. "We kept winning games nobody thought we would win, and at the end of it all, we got pretty confident we could take [the Packers]."

"We came from behind during the season, every game except one, that we won," Retzlaff said. "We were behind at halftime in every game. [After all that] I was not surprised we beat Green Bay. I knew they were a strong team, but after having that many games, coming from behind to win, we were undaunted. Nobody got excited, nobody panicked."

Actually, time has gilded Retzlaff's memories—the 10–2 1960 Eagles trailed at halftime only four times in games they won. But they trailed in the second half of 6 of their 10 victories.

"The feeling of the defense was, if we just get the ball back for Dutch [Quarterback Norm Van Brocklin] and the offense, we'll win this game," defensive tackle Ed Khayat recalled. "Some people would say that we had a defense that would bend and not break, and all that, but we had 30 interceptions in a 12-game season. We forced many turnovers." Despite this, the Eagles ranked just tenth overall in total defense for the season—in a 12-team league.

"We all realized this was no dynasty," Bednarik said at the twenty-fifth anniversary reunion, in 1985. "This was a team that would have its year and that was it. Most of these guys were gone in a year or two. How we won it I'll never know."

Tommy McDonald agreed: "Alex Karras said we were the worst team ever to win an NFL title. We might not have had the greatest personnel, but I never played on a team with more heart. That's what the fans remember."

As noted earlier, the 1948 and 1949 titles put the Eagles on the Philadelphia sports map, but until the A's left in 1954, this was a city with two major league baseball teams. The move to Franklin Field, at a time when the NFL was raising its national profile—many people believe the 1958 Colts-Giants title game, won by Baltimore in overtime, was a sort of rite of passage—and the 1960 championship really sealed the deal in Philly. After 1960, the Eagles weren't always good, but they were always at the forefront of sports discussion.

"I remember walking in downtown Philly and people hollering across the street and calling you by your name," said defensive lineman J. D. Smith at the fiftieth reunion of the 1960 team. "People knew who you were in Philly wherever you went. Someone was always picking up the tab. We loved the city, and the city loved us."

The title run began with a 41–24 home loss to the Browns that was not taken well by the fans, who turned out to the then-record tune of 56,303. Hall of Famers Bobby Mitchell (156 rushing yards) and Jim Brown (153) trampled the Birds' defense.

"The headlines read, 'Here We Go Again,'" Retzlaff recalled.

Shaw was peeved enough to repeat (not for the first time, apparently) his "one team coming, one team going, one team playing" warning.

The next game came just five days later in Dallas, because the Cowboys didn't have weekend dibs on the Cotton Bowl back then. Van Brocklin threw three interceptions, for the second week in a row, but a couple of blocked extra-point kicks provided a 27–25 victory margin. It didn't hurt that Dallas QB Eddie LeBaron threw five interceptions, either.

There's no doubt that Chuck Bednarik was a fearsome gridiron warrior, but just in case, he donned the full armor of a medieval knight, along with his Eagles helmet, to prove it. *Arthur Rickerby/Diamond Images/Getty Images*

MVP Books Collection

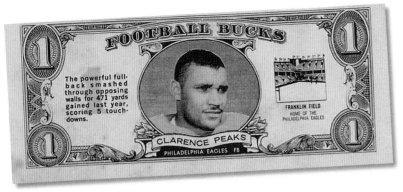

Running back Clarence Peaks was lost to injury during a 1960 victory over the Redskins, but the Eagles were fortunate to have had both Timmy Brown and Ted Dean to carry the load on their way to a championship season. *MVP Books Collection*

The next game, at home against the St. Louis Cardinals, the Eagles trailed 27–24 with less than six minutes remaining. Retzlaff caught a pass to convert a third-and-25 on what turned out to be the game-winning drive, with Van Brocklin hitting McDonald for the TD.

The Birds finally started looking like contenders the next week when they disposed of the Lions, 28–10, at Franklin Field, intercepting four passes in the process.

The next effort was seminal: a 31–29 victory over their longtime tormentors, the Browns, at Cleveland. The Eagles scored on the first play of the game but went down 22–7 in the third before scoring three touchdowns in a row. A Bobby Mitchell TD put Cleveland back on top, 29–28, but Bobby Walston, who had scored that first-play touchdown, booted a 38-yard field goal with 16 seconds left for the win.

The Birds followed that with a 34–7 pounding of the Steelers, giving them a five-game winning streak; the defense was starting to find itself.

The winning continued with a 19–13 victory over the Redskins, though running back Clarence Peaks went down for the season with a broken leg.

Nicknames like "Concrete Charlie" aren't awarded without good reason. Chuck Bednarik looks up after delivering a devastating hit on the Giants' Frank Gifford. The resulting fumble was recovered by Chuck Weber, and Gifford was out cold on the field at Yankee Stadium. He would miss the rest of the season and the entire next season as well. *NFL Photos/AP Images*

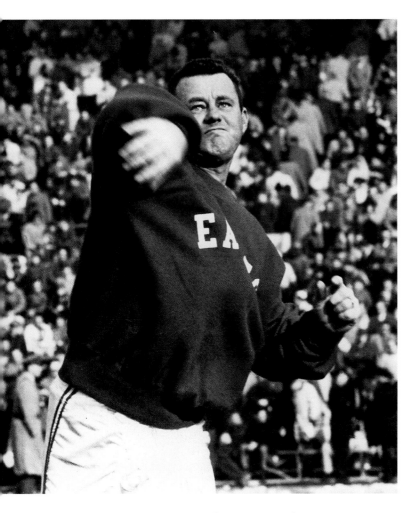

Quarterback Norm Van Brocklin tosses a few practice passes as he prepares for the biggest game of his life—the 1960 NFL Championship Game against the favored Green Bay Packers. *Vernon Biever/NFL/Getty Images*

Halfback Ted Dean runs past Packers linebacker Ray Nitschke during the 1960 NFL Championship Game. Dean played a pivotal role in the Eagles victory, returning a fourth-quarter kickoff for a big gain and capping off the drive with a five-yard touchdown run to put the Birds ahead for good. *Vernon Biever/NFL/Getty Images*

Bednarik, originally a two-way player, had decided to limit himself to center at age 35. Then linebacker Bob Pellegrini went down in the win at Cleveland, and Bednarik began playing both ways again. This adjustment led to one of the key moments in franchise history, on November 20.

The Giants were down 17–10 but were driving when star halfback Frank Gifford reached back and caught an underthrown pass. Bednarik was in his twelfth season and had played on the 1949 title team, but this moment would cement his legend. Or maybe "concrete" his legend. Bednarik hit Gifford with an explosive, concussive sound that echoed through Yankee Stadium. The ball squirted away as Gifford flopped to the turf, limp. Chuck Weber recovered the fumble for the Eagles. The photo of Bednarik exulting over Gifford's prone form has become an Eagles icon, often accompanied by Concrete Charlie's autograph.

Bednarik, not usually terribly sensitive about anything, bristled over the notion he was celebrating an injury that would cause Gifford to miss the entire 1961 NFL season.

"I didn't even know Gifford had not gotten up at the time," Bednarik told the *Inquirer* the next day. "I'm emotional. I knew we had the game won, because we had the ball. That's why I was jumping around."

A 20–6 return engagement with the Cardinals prefaced a 27–21 loss at Pittsburgh, the first since the opener and the last for the 1960 team. The Pittsburgh game was played in the snow, at Forbes Field.

"They lined the [snow-covered] field with coal dust. The referee called both coaches over and said, 'We can't see the markings. Don't argue the calls; they'll be fair, and whatever happens, happens.' That was just the way it was," linebacker Maxie Baughn recalled many years later.

Receiver Tommy McDonald is helped up out of the snow by security after scoring a touchdown in the 1960 NFL Championship Game. *NFL Photos/AP Images*

"I remember we couldn't fly home, so we took a train," defensive tackle Ed Khayat said. Khayat said once the team got back to Philadelphia, which also was snowed in, he was able to get to the hotel he stayed in at 39th and Chestnut, but he and roommate J. D. Smith had to accommodate teammates who lived in South Jersey, who couldn't drive across the bridge.

The Birds finished their regular season with a 38–28 win over the Redskins, then played the favored Packers for the championship.

"We knew we'd play Los Angeles or Green Bay in the championship game, and the people were asking which team I'd prefer," Bednarik recalled. "It sounds like a cliché, but I kept saying I didn't care, 'cause I knew we could beat either of them."

It was the day after Christmas, a Monday at noon; an odd time for a championship game, but the NFL didn't want to play on Christmas Day, and Franklin Field had

no lights. There was snow on the ground, but the day was clear, the temperature above freezing. Extra portable end zone stands allowed more than 67,000 fans to be packed into the venerable (even then) stadium.

The Eagles led 10–6 at halftime, but Green Bay took a 13–10 lead early in the fourth quarter on a seven-yard touchdown pass from Bart Starr to Max McGee.

Ted Dean ran the kickoff back 58 yards, to the Packers' 39. Dean scored the winning touchdown on a five-yard run, a play that was supposed to be a run by Billy Ray Barnes, but was changed at the line by Van Brocklin.

Nobody knows why Van Brocklin changed the play; he never said before he died in 1983. Dean has wondered if it didn't have to do with the fact that Dean was especially fired up after a rare fumble earlier in the game.

It wasn't necessarily the winning TD at the time; the Packers got three more possessions. On the final one, the clock ticking down from 12 seconds, fullback Jim

Halfback Ted Dean runs through the Packers' defense during the 1960 NFL Championship Game, as the façade of Franklin Field towers in the background. *NFL Photos/AP Images*

Taylor caught a pass and churned inside the Eagles' 10. He was met at the 9, first by Bobby Jackson, then Bednarik. Bednarik famously sat on top of Taylor until time expired, and exclaimed, "This [bleeping] game is over." In recent years, that has become the Concrete Charlie catchphrase.

"Everybody was afraid of Green Bay, but we beat 'em," Tommy McDonald recalled, on the fiftieth anniversary of the title. "What an experience! To do that was like being in the movies—a once-in-a-lifetime thing. It was the best Christmas present I ever had."

It was the only title game Vince Lombardi ever lost.

There were no victory parades in Philadelphia in those days, but the champions did celebrate.

At the fiftieth anniversary celebration, Barnes was asked what he remembered best about that day.

"About 7:30 the next morning, I was walking down Market Street, and I hadn't been to bed yet," Barnes said.

Coach Buck Shaw celebrates the championship victory with three of his stars, Bednarik, Van Brocklin, and Dean. *NFL Photos/AP Images*

TOMMY McDONALD

TOMMY MCDONALD was a man ahead of his time.

Had he played in the current era, McDonald might have changed his last name to "Veintecinco" (he wore No. 25) or exhorted fans to get their popcorn ready.

The smallest player ever inducted into the Hall of Fame, at 5-foot-9, 172 pounds, McDonald came to the Eagles from Oklahoma in 1957 as a running back but didn't flourish in the NFL until he was moved to wide receiver. He was a huge part of the Eagles' 1960 NFL championship team, leading the NFL in receiving yards that year. His career total of 84 touchdown receptions was second-highest all-time when he retired in 1968.

McDonald was a pioneer of the deep passing game, averaging almost 17 yards per catch over the span of his 495 career receptions, and an originator of the post-TD celebration. McDonald, wearing a distinctive short-sleeved uniform, frequently leaped into team-mates' arms or danced following touchdowns, things you didn't see all that much in the age of Unitas and Bednarik.

When McDonald was finally inducted into the Hall of Fame in 1998 after a tireless campaign by Hall of Fame writer Ray Didinger, he was extolled in Didinger's introductory speech as "an inspira-tion to every young person who has ever been told he wasn't fast enough or good enough. He's proof that you don't have to stand tall to stand for everything good in life as well as athletics."

McDonald's acceptance speech is worth looking up on the Eagles' website. Known for his oversized exuberance, McDonald, apparently fearing he would become too emotional giving a con-ventional speech, put on a memorable show.

Here is an excerpt from the *Inquirer*'s account: "In between his 'God almighty, I feel so good' opening and his 'Thank you, Canton, I love it' conclusion, the extra-exuberant McDonald careened around the stage like a drunken chorus girl, insulted his wife, drew a gasp from fans when he tossed his commemorative bust into the air, danced to Bee Gees music on a boom-box he had smuggled onto the podium, chest-thumped his four fellow inductees, and fell down.

"'That,' said fellow Hall of Famer Gene Upshaw, maybe only half-jokingly, after McDonald's stream-of-consciousness speech, 'is why they kept him out of here so long.'

"'That,' said former Minnesota coach Jerry Burns in his subse-quent introduction for ex-Vikings safety Paul Krause, 'is why he was with five different teams.'"

Didinger explained afterward why McDonald chose the outra-geous route in his Hall of Fame speech.

"Standing up there, remembering all that his mom and dad did for him and the fact that they couldn't be here . . . it would have been too much for him. He was afraid his emotions would get the

Hall of Famer Tommy McDonald may not have been the biggest guy on the field, but he was often the most exuberant. His nose for the end zone left him with a remarkable 84 career touchdowns, second only to Don Hutson's 99 at the time of his retirement. *MVP Books Collection*

best of him. So the only way he could avoid that was to have fun with it, let everyone have a good time. I know some people with the Hall of Fame were really nervous about it, and I'm sure they got really nervous when he picked up the bust and started tossing it in the air . . . but I guess when you've got great hands at 25, you've still got them at 60. He sure proved that today."

Didinger, a Philadelphia native, spoke of having witnessed every home game McDonald played with the Eagles.

"They were the best Sundays of my life," he said.

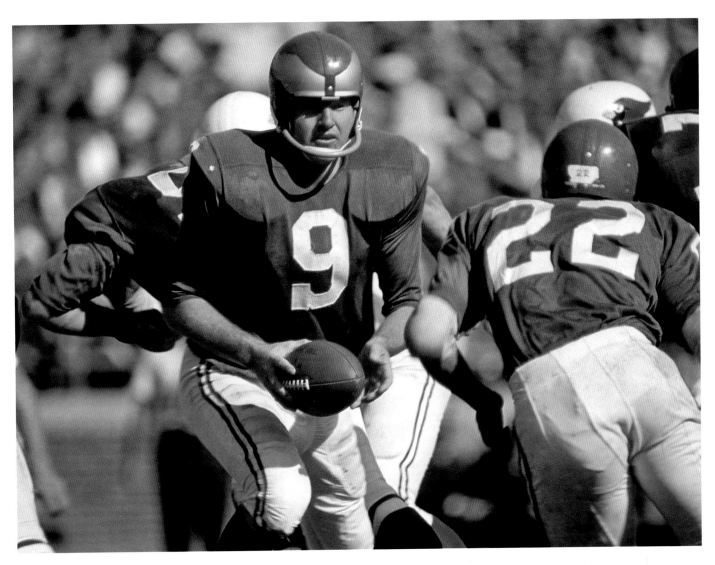

History has proven the difficulty of succeeding a highly regarded quarterback, and Norm Van Brocklin proved tough to replace. Sonny Jurgensen's time with the Eagles was plagued by injuries, and his best years in the NFL would ultimately be played in a Redskins uniform. *Focus on Sport/Getty Images*

INTO THE DARKNESS

The 1960 championship was unexpected, but maybe not as hard to foresee as what happened next: the Birds plunged into one of their darkest periods, right after going 10-4 in 1961 but managing only an appearance in the Playoff Bowl, for conference runners-up. Not only did they lose that meaningless postseason contest, 38–10 to Detroit, but quarterback Sonny Jurgensen, successor to Norm Van Brocklin, suffered a shoulder injury that would linger for the next two seasons, the last of his Eagles career. (Of course, in typical Eagles luck, after the Birds traded him to Washington in 1964, Jurgensen rebounded with 11 seasons strong enough to cement his Hall of Fame credentials.)

Some former Eagles still wonder what could have been if Jurgensen had stayed healthy. Defensive tackle Ed Khayat recalled a scene from 1961. "Chicago, they put a heavy rush on him from his throwing side. [Pete] Retzlaff was called in to pick up the blitz; they brought him in tight. They put that heavy rush on Sonny, so he just flipped the ball behind his back to Pete. It ended up being a 33-yard gain. It wasn't a 33-yard pass, but it was a 33-yard gain. He had an outstanding year, but we lost [the division] by half a game, and we had to go down and play in the Runnerup Bowl in Miami. That's where Jurgensen got hurt, J. D. Smith got hurt, Ted Dean got hurt. J.D. was supposed to go to the Pro Bowl and didn't get to go."

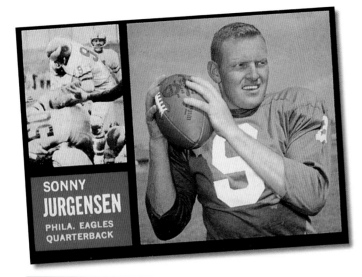

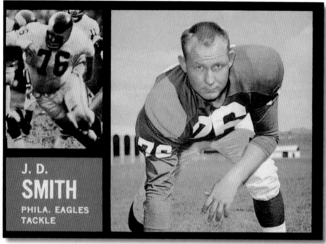

Sonny Jurgensen and J. D. Smith were two Eagles lost to injury in the meaningless "Playoff Bowl" following the 1961 season. *MVP Books Collection*

MVP Books Collection

A terrible broken leg also put an abrupt end to Tom Brookshier's career, another blow to the talent and leadership.

In the 16 years following 1961, the Eagles would put together just one winning season. That single winning campaign, in 1966, resulted in another trip to the fake playoff game between runners-up. The reasons were the usual ones that afflict losing organizations: a couple of ownership changes, uninspired drafts, and some really bad coaching hires. Joe Kuharich, the coach who traded Jurgensen in 1964, remains perhaps the most hated coaching figure in Philadelphia sports, more than 40 years after the end of his five-year, 28-41-1 reign.

The first jarring note sounded right after the 1960 title. Buck Shaw retired as expected, but Van Brocklin was surprisingly not named his successor. Team lore holds that ownership wanted Van Brocklin to serve a year as a player-coach before taking over. Van Brocklin felt he had a deal in place to coach the team, and left in a huff to coach the expansion Minnesota Vikings.

"That was his deal," Pete Retzlaff recalled at the fiftieth anniversary gathering of the 1960 team. "He was told that. What caused the change, I don't know."

Retzlaff said the planned succession was common knowledge in the locker room.

"I know that Van Brocklin, during the last part of the 1960 season, he distanced himself a little bit from some of the players, because he wasn't going to go from having drinks with you at the bar to being your head coach. He started to make that move. So it was a surprise to us that he didn't get the job, but no surprise to me that he went to Minnesota."

Stan Hochman, longtime *Daily News* sports editor and columnist, believes the hard times the Eagles experienced

The Eagles did some unpopular housecleaning in 1962, trading or releasing several experienced players. Among them was veteran offensive lineman Jess Richardson, who had been with the team since 1953. Richardson is believed to be the last offensive lineman to play without a facemask on his helmet. *MVP Books Collection*

Defensive lineman Ed Khayat talks with Browns tight end Johnny Brewer as the two walk off a foggy field after a 1965 game. Khayat was one of several veterans cut by the Eagles in 1962, though he'd return after a stint with the Redskins. *Al Messerschmidt/Getty Images*

after their 1960 title "began with reneging on the promise to Van Brocklin," who "was almost the coach under Shaw" in terms of the degree of authority he wielded over the offense.

A couple of decades later, when Dick Vermeil brought the Eagles back to championship contention, he invited Bednarik to spend time around his team, as a sort of talisman. Inevitably, reporters would ask for comparisons.

"Our secret wasn't in coaching, it was in Norm Van Brocklin," Bednarik told the *Daily News*. "When Dutch retired after the championship year, I knew the team was goin' downhill. I knew we were done without him.

"He's the most knowledgeable guy I ever played with. He's the reason the Eagles were a one-shot team. If he had stayed on, we'd have been in contention for two, three more years. We had a lot of good players, especially guys who were dying to get on the special teams, do whatever was necessary. But Dutch was the one that made it all go."

In 1962, their second season under coach Nick Skorich, the Birds went 3-10-1. Seven prominent offensive players suffered serious injuries, including an amazing trifecta of receivers—Retzlaff, Bobby Walston, and Dick Lucas all suffered broken arms. The low point was a November 11 49–0 loss to the Packers at Franklin Field, less than 23 months after the Birds' 1960 Championship Game victory there over the Pack. This time Green Bay rolled up 628 yards of total offense and 37 first downs.

"In 1962, they got rid of a lot of guys," recalled Khayat, who was one of those guys, getting traded to the Redskins

Timmy Brown set an NFL record in 1963, single-handedly racking up 2,346 yards of total offense. *MVP Books Collection*

(although he eventually returned). "[Billy Ray] Barnes was gone, Bobby Freeman, Bob Pellegrini. They cut Jesse Richardson, cut Will Renfro."

The next season featured more key injuries and more disappointment. The Eagles went 2-10-2, and didn't win after October 13, going 0-8-1 in their final nine games. As usual in such situations, there was a valiant warrior who persevered through the futility—Timmy Brown set an NFL record for total offense in a season, 2,346 yards. Forty years later, when Sylvester Stallone was the surprise featured guest for the opening of Lincoln Financial Field, he wore a No. 22 Eagles jersey, explaining that it was not in honor of Duce Staley, the popular No. 22 of that era. It was Stallone's homage to his childhood hero, Brown.

In retrospect, Brown said the special atmosphere that led to a team winning a championship as an underdog deteriorated rapidly, once a few key figures left.

"That camaraderie and getting together as one—you can have all the individual stars in the world, but when you get the team working together, playing together, going out and having fun together—we ate together—it was like a special thing. We didn't have that after [1960]. It became like we just had to go out and do the best we could individually, because the camaraderie wasn't there, and the owners weren't keeping everything like it should have been. Coaches changed; everyone wants to prove their own [way of doing things] is right. [Players] are the last ones that have any choices."

TRADER JOE

Kuharich came aboard in 1964, courtesy of new owner Jerry Wolman, and immediately started trading away key pieces, most notably Jurgensen and McDonald. Kuharich's explanation for the straight-up quarterback trade with Washington, Jurgensen for the less impressive Norm Snead, didn't explain much.

"Trading quarterbacks is rare, but not uncommon," he said. Presumably, he meant "not unheard of."

A couple of decades later, Philadelphia *Daily News* columnist Jack McKinney offered this assessment: "What

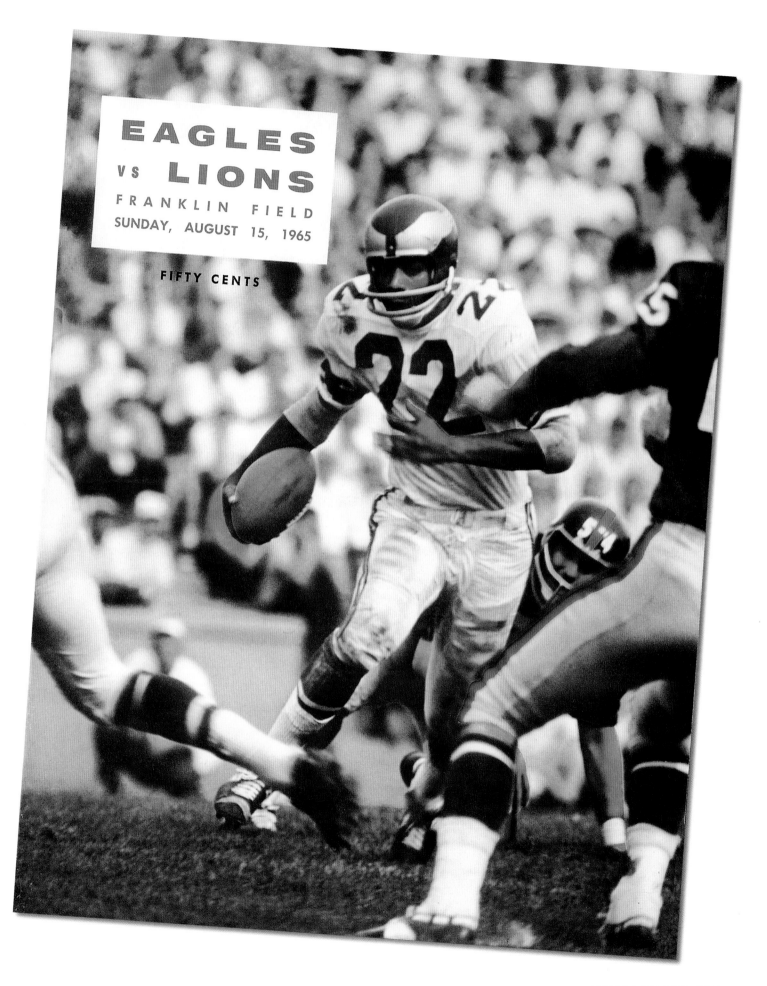

EAGLES
VS LIONS
FRANKLIN FIELD
SUNDAY, AUGUST 15, 1965

FIFTY CENTS

PETE RETZLAFF

NOBODY IN NFL history made an impact in more areas of the sport than Pete Retzlaff. He was a running back, wideout, and tight end for the Eagles, playing 11 seasons, making five Pro Bowls, and serving as an early president of the NFL Players' Association. After his playing days he worked in Philadelphia radio and TV broadcasting, and he was the team's general manager from 1969 to 1972.

Retzlaff never caught a pass at South Dakota State, but he did rush for 1,000 yards in 1951. He was drafted by the Lions but went into the army. Sold to the Eagles two years later, he felt his career really blossomed when the team acquired quarterback Norm Van Brocklin in 1958. In their first year together, Retzlaff had 56 receptions, good enough to tie the Colts' Raymond Berry for the league lead.

"I'll just give you an example of the stature he held on our team," Retzlaff said, when asked about his partnership with Van Brocklin. "When we were in training camp, coach Buck Shaw would put a new play up on the blackboard. When he finished explaining why it was there, what we were supposed to do, he would turn to Van Brocklin, sitting down with the rest of us, and say, 'Is that OK with you, Dutch?'"

Although Tommy McDonald was the most colorful receiver on the 1960 championship team, Retzlaff led the Eagles with 46 catches for 826 yards, good for 18 yards per catch.

In recent years, since Van Brocklin's passing, Retzlaff has become the unofficial spokesman for the 1960 team. Still sharp and polished as a public speaker, he's the guy the current management invites to say a few words whenever the champs are honored.

At such a function during the fiftieth anniversary celebration in 2010, Retzlaff said: "I think that was the season where the love affair between the fans and the Philadelphia Eagles got started."

Retzlaff recalled a specific moment he felt was a turning point for the team, an October 23 victory in Cleveland that avenged an opening-game loss at home.

"Bobby Walston kicked a field goal in the last minute, and we won it 31–29," Retzlaff recalled. "We went on to win nine straight games [four after Cleveland]. And when we came back from St. Louis [December 4] . . . [t]here were 15,000 people at the airport to greet us when we came home. . . .They surrounded that plane, and we weren't sure how we were going to get off."

Retzlaff takes pride in the fact that the 1960 Eagles produced three NFL GMs and 11 NFL head coaches.

"It was a great team. We developed a very close social bond, which still exists today," he said.

Retzlaff moved to tight end late in his career, in 1964. Along with Mike Ditka and John Mackey, he helped redefine that position. Had

Pete Retzlaff teamed up with Tommy McDonald to form a dangerous receiving duo for the Eagles in the early 1960s. Later in his career, he transitioned to tight end, and his impact on that position is still seen in today's game. *NFL Photos/AP Images*

he not retired following the 1966 season, he probably would be in the Pro Football Hall of Fame. The Eagles retired his No. 44; when he took it off, he had just about every Eagles receiving record, including catches (452), yards, (7,412), catches in a season (66), and yards in a season (1,190).

Though beloved as a player, Retzlaff was not a success as the Eagles' GM, having had no real training for the job.

Jurgensen did to the Eagles the first time Kuharich took them down to D.C. was not destined to be uncommon, either. The redhead was like a mouse eyeing Swiss cheese when he beheld a secondary that Kuharich had perforated by trading All Pro Irv Cross to the Rams for a gun-shy stiff named Aaron Martin.

"Sonny explored the holes in the cheese with five touchdown passes. And when it was over, Kuharich said he'd still take Snead over Jurgensen '99 times out of 99 times. Absolutely.'"

The team lost that day, 35–20, and ultimately went 6-8, which somehow inspired Wolman to give Kuharich a 15-year contract, even more unheard-of then than it would be today. It has long been rumored that Wolman's ardor for Kuharich was inspired by then–NFL commissioner Pete Rozelle, who had worked with Kuharich at the University of San Francisco and considered him a friend.

The Eagles went 5-9 in 1965, despite Retzlaff's 66 catches for 1,190 yards and 10 TDs at tight end. How many tight ends ever averaged 18 yards per catch? But the defense gave up 28 points or more five times, even if it did intercept nine passes in a game against the Steelers.

In 1966, the Birds somehow went 9-5 and returned to the Playoff Bowl, though Kuharich kept juggling QBs

MVP Books Collection

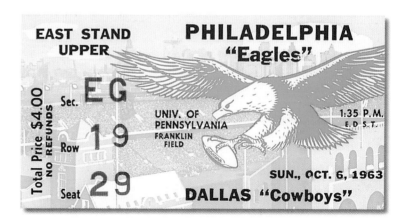

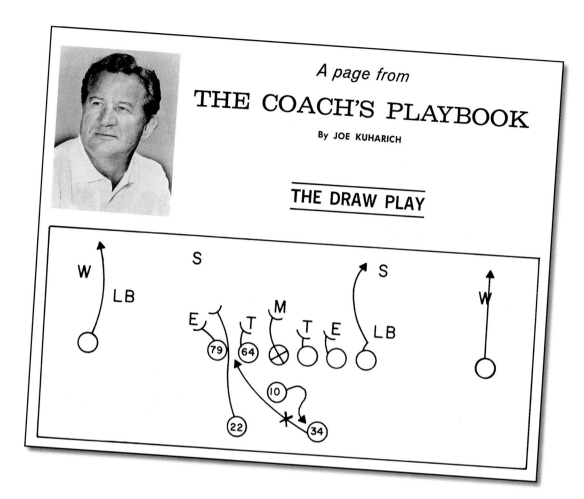

A diagram of Coach Kuharich's draw play, as featured in a game program from 1966. *MVP Books Collection*

A page from
THE COACH'S PLAYBOOK
By JOE KUHARICH

THE DRAW PLAY

Snead, King Hill, and Jack Concannon. Concannon was a better runner than passer, gaining 195 yards on 25 carries and completing 21 of 51 passes for 262 yards, one touchdown, and four picks.

The next season was back to more familiar futility, again largely because of the defense (409 points allowed in 14 games). The Eagles went 6-7-1, winning just 3 of their last 10. Wideout Ben Hawkins caught 59 passes for 1,265 yards—a lot of yards in a 14-game season—but only twice all year did an Eagles opponent score less than 21 points.

JOE MUST GO

It was 1968 when the popular revolt against Kuharich really erupted. An 0-11 start does tend to make folks testy. Someone hired a plane to trail a "Joe Must Go" banner over Franklin Field. The popular slogan spread via buttons. Tight end Mike Ditka, who later would do something Kuharich never came close to doing as a coach—winning the Super Bowl with the Bears—was suspended for telling a banquet audience the team lacked discipline.

Late in the year, it appeared the Eagles might just be bad enough to earn the first pick in the next year's draft and a chance to sign O.J. Simpson, the Heisman Trophy winner from USC. As luck would have it, they won two of their last three games, and that pick went to the Buffalo Bills. Instead, Philly ended up with Leroy Keyes, a running back from Purdue. Keyes eventually made the National Collegiate Hall of Fame and was voted Purdue's top player ever in 1987 (well before Drew Brees), but he was not a great pro, especially after suffering a ruptured Achilles tendon near the end of his rookie season. Keyes wound up being moved to safety, left the Eagles in 1972, and was out of the NFL a year later.

"If I was a horse, I'd have been shot, so it could have been worse," Keyes said, recalling his injury for the book *Eagles: Where Have You Gone?* by Fran Ziminuch. "Sometimes I sit in the dark and wonder what might have happened had I not gotten hurt. But I'm very thankful. Only a few people get to play in the National Football League.

"I did the best I could. I tried and didn't quit. I played hurt and I ruptured my Achilles tendon two times. I hope my teammates appreciate what I tried to do, to be a team player who didn't make waves, and I tried to be a good force in the community.

"I'm not ashamed of my five years in the NFL. A long career wasn't meant to be. But I left some skin and blood on the field."

Keyes spent 17 years working with Philadelphia schools and now is a fund-raiser for Purdue. You'd have to say his post-football career has turned out better than Simpson's, anyway.

SNOWBALLS FOR SANTA

December 15, 1968. A lot has been written about the events that took place at Franklin Field on this day, and though it wouldn't be exactly right to call it "urban legend"—those are myths, apocryphal stories that are widely repeated—the accounts aren't always totally accurate, either. It's true, Eagles fans really did pelt Santa Claus with snowballs. But it wasn't quite the "these people will boo anything" cautionary tale it has grown into. Over the years, the incident has repeatedly been referenced during network broadcasts from Philadelphia, almost as often as cheesesteaks, Ben Franklin, and *Rocky*.

The real story is this: On December 15, 1968, the Eagles closed the books on a 2-12 season with a 24–17 loss to the visiting Minnesota Vikings at Franklin Field. They had gained those two victories the previous two weeks, against the Lions and Saints, knocking themselves out of the top position for the 1969 draft, spoiling their chance at bringing phenom O.J. Simpson to the city of brotherly love.

There was a winter storm, and fans were unhappy. One of them, 19-year-old Frank Olivo, had worn a Santa suit to the game, as a lark. He arrived early and ran into an Eagles marketing guy named Bill Mullen, who was upset. There was supposed to be a Santa appearance at halftime, but the designated Santa couldn't make it in from Atlantic City because of the storm. Mullen asked Olivo—thin at the time, with no extra padding in his suit—if he would step in. Olivo agreed.

Alas, the skinny Santa parading along the Franklin Field track bore the brunt of a fan rebellion that was initially focused on head coach Joe Kuharich as he left the field at halftime.

Today, Eagles fans still dress up as Santa Claus to playfully honor one of the stranger moments in team lore. *Doug Pensinger/Getty Images*

Olivo has become something of a local celebrity over the years; in 2003, the Sixers tried to get into the *Guinness Book of Records* for having the most people dressed as Santa, at a December 22 game against Orlando. Olivo was a special guest, 35 years after his moment of fame.

Interviewed at his Sixers appearance, where fans mock-booed but had nothing handy to throw, Olivo recalled having been hit by 100 to 150 snowballs.

"I got hammered," he told the Philadelphia *Daily News*. "They were on top of you at Franklin Field. I was carrying an equipment bag they gave me as a Santa bag. And as I was walking back, I actually watched a guy, in the third or fourth row, making a snowball to throw it at me. We made eye contact. And I still couldn't get out of the way of it. I told him he wasn't getting anything for Christmas."

Eagles guard Jim Skaggs leads the way for Hall of Famer Ollie Matson during a muddy game against San Francisco in 1966. *Frank Rippon/NFL/Getty Images*

Pictured on the cover of a 1966 game program, the Eagles defense, including John Meyers, Al Nelson, and Floyd Peters, works together to wrap up Giants QB Earl Morrall. *MVP Books Collection*

Olivo wanted to stress something that still gets lost in the use of his experience to reinforce the theory that Philadelphia fans are horrible people. He said the folks throwing the snowballs weren't doing it maliciously; they thought they were being funny. They were displeased by the Eagles and saw the skinny Santa as an excuse to vent.

"It was humor," he said. "And I took it humorously. The team stunk. As I remember, someone climbed up the flagpole and turned the Eagles flag upside down. They were angry because the Eagles were so bad."

Olivo also disclosed that when he staggered to safety in the tunnel, Mullen asked him if he would be Santa the next year, as well.

"I remember I said, 'I don't think so, because if it don't snow next year, they may throw beer bottles at me.'"

Like many Philly fans, Olivo has grown tired of hearing the snowball tossing casually referenced by people who don't know what happened and aren't from Philadelphia. In 2009, he dressed in the suit at an Eagles game and took pictures with fellow fans who knew of his legend. Olivo told the *Daily News*: "It was cool to hear it back then when it went national and Howard Cosell is saying your name on TV, but today when you hear it [on a broadcast], it's like, 'Shut up already.'"

MAKING AN EXIT

Mercifully for the fans, Wolman ran into money problems because of trouble with a Chicago skyscraper project. Shortly after the 1969 draft, he lost control of the Eagles and of the Spectrum, which he'd opened in 1967 to house Philadelphia's NHL expansion team, the Flyers, as well as the 76ers of the NBA. Former Eagles official Ed Snider took a leading role with the Flyers, while new Eagles owner Leonard Tose fired Kuharich and hired Jerry Williams.

Williams's experience running the Birds' defense for Buck Shaw in the 1960 championship season proved he knew how to win, but Tose gave him very little to work with, and he went 7-22-2 before being fired after an 0-3 start in 1971.

Although many were happy to see Kuharich go, the one Eagle who seemed to really love Joe Kuharich was future Hall of Fame offensive tackle Bob Brown, one of the most celebrated blockers in NFL history. Unfortunately, Brown demanded a trade after Kuharich's dismissal and was quickly dealt to the Raiders.

"He was the most dominant offensive tackle I've ever seen," newspaperman Hochman recalled. "Third-and-1, the entire stadium knew they were going to his side. They'd get it anyway."

After Brown was inducted into the Hall in 2004, the Eagles honored him at a preseason game. "I think sometimes old guys like to talk about how great old guys were. I believe that I was very competitive when I was working," Brown said. "I believed that I could block anything that was born from a woman, walked upright, and called himself a man."

Coach Joe Kuharich talks things over at training camp with Harry Jones, the Eagles' top draft pick in 1967, and tight end Mike Ditka. *Paul Vathis/AP Images*

Bob Brown was a monstrous, dominant offensive lineman who felt there was no one he couldn't block—and most of the time, he was right. *Tony Tomsic/NFL/Getty Images*

The Eagles' Victory Song

Words and Music by,
CHARLES BORRELLI, ROGER COURTLAND

Fight, Ea-gles Fight,—On your way to vic-to-ry,—
Fight, Ea-gles Fight,—Score a touch-down, One,—Two,—Three.—Hit 'em
—Hit 'em high,—Let us see our Ea-gles fly.—Come on and
—Ea-gles Fight,—On your way to vic-to-ry.—

MVP Books Collection

Hit 'em low, hit 'em high, let us see our Eagles fly! *MVP Books Collection*

Brown added, "When Joe Kuharich was fired, I kind of protested at the time and asked to be traded. I didn't think it was fair that he took all the blame because we had some veteran players—myself included—who should have stepped up and shown more leadership. I didn't support the firing."

Kuharich, who became an NFL supervisor of officials, died at age 63 in Philadelphia's Graduate Hospital while the Birds were playing in their first Super Bowl, on January 25, 1981. He had sent his best wishes to the Eagles a week or so earlier, calling them a "team of destiny." Head coach Dick Vermeil had employed Kuharich as a special consultant.

At Kuharich's funeral, Pete Retzlaff recalled the "Joe Must Go" days.

"He never let it affect his rapport with the team. He put it in its proper perspective. He had an admirable set of values and didn't compromise them in the face of adversity," Retzlaff said. "That's one of the things I learned from him. I'll remember him as a highly principled man."

1960s Philadelphia Eagles
Year by Year

Year	Record	Finish
1960	10–2	1st in NFL East Division, 1960 NFL Champions
1961	10–4	2nd in NFL East Division
1962	3–10–1	7th in NFL East Division
1963	2–10–2	7th in NFL East Division
1964	6–8	3rd in NFL East Division
1965	5–9	5th in NFL East Division
1966	9–5	2nd in NFL East Division
1967	6–7–1	2nd in NFL Capitol Division
1968	2–12	4th in NFL Capitol Division
1969	4–9–1	4th in NFL Capitol Division

5 LIGHT AT THE END OF A LONNNG TUNNEL

The 1970s

MVP Books Collection

THE COLLECTIVE FEELING among the Eagles' fan base is that almost every decade has been an incredibly frustrating time to be a Birds fan, but the 1970s were especially tough.

The team went 3-10-1 in 1970 in their second season under head coach Jerry Williams and owner Leonard Tose. Losing the first seven games of the season kind of dampened expectations. The highlight of the season might have been winning the first Monday Night Football game in franchise history, 23–20 over the Giants.

While few fans probably remember the details of that game or even the season, almost everyone has heard the story of how Howard Cosell left the broadcast at halftime. Local legend holds that Cosell had been drinking quite a bit to ward off the intense cold in the open-air broadcast booth. Another version of the story maintains that he had complained of flu-like symptoms. Whatever the case may have been, as the book *Monday Night Mayhem* recounts, Cosell tossed his cookies on Don Meredith's cowboy boots and was not heard from again that night.

That sort of thing defined the first half of the decade for the Eagles—oddities and footnotes. Just about the only Eagle who got a lot of national attention was defensive end/linebacker Tim Rossovich, who ate glass and set himself on fire for fun.

In a September 20, 1971, profile in *Sports Illustrated*, NFL Films president Steve Sabol (a friend and contemporary of Rossovich), said: "When the organ grinder goes, he goes. He'll do anything. He puts things in his mouth I wouldn't put in my hand. He was going to have a footrace with this guy. To get ready he drank a quart of motor oil. I didn't see it, but it must have been awful. He likes to 'hang out.' We do that a lot around Philadelphia, hang out. We were hanging out at Rittenhouse Square, where they were having a concert. He saw this big box a guy had taken a tuba out of. He dragged it out into the middle of Walnut Street, crawled inside, and curled up. People stopped and

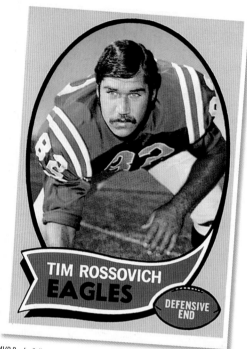

TIM ROSSOVICH
EAGLES

DEFENSIVE
END

Above: The eccentric Tim Rossovich didn't last long as an Eagle, but he was entertaining for almost every minute of his tenure. Fittingly, he went on to a career in acting after leaving the NFL after the 1976 season.

A trifecta of Philly sports venues, circa April 1971: the newly built Veterans Stadium in the foreground, and The Spectrum and JFK Stadium behind it. *AP Images*

HAROLD CARMICHAEL

WHEN HAROLD CARMICHAEL arrived in the seventh round of the 1971 draft from Southern University, the assumption was that he had to be a tight end. There were no 6-foot-8, 225-pound wide receivers in the NFL at that time. Of course, there were no 6-foot-8, 225-pound tight ends either, but that notion seemed less ridiculous in an era when men six inches shorter were considered big wideouts.

Head coach Jerry Williams started Carmichael out at tight end, and it was apparent, with Carmichael's basketball physique, that he lacked the physicality for that position; in fact, Carmichael quickly suffered a knee injury that ended his rookie season.

In 1973, Carmichael was moved to wide receiver and his career really got going as part of the "Fire-High Gang," along with 6-foot-5 Charles Young and 6-foot-4 Don Zimmerman, catching passes from Roman Gabriel, who was rejuvenated after coming over to the Eagles from the Rams. Carmichael led the NFL in 1973 with a then team record 67 catches for 1,116 yards.

The next few years weren't as good; Gabriel never recaptured his 1973 magic. Carmichael didn't start playing to his potential again until after Dick Vermeil began the Eagles' turnaround and Ron Jaworski took over as the starting quarterback in 1977.

In 1978, Carmichael caught 55 passes for 1,072 yards, and the Eagles produced a winning record for the first time in the 1970s. The next year he scored 11 touchdowns.

After a 1979 playoff win over Chicago, receivers coach Dick Coury said of Carmichael: "Harold is a real pro. You talk about all the things that go into being a superstar, he's got 'em. A tremendously gifted athlete. He is so big, so graceful.

"What he is, is a big, graceful basketball player playing football."

Vermeil observed that Carmichael sometimes was too harsh on himself, would brood when he played badly.

Asked by reporters about that observation, Carmichael said: "I am a team player. I don't want to let 'em down. I pride myself in doing what I have to do, the way the coaches want it done. I can't help being like that."

Carmichael started a team record 162 games in a row from 1972 through 1983, the streak ending only when the team released him. Carmichael signed with the Jets, was cut, and ended up with Dallas, where he played in only two games and caught one pass before retiring.

"I love Philadelphia," Carmichael said at his teary-eyed retirement press conference in June 1985. "The people here are the nicest and warmest in the world. . . . The fans are the greatest and the most knowledgeable."

Focus on Sport/Getty Images

Actually, as the biggest and sometimes most prominent Eagle, Carmichael was a target of boos in the mid-1970s, when fans were frustrated by a wretched team that was going nowhere.

"Nobody likes to be booed," Carmichael said that day. "I didn't like it, it hurt me. But I always tried my best. The best thing that could have happened was Dick [Vermeil] came in and built my confidence back up."

One tangible thing Vermeil did was tell Carmichael to cut out his trademark "dice-roll" touchdown celebration, which today seems pretty tame.

"I guess that's OK when you win," Carmichael said, "but we weren't winning, so I cut it out. After that, I just handed the ball to the referee and pointed into the stands to [agent] Jim Solano. Just my way of saying thanks for everything."

Carmichael caught at least one pass in a 127 successive games, an NFL record at the time.

looked in. 'How are you?' he said. 'I'm Tim Rossovich.' 'What are you doing in there, Tim?' 'Well, we had a tough practice today and I'm relaxing.'"

The 1971 season was Rossovich's last with the Eagles. It was also the inaugural season at Veterans Stadium, the first brand-new facility the team had ever played in. Although the building's unforgiving artificial surface would become infamous in a sport where what you land on matters, everyone was thrilled initially. The Eagles even went 6-7-1, rousing a faint glimmer of hope, though they were beaten 42–7 by Dallas in their first game there. In fact, they started out 0-5, getting Williams fired three games in, in favor of assistant coach and former Eagles defensive tackle Ed Khayat. Khayat had played on the 1960 championship team, with Williams as his coordinator.

CRACKING DOWN ON FUN

Oddly for a former player who hadn't been off the field that long, at 36, Khayat was a disciplinarian with little feel for the era. His strict rules on things like hair length bothered the team's free-spirited players, who also tended to be its *better* players. Training camp in 1972 got off to a bad start, with Rossovich and safety Bill Bradley—another of the franchise's all-time greats—holding out, basically to be nonconformists. The team ended the impasse by trading Rossovich to San Diego for a first-round draft pick.

Today, Khayat emphasizes that those differences are long past, and he isn't really interested in analyzing them.

"Bradley was an outstanding player, really smart," Khayat said. Bradley played in the Pro Bowl three times. "I see Bradley now and then, at the Senior Bowl and things like that. . . . He's been an outstanding coach."

Khayat acknowledges that he was really an emergency coach. When the team went 6-2-1 down the stretch, he got another year.

"It was not like the first one," Khayat said.

The Eagles managed another 0-5 start in 1972, but this time Tose waited until the season was over to fire his coach. Pete Retzlaff, the elegant receiving legend who had ascended to the general manager's spot when Tose bought the team (despite the fact that he had no personnel background),

Bill Bradley was a jack of all trades—he led the league in interceptions in back-to-back years while playing safety for the Birds, and he punted and returned kicks as well. *Ed Mahan/NFL/Getty Images*

HAIG | **PHILADELPHIA EAGLES** 1971 SCHEDULE

SEPT. 19	CINCINNATI BENGALS
SEPT. 26	DALLAS COWBOYS
OCT. 3	SAN FRANCISCO 49'ERS
OCT. 10	MINNESOTA VIKINGS
OCT. 17	OAKLAND RAIDERS
OCT. 24	NEW YORK GIANTS
OCT. 31	DENVER BRONCOS
NOV. 7	WASHINGTON REDSKINS
NOV. 14	DALLAS COWBOYS
NOV. 21	ST. LOUIS CARDINALS
NOV. 28	WASHINGTON REDSKINS
DEC. 5	DETROIT LIONS
DEC. 12	ST. LOUIS CARDINALS
DEC. 19	NEW YORK GIANTS

HOME GAMES IN BLACK   *NIGHT GAMES

HAIG THE OLDEST NAME IN SCOTCH
BLENDED SCOTCH WHISKEY. 86 PROOF. RENFIELD IMPORTERS, LTD., N.Y.

MVP Books Collection

Running back Tom Sullivan powers his way through a muddy scrum to find the end zone in a 1974 game against the Giants. *Ed Mahan/NFL/Getty Images*

resigned as the Eagles finished 2-11-1, going winless at home (0-6-1).

The next year was the one in which O.J. Simpson—the back the Eagles couldn't draft because they won two meaningless games in 1968—rushed for a record 2,003 yards as a Buffalo Bill. The Birds' top rusher was the less-celebrated Tom Sullivan, who gained 968 yards on 217 carries, a solid 4.5 yards per carry. His team went 5-8-1, though, under first-year coach Mike McCormack.

McCormack was a coaching disciple of the Rams' and Redskins' George Allen, and he went the Allen route, trading draft picks for veterans. Alas, Allen was a unique coach, one of very few who has ever won in the NFL by eschewing young talent. The tried-and-true way to win in the league, then as now, is largely through drafting and developing good players.

EVERYTHING OLD IS NEW

Quarterback Roman Gabriel, linebacker Bill Bergey, and running back Norm Bulaich were among the veterans in green jerseys over the next few years. The Birds went 5-8-1 in 1973—which looked like progress considering their recent performances—and they beat Dallas twice, after not having done so at all since 1967. Wideout Harold Carmichael, who'd managed not to get traded for a veteran player, led the NFL with 67 catches for 1,116 yards and nine touchdowns. Carmichael, at 6-foot-8, 225 pounds, got off to a slow start in his career because everyone assumed a guy that size had to be a tight end. Carmichael was a better fit at wideout, as incongruous as that seemed, especially at the time. Khayat, the coach when Carmichael was drafted in the seventh round from Southern, recalled that he was billed as a defensive back/wideout.

BILL BERGEY

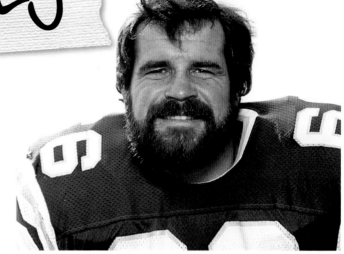

NFL Photos/AP Images

BILL BERGEY MIGHT HAVE BEEN the best middle linebacker in the NFL in the mid-1970s. Unfortunately, the Eagles weren't the NFL's best team then, or anything close to it.

Bergey arrived from the Cincinnati Bengals in a 1974 trade. Unhappy with the Bengals, Bergey attempted to jump to the World Football League, and the team sent him to Philadelphia in exchange for two first-round picks and a second-round pick. He was huge for his time, 6-foot-2, 245 (and as much as 260 later in his career), but agile, able to roam the field making plays. Bergey made four Pro Bowls for the Eagles, but was running on fumes in 1980 when the Birds finally went on a Super Bowl run.

Bergey was never the same after a devastating 1979 knee injury. His last game that counted, it turned out, was Super Bowl XV, though Bergey didn't officially retire until the spring of 1982. He went through training camp in 1981, then went on injured reserve, got second opinions, but had to finally acknowledge he was done at age 37.

"The week before the Super Bowl, I kept ice on it all the time," Bergey said afterward. "I kept thinking, 'Just one more [game], that's all. Give me this one more.' I tried to be upbeat, but it was hard. I was playing at about 65 percent. I couldn't even walk after the [NFC Championship Game]. There was so much fluid built up in my knee that when the doctor stuck his needle in there, he didn't even have to draw the fluid out; it just started gushing into the needle, filling it up."

Dick Vermeil said, "The fact that [Bergey] was so gifted allowed him to play a year on it." In other words, Bergey could get by with reduced mobility for a while because he was so good.

Marion Campbell, defensive end on the 1960 championship team, was the Eagles' defensive coordinator when Bergey retired.

"I wish we had more of this kind of people," Campbell said. "If we did, I know we would be able to get to the ultimate and win the Super Bowl. Sometime when I sit down and write my all-time NFL team, this guy is going to be the captain."

The injury happened in the Superdome, against the Saints, breaking Bergey's string of 75 successive Eagles starts and teaching him he wasn't invulnerable after all. He'd seemed that way to team-mates, and even to himself.

"I feel like I've got a knack to roll with a play. I can almost act like a drunk and go limp. Instead of fighting a hit, I roll with it," Bergey told Gary Smith of the *Daily News*, from his hospital bed after sur-gery. "But this time I had my feet planted in the turf. Conrad Dobler hit me up high, a clean shot, but I couldn't pick my foot up off the turf. It was locked. AstroTurf is a filthy, terrible thing to play on."

Bergey had arrived with a bang, notching 18 tackles in his first regular-season game at Veterans Stadium, a Monday night affair

Bill Bergey was a warrior of a linebacker for the Eagles in the 1970s. His tough-as-nails dedication to the team made him a fan favorite at Veterans Stadium

Focus on Sport/Getty Images

against the Cowboys in which he thrilled fans by drilling running back Doug Dennison and causing a fumble. Eagles corner Joe Lavender picked the ball up and ran 96 yards for a touchdown in a 13–10 Eagles victory.

The year after the knee injury, Bergey played in the opener, September 8, 1980, against the Broncos. When he sacked Denver quarterback Matt Robinson, the crowd at the Vet began chanting "Ber-gey! Ber-gey!"

"All of a sudden the place just lit up," said Jerry Robinson, who was to replace Bergey as the team's dominant linebacking force, after the game. "Down on the field you could sense how genuine the feeling was. The fans know what he's done, what he means to the team. They really like him."

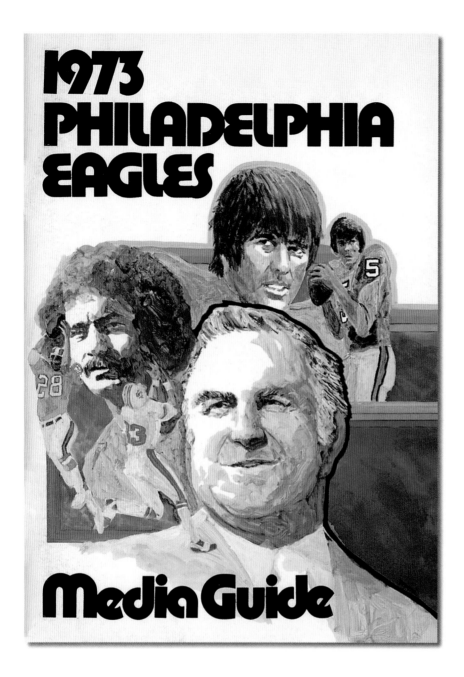

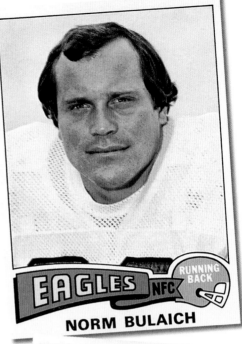

NORM BULAICH

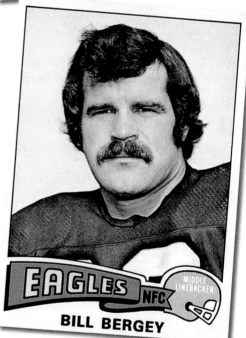

BILL BERGEY

Bill Bergey and Norm Bulaich provided veteran leadership for the Eagles in the mid-1970s. *All MVP Books Collection*

In 1974, the Eagles won four of their first five games, with Bergey leading an improved defense. Six successive losses dampened the enthusiasm there, and the team finished 7-7. Gabriel angered some teammates by reporting to training camp during a preseason players' strike. Gabriel said he had always been a slow starter and needed the extra time.

Any thoughts that McCormack might be building something were erased when his team lost seven of its first eight in 1975. A 4-10 season ended his tenure, bringing on Dick Vermeil and, eventually, a long-anticipated return to winning.

"We were never the same team after that strike," McCormack said after his dismissal. "It left a wound that never healed."

You could tell right away that Vermeil, hired from a successful tenure at UCLA, was young and intense. "His glare would set your eyebrows on fire," Tom Cushman

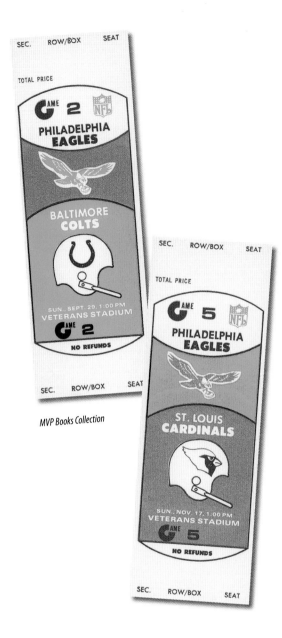

MVP Books Collection

Quarterback Roman Gabriel's valuable veteran presence was diminished when he crossed the picket lines during the 1974 players' strike. After that, he had mud on his face—literally. *Ed Mahan/NFL/Getty Images*

wrote in the Philadelphia *Daily News*. You couldn't tell right away that he was going to get better results. The Eagles went 4-10 in 1976 and 5-9 in 1977, but 1977 marked the arrival of quarterback Ron Jaworski to replace Gabriel, who retired following his sixteenth NFL season.

In Jaworski, Vermeil had a kindred spirit, an over-sized personality with corresponding oversized drive and intensity.

"Actually," Jaworski once told a *Philadelphia Inquirer* reporter, "it's not so much that I love to win. I just hate to lose."

Jim Murray, general manager at the time, later declared the acquisition of Jaworski, available after the Rams

decided to go with Pat Haden at QB, "a turning point for this franchise."

"We've tinkered around at different times with psychology tests for players, trying to judge a specific type of personality," Murray said. "But with Ron, we didn't bother with that. All we had to do was look in his eyes."

Murray's sentiment eventually found agreement with Norm Van Brocklin, who was interviewed by *Daily News* columnist Jack McKinney after Jaworski became the first Eagles QB since the Dutchman to lead the Birds to an NFL title game.

"I like Ron Jaworski," Van Brocklin said. "When Vermeil got Jaworski, I think that was the turning point

Dick Vermeil brought inspiration, youth, and exuberance back to an Eagles team that was in desperate need of all three. *MVP Books Collection*

Known as "the Polish Rifle," Ron Jaworksi is one of only two Eagles quarterbacks to lead his team to the Super Bowl. *Focus on Sport/ Getty Images*

for the franchise. You've got to have that quarterback. Jaworski is a great competitor and a real good pure passer. This season will give him the confidence of knowing he's as good as anyone in the league."

INVINCIBLE

One of the things Vermeil did to try to change the atmosphere around the team was hold an open tryout,

something you're unlikely to see in today's NFL. A 30-year-old receiver named Vince Papale, a teacher and bartender from the Delaware County suburbs who had been a pole-vaulter at St. Joe's, which didn't have a football team, stood out among the wannabes. Papale had played two seasons, 1974 and '75 for the Philadelphia Bell of the World Football League (though this background was overlooked for dramatic effect in the Hollywood movie *Invincible*, starring Mark Wahlberg as Papale and Greg Kinnear as Vermeil).

DICK VERMEIL

Dick Vermeil was a natural leader, and his discipline and vision were a big part of the Eagles success during his tenure as head coach. *Rusty Kennedy/AP Images*

WHEN DICK VERMEIL ARRIVED in Philadelphia from UCLA and started laying down the law, linebacker Bill Bergey, for one, was not impressed.

"In 1976 we got this little fellow from Napa Valley. I'll tell you the truth, after the first two weeks of training camp I was thinking, 'This has to be the Harriest-high-school guy I've ever seen.' I was so tired at night I couldn't roll over in my bunk," Bergey recalled when he was presented the Wanamaker Award at a 1979 banquet, with Vermeil in attendance. "I'll tell you something else—last year was by far the best year of pro football I've ever had. When you're 9-7 and get beat in the playoffs, it beats hell out of being 4-10 and stinking all year long."

Vermeil, asked that night for a reaction, was unsurprised. "I knew they thought I was crazy," he said, "but I wanted them to think that way. We still work them just as hard, but it's better directed now. The guys you lose because of the work don't make any difference. I don't want to have a football team that anybody can belong to."

Today, the workaholic, sleep-in-the-office football coach is a cliché, but it might have been Vermeil who invented that cliché. He also might have invented "burnout," when he stepped away from coaching for a decade and a half after the 1982 season.

During the 1979 season, Vermeil talked about celebrating his October 30 birthday during football season every year. That day, Vermeil said, he'd told his wife, Carol, "Someday we'll take 10 days off and go somewhere and really celebrate my birthday."

"She said, 'Yeah, when that happens I'll be living in a room at an old people's boarding home, and you'll be in the room next to me,'" he said.

When the Eagles made it to the first Super Bowl in franchise history following the 1980 season, owner Leonard Tose gave Vermeil all the credit.

"Jimmy Murray [the general manager] and I were lucky enough to pick the right coach," Tose said. "It's that simple. Luck had to be involved, because look at how many wrong ones I'd picked before. The Dick Vermeils are rare. There's been a great deal written about the authority he was given here, but the truth is he has no more authority than Mike McCormack did before him. The difference is, Dick took it and used it.

"All the positive things that have happened began with the day we hired Vermeil. Firing Mike McCormack was not a difficult decision—the press made it seem difficult—but we were going nowhere. It was my feeling that one thing we needed was discipline, and Dick has since proven me right.

"I still remember watching him walk off the field the day his UCLA team beat Ohio State in the Rose Bowl. There was something in his manner that suggested the kind of strength we were looking for. Then we called him—he was five minutes from our hotel, and he said he wasn't interested. I told Jimmy, 'You certainly picked a fine guy. How bright can he be if he won't walk cross the street to talk about an opportunity?' Then he called back. We didn't bull him. We told him that what we had was one of the toughest jobs ever offered to a man. Looking back on it now I kind of think that's the real reason he took it."

Vermeil remains a beloved figure in Philadelphia, one of the region's most revered sports icons. He almost coached the Eagles twice—after the 1994 season, owner Jeffrey Lurie was about to make his first coaching hire, having dismissed Rich Kotite, whom Lurie had inherited when he took control of the team. After more than a decade in broadcasting, Vermeil was starting to think about coaching again. They came very close to striking a deal, a prospect that had fans giddy. But Lurie and team president Joe Banner were not comfortable with the money and level of control Vermeil wanted. Lurie maintained that Vermeil's agent asked for $10 million over five years, plus 5 percent of the team, the salary still to be paid even if Vermeil decided he wanted to go back to broadcasting before the deal was up.

Lurie hired Ray Rhodes instead, and Vermeil returned to coaching with St. Louis in 1997, winning Super Bowl XXXIV before retiring. This retirement only lasted a year, with Vermeil moving across Missouri to take over the Kansas City Chiefs. He retired for good after the 2005 season.

RON JAWORSKI

Ron Jaworski credits his coach, Dick Vermeil, for molding him into a successful NFL quarterback. *George Gojkovich/Getty Images*

YOUNGER FANS MIGHT BE SURPRISED to learn that Ron Jaworski, the avuncular NFL analyst and co-host of ESPN's Monday Night Football broadcasts, was once a brash young quarterback, a cocky kid with a big arm.

"Jaws" or "the Polish Rifle" came to the Eagles in 1977 after losing a battle for the starting job in Los Angeles to Pat Haden. Jaworski would ultimately prove to be both a better quarterback and a better TV analyst than Haden, the former USC star.

The move was a good one for Jaworski, though, who credited head coach Dick Vermeil for rounding off his rough edges and making him a complete quarterback. Released by Buddy Ryan in 1987, Jaworski still lives in the Philadelphia area and has developed a variety of local business interests, including part ownership of the Philadelphia Soul of the Arena Football League.

Jaworski led Vermeil's Birds to Super Bowl XL after a tremendous 1980 season, highlighted by 27 touchdowns, just 12 interceptions, and the only Pro Bowl appearance of his career. Despite these accomplishments, Jaworski was booed a lot in his Eagles years.

In subsequent seasons, fans were displeased with the crumbling of the Vermeil success standard, and Jaworski was an easy target. Eventually he gained some hard-earned respect for taking a terrible pounding behind porous offensive lines, absorbing the boos without complaint; it helped that Jaworski, raised in the steel town of Lackawanna, New York, understood the Philadelphia vibe. But there were still some bleak moments, even some bleak years: Jaworski was sacked 53 times in 1983.

After his release in 1987, Jaworski was asked in an *Inquirer* interview how he wanted to be remembered.

"I hope they'll remember me for the thing that I'm most proud of, and that's playing 116 straight games. Maybe I wasn't the most talented guy, maybe I wasn't blessed with the ability of a Bobby Clarke, a Julius Erving or a Mike Schmidt," Jaworski said. "So I want to be remembered as a guy who just kept getting up, a guy who never said die," he said.

That was, indeed, his legacy. The following August, Jaworski returned to Veterans Stadium as a Dolphins backup. He was greeted with cheers and signs indicating support; in being cast aside by Ryan, Jaworski had become a sympathetic figure for Eagles fans.

Jaworski's wife, Liz, was asked that night about the reception.

"It was very gratifying to hear the cheers," she said. "It helped mend the ulcer the [fans] gave me the last 10 years."

At the farewell press conference Jaworski held after his release, Wilbert Montgomery said: "Ron was the one who made things go. He was our leader, on and off the field. He was a guy who would say something crazy to pick everybody up. He'd come up with the big play when we needed it.

"He took me under his wing the first few years. He sat next to me during film study. He'd say, 'Wilbert, watch for this. Be alert for that.' He did the same thing for other young players later on. He knows the game as well as any offensive coordinator in the league."

Jaworski's Eagles made the playoffs four years in a row, when Vermeil was in charge, but they fell just short in their one great shot at immortality.

"I still believe if we played that [Oakland] team best-of-seven, we'd win four or five," Jaworski said at a tenth anniversary celebration. "I think we were the better team, but the fact that some of their players had been in a Super Bowl before made a difference. They knew how to handle the pressure."

Vince Papale (left, *George Gojkovich/Getty Images*) and actor Mark Wahlberg (right, *Coke Whitworth/AP Images*), who plays Papale in the film *Invincible*.

Papale was a training-camp sensation, leading the Eagles in receptions during the 1976 preseason.

After *Invincible* came out, in 2006, Papale often recalled the moment after Vermeil told him he had made the team.

"I asked him if I could make a phone call," Papale said. "I ran up the ramp to a pay phone. Called Westinghouse, where my dad was working. Told the foreman I'd made the team and to tell my dad, Frank. I could hear the guys cheering in the background. A *Rudy* moment."

Vermeil thought Papale could help out on special teams. His first home game, his second game in the NFL, he forced a fumble on a punt return and recovered, setting up a touchdown in a 20–7 Eagles victory over the Giants. Papale had proven he was more than a sideshow; he ended up staying three years.

When the movie debuted, Vermeil recalled the origins of the story: "The tryout wasn't a publicity stunt," he said. "We were hoping to find two or three guys who would

MVP Books Collection

at least be good camp players—and just maybe one plum who would make the team. All kinds of people turned out in all different shapes and sizes. We had a doctor, guys with big bellies, kids right out of high school. The Eagles hadn't been to the playoffs in a long time, and I came in there wanting to do whatever it took to rebuild the team. Vince had talent and a great attitude, and those were things we were looking for."

FINALLY, PROGRESS—AND A MIRACLE

The next season was a milestone. The 9-7 record of the 1978 Birds might not seem like that big a deal, but it was their first winning season since 1966, and it was good enough to catapult them to the playoffs (the *real* play-offs, not the now-defunct runner-up affair) for the first time since 1960. Wilbert Montgomery, among the most beloved Eagles of all time, burst onto the scene with 1,220 rushing yards.

One of the oddest quirks in Eagles history is how many times the team has won in bizarre, unlikely fashion on the road against the Giants. This tradition, so to speak, started on November 19, 1978, at the Meadowlands. The Giants were running out the clock with a 17–12 lead. Bob Gibson, offensive coordinator for the Giants, made a play call that led to his firing: a handoff from quarterback Joe Pisarcek to fullback Larry Csonka, with 31 seconds left. Pisarcek flubbed the handoff, perhaps because Csonka lined up in the wrong spot. The ball took a fluky bounce on the artificial turf. Eagles corner Herm Edwards scooped it up and ran 26 yards for the game-winning touchdown, the play Eagles fans dubbed "the Miracle at the Meadowlands."

Edwards found himself talking about that play more than 32 years later, when DeSean Jackson made the TV networks dig out the Edwards footage. Jackson returned a Giants punt 65 yards for a game-winning touchdown on the final play of perhaps the most amazing game in Eagles history, a 38–31 victory over the New York hosts in which the Birds had trailed 31–10 midway through the fourth quarter.

"His was different in the sense that he had to make people miss," Edwards, who was watching Jackson on TV, told the Philadelphia *Daily News*. "All I had to do was pick it up on the hop and run my heart out."

Edwards credits the boost from his "miracle" for pushing the Eagles into their first playoff berth in 18 years.

"We were a team trying to figure how to win, and that win gave us some energy," Edwards said.

Jackson's dash wasn't the first occasion Eagles fans had to reminisce about Edwards. On November 20, 1988, the Eagles had a potential game-winning field goal blocked in overtime, by Lawrence Taylor. But they won the game on that play anyway, when Eagles defensive end Clyde Simmons, on the field to block for kicker Luis Zendejas, alertly picked up the ball and ran 15 yards for a game-winning touchdown. Again, the victory was a catalyst, the Eagles going on to win the NFC East for the first time in eight years.

In the book *Game Changers*, Simmons recalled that even though he thought he held his block, teammates told him afterward Taylor was his responsibility. As with Edwards, the bounce was the key—Simmons recovered behind the line of scrimmage, so he was able to advance the ball.

Edwards's name was invoked again on October 19, 2003, when Brian Westbrook turned another sure defeat into victory, returning a punt 84 yards for a touchdown in a 14–10 win with 1:16 left, which made a team that was about to be 2-4, 3-3 instead. It would be the first of nine victories in a row, as the Eagles powered their way to the NFC Championship Game.

When the old Giants Stadium was torn down, you had to figure the Eagles' swamplands magic would go with it. But in their first visit to the New Meadowlands Stadium, Jackson made history with the NFL's first "walkoff" punt return. The back page of the Philadelphia *Daily News* was headlined: "Miracles Never Cease."

The Miracle at the Meadowlands: Herman Edwards scoops up a fumble by the Giants' Joe Pisarcik (Left, *Burnett/AP Images*) and takes it the distance to win the game. (Below, *Ed Mahan/NFL/Getty Images*)

Leroy Harris fights for yardage against the Bears' Allan Page in the 1979 wild-card game at Veterans Stadium. *Ed Mahan/NFL/Getty Images*

The Buccaneers' Ricky Bell was too much for the Eagles' D in the 1979 playoffs. Here, Frank LeMaster tries to bring him down. *Ed Mahan/ NFL/Getty Images*

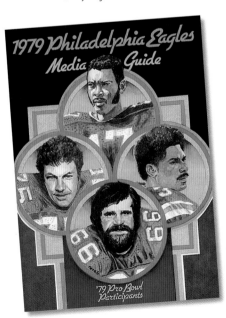

Harold Carmichael used his size, strength, and pass-catching ability to change the way people viewed the wide receiver and tight end positions in the NFL. At his size, nobody thought he could play wide receiver—he proved them wrong, and then some. *A. Neste/NFL/Getty Images*

WILBERT MONTGOMERY

Wilbert Montgomery runs away from a Tampa Bay defender during the Eagles' 1970 divisional playoff game, a loss to the Buccaneers. *Ed Mahan/NFL/Getty Images*

ON SEPTEMBER 9, 1984, Wilbert Montgomery surpassed Steve Van Buren (5,860 yards) as the franchise's all-time leading rusher. The Eagles had intended to stop the game to honor his accomplishment, but the circumstances made that impossible. The Eagles were trailing the visiting Vikings when Montgomery's record breaker came on a 15-yard dash that set up a first-and-goal for the Eagles inside the two-minute warning. The accomplishment was noted on the video board at Veterans Stadium, and referee Jim Tunney gave Montgomery the ball, which he quickly tossed to the sideline for safekeeping. And the game went on.

"You don't want to break momentum in that situation," Montgomery said afterward. "I'm glad it worked out that way. I would have felt funny if they held up the game for that. The way it was was fine. There was nice applause, the fans let me know how they feel, then the game went on and we won. That's the most important thing. [Winning] means more to me than the record."

It all seemed pretty fitting for a soft-spoken star who arrived as a sixth-round draft choice and never wanted to make a fuss.

"I never thought I'd be in this position," Montgomery, 5-foot-10, 195, said that day. "One team [New England] gave me a physical and said I'd never play in the NFL. They said I'd be hurt all the time."

Apparently, scouts felt Montgomery, who played at Abilene Christian, was too slightly built.

"I owe a lot to Dick Vermeil for sticking with me that first year when I made so many mistakes. I owe a lot to the linemen who opened the holes for me," he said. "I wish they could all be here because they have a share in this. I'm just one man. I didn't do any of this alone."

Under Vermeil, Montgomery got into NFL coaching with the Rams in 1997, staying eight years before going to the Lions and then to the Baltimore Ravens, where he coaches running backs. His return to Philadelphia, in whatever coaching colors, is always noted by fans who credit him with one of the franchise's signature moments, the NFC Championship Game victory over hated Dallas following the 1980 season.

Montgomery ran for 194 yards on 26 carries on that arctic-cold day. Most famously, after not being able to take the field for the pre-game warmup on his battered legs, he ran 42 yards for a touchdown on the Eagles' second play from scrimmage. Montgomery started left, cut right, and carried the Birds to their first-ever Super Bowl appearance.

Montgomery's career numbers (6,538 rushing yards as an Eagle, 6,789 overall, after a final year with Detroit in 1985) would have been more impressive if not for injuries and the strike-shortened 1982 season. His last great year was 1981 (286 carries, 1,402 yards), when he was only 27 years old. He remains the team's all-time leading rusher, and its single-season leader, with 1,512 in 1979.

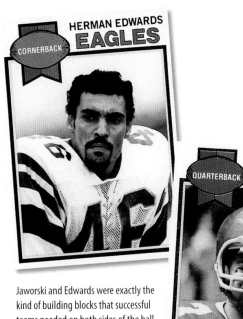

Jaworski and Edwards were exactly the kind of building blocks that successful teams needed on both sides of the ball.
MVP Books Collection

Not everything that happened the day of the original "miracle" turned out well for the Birds, however. Kicker Nick Mike-Mayer took a hit that damaged his ribs, and he had to go on injured reserve. That injury would resonate when the Eagles played their wild-card playoff game at Atlanta; replacement kicker Mike Michel missed the potential game-winning field-goal attempt from 34 yards out, with 1:34 left. Michel also missed another field-goal try and an extra point in a 14–13 loss that just about everyone around the team felt should have been a win.

The 1979 season started off beautifully, with six wins in seven games, but the Eagles followed that with three losses in a row, which got fans wondering what kind of team they really had. The losing streak ended in the best possible way, with a 31–21 victory over Dallas, the start of a four-game win streak that took the team to 10-4 before it split its final two. The loss, alas, was to Dallas, giving the Cowboys the NFC East title. Wilbert Montgomery set a franchise record, rushing for 1,512 yards on 338 carries, and Harold Carmichael livened up a November 4 loss to the Browns by catching a pass in his 106th consecutive game, an NFL record.

The Birds made the postseason as a wild-card team, and Philadelphia would host a playoff game for the first time since the 1960 NFL Championship. The Eagles defeated the Chicago Bears, 27–17, cementing Vermeil's credentials as Coach of the Year. It seems almost quaint today that a big deal was made of it, but the boos that rained down on Jaworski after a third-quarter interception were a big post-game topic.

"You don't always know who they're booing," Harold Carmichael suggested. "They could be booing someone who fell out of the stands and didn't fall just right."

Vermeil found the booing less humorous. The coach, now one of the area's most beloved sports figures, did some scolding that afternoon.

"Sometimes a team becomes a loser because its fans are losers," Vermeil told reporters. "When they were booing Ron, my sincere thought was that these fans have been losers so long, they better not turn back to losers before the game's over. This [game] might be a lesson for them, too."

The Eagles had to go to Tampa for the next round of the playoffs, and the Bucs handled them, 24–17, the first playoff victory in the history of a then-bedraggled franchise. Vermeil had set winning the Chicago game as the standard for calling the season a success; anything more, he said going in, would be "frosting on the cake." In retrospect, that might have been a mistake.

In the *Daily News*, Gary Smith wrote that the Birds "came out dead and stayed that way."

Eagles fans would have to wait for a new decade to see their team play in the Super Bowl.

1970s Philadelphia Eagles
Year by Year

1970	3–10–1	5th in NFC East Division
1971	6–7–1	3rd in NFC East Division
1972	2–11–1	5th in NFC East Division
1973	5–8–1	3rd in NFC East Division
1974	7–7	4th in NFC East Division
1975	4–10	5th in NFC East Division
1976	4–10	4th in NFC East Division
1977	5–9	4th in NFC East Division
1978	9–7	2nd in NFC East Division
1979	11–5	1st in NFC East Division

6 ALMOST SUPER
The 1980s

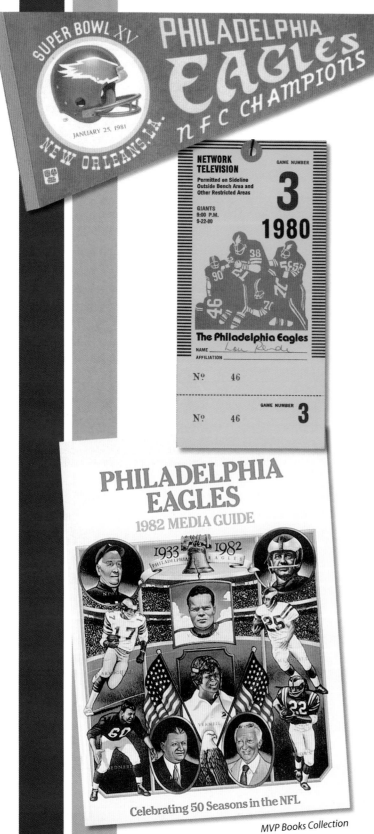

Celebrating 50 Seasons in the NFL

MVP Books Collection

THE DEFINING MOMENT of the Eagles' first Super Bowl season, for any fan, is Wilbert Montgomery romping 42 yards on his first carry of the 20–7 NFC Championship Game victory over Dallas at Veterans Stadium. That's because Super Bowl XV produced no happy memories, but getting there was indeed a lot of fun.

Jaworski threw for 3,527 yards and 27 touchdowns, despite lacking great receivers (Harold Carmichael, in his tenth year at age 31, caught 48 passes, but Jaworski's top target was Montgomery, with 50.) Jaws was named the Maxwell Club's NFL Player of the Year, and the Birds won 11 of their first 12 games. Carmichael's streak of 127 consecutive games with a catch came to an end in the regular-season finale at Dallas, a 35–27 loss that set the Eagles' record at 12-4; Carmichael hurt his back in the first half. The Birds had to lose that game by less than 25 points in order to come out ahead of the Cowboys in the division title tiebreakers. They trailed 35–10 in the fourth quarter before Jaworski pulled them together for a late rally.

A popular newspaper topic from that season was the team's lack of pedigree; Vermeil had all sorts of stats about championship teams and the number of high-round draft picks they'd assembled. Improving the Birds' standing in that regard was something he started working on when he got the job, but he hadn't produced immense change by 1980, at least partly because management had traded away so many draft picks in the mid-1970s. Only three players on the 1980 roster were first-round picks.

There were some high-profile youngsters, like Jerry Robinson, the 1979 first-round pick (who remains the last linebacker taken by the Eagles in the first round, by the way). But most of the Eagles had been around, and many had played elsewhere; Claude Humphrey, famous as an Atlanta defensive end, came to Philly and recorded 14 sacks at age 36.

The way that team came out of the gate, the Super Bowl berth wasn't a shock. The first five wins were all by double digits. Montgomery was the key to the offense, but he missed four games with injuries. The Eagles won all four, as well as two of the three games in which Montgomery was significantly limited. Vermeil's nephew, hardscrabble Louis Giammona, filled in capably.

In the first round of the playoffs, the Minnesota Vikings grabbed an early 14–0 lead, but the Eagles forced eight turnovers and cruised to a 31–16 victory. They intercepted Vikings quarterback Tommy Kramer five times in the second half. Linebacker Frank LeMaster recalled that at half-time, the Eagles scrambling, defensive coordinator Marion Campbell was less than ecstatic. "He told us, 'You're a great defense. Now play like one,'" LeMaster said.

Montgomery kept aggravating injuries, leaving the game, and coming back stronger.

Claude Humphrey's 14 1/2 sacks helped lead the Eagles to the Super Bowl in 1980. *Sylvia Allen/NFL/Getty Images*

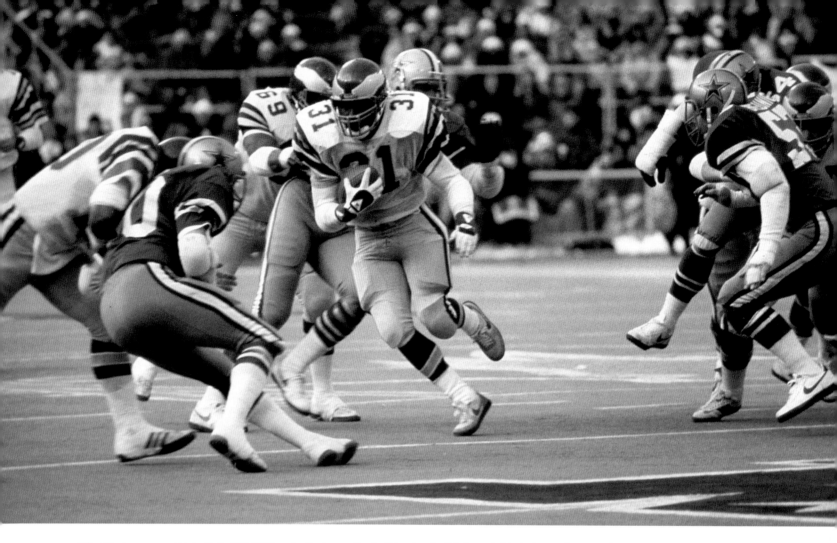

Wilbert Montgomery was at his best in the 1980 NFC Championship Game, rushing for 194 yards as the Birds dismantled the Cowboys on their way to the Super Bowl. *Ed Mahan/NFL/Getty Images*

"I don't consider myself a super tough guy," Montgomery said afterward. "I don't think I'm any blood 'n' guts hero. I just feel, if you want to go, you'll go. Pain? Every guy in this room has pain, but we know we have a job to do. You can't play on a broken leg, but, hey, the stuff I got wasn't much. Just little naggy hurts. That's what I've been getting all year. It's frustrating. You feel like you're never quite going full-blow."

Montgomery's health dominated the buildup to the NFC title matchup with the Cowboys. The Eagles spent four days in Tampa preparing, to get away from the Philly winter weather (this was before state-of-the-art indoor practice facilities). The crush of national media that descended to chronicle every moment (including when Montgomery's knee buckled in a Wednesday drill) was something new to a team that hadn't spent much time in the national spotlight.

"The locker room was closed for 10 minutes after practice yesterday because guys got tired of tripping over

reporters on their way to the showers," Bud Shaw wrote in the *Daily News*. "It seems there are more things tightening up than just locker room space."

But when game day arrived at the Vet along with a 16-degree temperature and howling wind, it wasn't the Eagles who looked tight. Montgomery shook off everything, even having to undergo treatment in the locker room as the game was starting, and ran for 194 yards on 26 carries. The underdog Eagles won easily, even with the wind limiting Jaworski to a 9-for-29 performance.

Montgomery ended up just two yards shy of the championship game record, set by Steve Van Buren in 1949. At least one interested observer was able to make a knowledgeable comparison. Norm Van Brocklin, the QB of the NFL Champion 1960 Eagles, had been the Rams' QB in 1949.

"Ol' Steve split about three shoulders that day," Van Brocklin told *Daily News* columnist Jack McKinney. "But Montgomery isn't the punishing type runner Steve was.

Dick Vermeil led the Eagles to their first-ever Super Bowl after the 1980 season, but he was left grimacing at the scoreboard for much of the game. Vermeil resigned and retired after the 1982 season, citing "burnout" as his reason for leaving the game. He returned to coach the St. Louis Rams in 1997, eventually leading them to a victory in Super Bowl XXXIV. *Al Messerschmidt/ Getty Images*

MVP Books Collection

Montgomery does it on quickness. He gets through that hole as quickly as any back I've seen."

Montgomery's 42-yard TD ramble on the sixth play of the game set the tone.

"As soon as I turned I could see the end zone," Montgomery said afterward. "I knew I was going all the way."

It was his first 100-yard performance since a game in Minnesota on September 14, a reflection of the many dings he'd suffered over the course of the season.

Dallas, peeved over having to wear its "unlucky" blue jerseys, gained just 202 total yards and managed only 11 first downs. Quarterback Danny White completed 12 of 31 passes for only 127 yards.

"I don't think I've ever played against a team that was so pumped up. They swarmed all over us," Cowboys halfback Tony Dorsett said afterward.

"We just beat 'em," said linebacker John Bunting, an Eagle since 1972, who hadn't often been able to say that about Dallas. "Take a look at the stats. Take a look at the scoreboard. Case closed."

TO THE BRINK AND THEN, A BLINK

The buildup for the Super Bowl in New Orleans was delirious. The Birds were actually favored over the Raiders, and the way Al Davis's renegades kept getting caught on Bourbon Street in the wee hours of the morning only reinforced that notion. Vermeil, who had worked so hard to get there, was all business, perhaps too much so. At least, that became a popular theme after the Eagles lost.

The Eagles had hosted the Raiders on November 23 and won, 10–7, sacking quarterback Jim Plunkett eight times. Alas, this wasn't much like that.

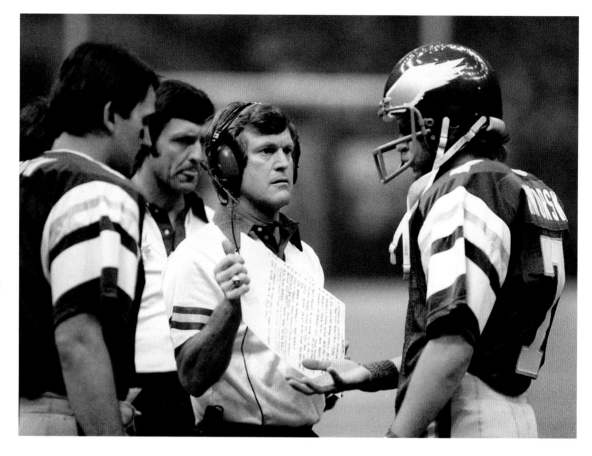

Ron Jaworski talks things over with coach Vermeil during Super Bowl XV. Unfortunately, the Raiders' defense was in dominant form all day, and Jaws threw three interceptions in the Eagles' 27–10 defeat.
AP Images

"All day long he has to pass," John Cardinal Krol, Archbishop of Philadelphia, complained to *Daily News* columnist Larry McMullen. Krol was sitting in the Eagles' owner's box at the Superdome as Plunkett forged his MVP credentials; he completed 13 of 21 passes for 261 yards and three TDs. "What can you do?"

Krol noted to McMullen that God answers all prayers, but that the answer isn't always yes.

"We let him stand back there all day and pick us apart," said Frank LeMaster. "They were the same team they were last time, but we weren't anywhere near the same. It's a hard thing to explain."

For reasons that have been much speculated upon over the years, the Eagles came out flat and stayed that way. They were down 7–0 early when Jaworski hit Rodney Parker for a 40-yard game-tying touchdown. Unfortunately, Carmichael, in motion, had broken toward the line too early.

"I still can see the flag they dropped on me," Carmichael said in a *Daily News* story commemorating the tenth anniversary of the Super Bowl. "I was in motion and all

I did was this [rolling his shoulders] as I turned upfield. I thought it was kind of a cheap call. I see receivers now spinning 360 degrees, going this way and that way and it's OK."

Soon it was 14–0, and then 21–3. Jaworski, never great at throwing on the run, tossed three picks to Raiders line-backer Rod Martin, who, it turned out, was not one of those partying Raiders who made all the pre-game headlines.

"I didn't miss curfew all week," Martin said afterward. "I was in my room every night, studying film on the Eagles. I felt like I had a real good handle on their offense. They like to run Carmichael deep, then bring the tight end across to the sideline. That's what they did on the first pass I intercepted. I saw it coming all the way. The other two interceptions, I was playing off in a kind of prevent coverage. How good are my hands? Not usually as good as they were today."

"We weren't the same team we were two weeks ago," Montgomery said. "I came into the clubhouse and it was kind of silent. There wasn't all the hollering we usually have. I felt it in the air, that the team might be a little timid playing in this game. And on the sidelines, we weren't making a lot of noise. There wasn't that much life."

Ten years later, Vermeil was asked to reflect.

"I don't think [the outcome] was the result of overwork. I didn't work the team any harder that week than I did the rest of the year. . . . We beat Dallas and everyone said it was because of our great work ethic. Then we lost to Oakland two weeks later and the same people were blaming our work ethic. It doesn't make sense," he said. "When you lose a big game, everyone looks for reasons. Sometimes people think they see things that aren't really there. We didn't play at the level we played most of the season, but that's because the Raiders didn't let us. They flat whipped our butts that day. That's football; it happens."

Jaworski had similar memories: "As a player, you keep telling yourself, 'This is just another game,' but it's not. I think it really hit us that day at the Superdome. I saw some of our guys looking around like this [wide-eyed] during pre-game warmups. That's when I began to think, 'Uh-oh . . .'

"I felt myself pressing, too. On our first series, I threw an interception I never should have thrown. I read the coverage, I knew I should lay the ball off to Wilbert, like I'd done all year, but instead, I tried to force it in to John [Spagnola] and I got it picked off.

"I was trying too hard to make a big play," Jaworski noted. "I think that happens to a lot of teams in their first Super Bowl. Instead of sticking with the [basic] things that got you there, you try to do more, and it backfires."

ANOTHER DECLINE

The aftermath of the 1980 season unfolded a little like the aftermath of 1960, except, of course, this time the Eagles hadn't won a championship. In 1981, the Eagles started out 9-2, fueled by the NFL's top-ranked defense and a much healthier Montgomery, who would finish the season with 1,402 rushing yards on 286 carries, a healthy average of 4.9 yards per carry. Things turned sour down the stretch, though, with the team losing four in a row before finishing with a 38–0 walloping of the Cardinals that they thought might restore their playoff mojo.

Three of their four end-of-season losses were to divisional foes, which made it even harder to swallow. The Week 15 loss to Dallas on December 13 was particularly tough, because it gave the NFC East title back to the Cowboys for the twelfth time in 16 years. The previous

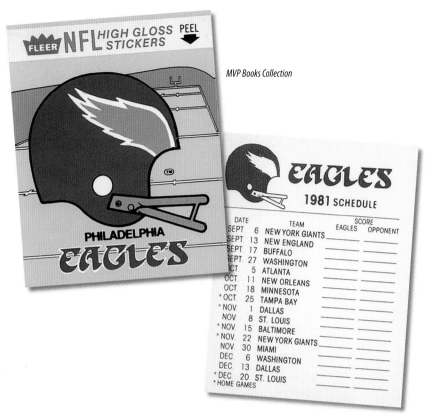

MVP Books Collection

year, when the Eagles won the division and vanquished Dallas in the NFC title game, there was a lot of talk about ends of eras and turning tables. One year later, the tables were right back where they had been for so long.

"We're about at the bottom right now," Frank LeMaster said of a team that had been outscored 43–3 in the second half during its losing streak, 36–0 in the fourth quarter. "Maybe there's nowhere to go but up. The Cowboys played like NFC champions. We sure didn't. We haven't done it for four weeks.

"The only thing that sheds any ray of hope on this is that as badly as we're playing, we can still make the playoffs. That's the one thing we can hold onto. Right now, maybe it's the only thing."

They did indeed make the playoffs, backing in as a wild-card team the very next day. Then they seemed to put it all back together again at home against St. Louis in the final game of the regular season. But all the problems came home to roost in the wild-card game, a 27–21 loss to the Giants.

Wally Henry, the plucky returner and wideout who had to have his spleen removed during the Super Bowl season, fumbled away both a punt and a kickoff early, helping the Giants to a 20–0 lead. The Eagles, built around defense and ball control, were way out of their comfort zone.

Years later, rumors surfaced of a drug party that three or four key players allegedly attended the night before the

John Spagnola caught a lot of balls during his nine-year run with the Eagles. In 1985, he and Mike Quick combined for 135 catches and more than 2,000 yards. *Ed Mahan/NFL/Getty Images*

playoff loss. Tight end John Spagnola made them public in 1987, speaking at a symposium at the Philadelphia Psychiatric Center. When a furor erupted, Spagnola backed off a bit.

"I am not sure whether or not it took place, whether or not players actually did take drugs before that game," Spagnola told the *Daily News*. "I certainly am not aware of

who the players would be. It was simply rumor, innuendo. I used it to highlight a point I was trying to make [about the pervasiveness of drug use in sports]."

DELAY AND THEN BURNOUT

The 1982 season was only two weeks old when an NFL players' strike stopped everything for eight weeks. The

Eagles, 1-1 when the strike began, lost four in a row coming back, and at the end of a 3-6 season, they lost much more. Vermeil resigned, citing burnout.

Mike Quick, who was to become a Pro Bowl wideout, was an Eagles rookie that year. Quick now says he wasn't really surprised to see Vermeil step down.

"As a young kid coming out of college, I did not expect to see my head coach breaking down in every meeting, and that's what I saw," Quick said.

Vermeil's emotional side is a well-known part of his persona—today, Philly comedian Joe Conklin still does a Vermeil impression that features the beloved ex-coach crying over just about anything—but Quick felt Vermeil was walking the ragged edge in 1982, unable to fix organizational problems that later became apparent.

The *Daily News*'s Stan Hochman believes "the strike hurt Vermeil emotionally" but that the burnout issue was real—Vermeil had worked too hard for too long.

Marion Campbell, Vermeil's defensive coordinator and a defensive end on the 1960 championship team, ascended to the head coaching job. "The Swamp Fox" was popular with players but a disaster as a head coach, both in Philadelphia and later in Atlanta, going 34-80-1.

"He was not a good head coach, in my opinion," Quick said. "I thought he was a great defensive coordinator, but I didn't think the team was really focused, when he was the head coach. I didn't think the team was particularly prepared. Dick was such a detailed guy, had every minute of the day detailed, where you were supposed to be and what you were supposed to be doing. I didn't feel that same sense of detail with Marion as coach. I thought the guys were a little more lax, spent a little too much time playing grab ass when he was the head coach."

As had become customary during pervasive periods of losing, there was a backdrop of financial trouble and ownership instability within the Eagles organization.

1982 was the 50th Anniversary of Eagles football. Unfortunately, it was also a strike-shortened season that took an emotional toll on Dick Vermeil, who cited "burnout" as his reason for resignation at the end of the year. *MVP Books Collection*

The Birds' 5-11 finish in 1983 included a seven-game losing streak, despite a team-record 1,409-yard receiving year from young standout Quick, who caught 69 passes for 13 touchdowns. The offensive line that had taken the Eagles to the Super Bowl was crumbling, as was Montgomery, who suffered a knee injury and gained just 139 yards on 29 carries.

When the season ended with a 31–7 loss at St. Louis in the snow, placekicker Tony Franklin sensed the Vermeil

In 1982 Ron Jaworski began throwing to receiver Mike Quick, a connection that would ultimately combine for the longest pass in Eagles history, a 99-yarder during overtime of a 1985 game against the Atlanta Falcons. *Al Messerschmidt/ Getty Images*

Al Messerschmidt/ Getty Images

gang was breaking up. "Nineteen eighty seems like the Stone Age," he said.

Jaworski, sacked 11 times in the finale, threw 18 interceptions to go with his 20 touchdown passes.

A MOVING EXPERIENCE

The Birds started the 1984 season 1-4 but got better; a 60-sack defense provided a little stability and helped the team recover to a 6-9-1 record. For once, though, fans were more riveted by what was happening off the field.

Flamboyant owner Leonard Tose had been fairly popular, having hired Dick Vermeil and shepherded the run to Super Bowl XV after several early missteps. Philadelphia likes outsized, hard-living personalities, and Tose, known for his lavish lifestyle and impulsive generosity, definitely fit this bill. But Tose's image changed forever on December 11, when a Phoenix newspaper broke the news of a verbal agreement to move the Eagles to that city.

It wasn't a secret that Tose, accustomed to regularly wagering high stakes in Atlantic City casinos, was deep in debt. Everyone also knew that Phoenix was actively seeking a team (they ended up luring the Cardinals away from St. Louis). But Tose had responded to speculation

that season by declaring the Eagles would move "over my dead body." In fact, the day before news of the agreement broke, the *Inquirer* ran an analysis of Phoenix's attempts to lure a franchise that indicated the Eagles probably weren't going there.

And of course, the team ultimately didn't move, but that outcome didn't become clear for a week. It was perhaps the most frantic, confusing week in the history of the franchise, as Mayor Wilson Goode brokered a deal to build Veterans Stadium skyboxes and make other improvements to the venue, along with deferring rent and sharing parking money.

This was not as lucrative for Tose as moving the team might have been, and like his other financial fixes,

KEVIN ALLEN

THE EAGLES, LIKE MOST FRANCHISES, have had their share of draft-day failures. There are bad-luck stories, such as losing out on the O.J. Simpson sweepstakes in 1968. There are couldn't-stay-healthy stories, such as 2003 first-round defensive end Jerome McDougle, whose travails included a career-threatening gunshot wound suffered the night before he was due to report to training camp in 2005.

And then there is Kevin Allen. Whenever Eagles fans sit down to compare draft-day disasters, Allen is the trump card, the man whose name pretty much ends the discussion.

The offensive lineman from Indiana wasn't very good, despite having been drafted ninth overall in 1985. The Birds had counted on getting an offensive tackle, aiming for one of the top three that year—Bill Fralic, Lomas Brown, or Ken Ruettgers. Officials panicked when all three vanished in the first eight picks, and reached for Allen, who was never a first-round talent. Had they not been so locked in at offensive tackle, they could have taken, say, wide receiver Jerry Rice, who would have gone nicely with their second-round pick that year, quarterback Randall Cunningham.

But the Eagles had a brand-new owner, Norman Braman, and an embattled coach, Marion Campbell. Nobody was looking down the road; the team had given up 60 sacks and had the league's worst running game the previous season. They needed a left tackle, period.

"He's ready to play," Campbell said on draft day. "I expect him to come in and make a real big mark with us this year."

Allen made his mark, all right, by testing positive for cocaine around the time of the draft. Then he held out for 35 days, signing less than two weeks before the opener. Allen gave up 8.5 sacks in his first four starts, forcing Campbell to bench him.

When the Birds changed coaches from Campbell to Buddy Ryan after Allen's rookie season, Ryan made Allen a source of ridicule, asserting that his main talent was for standing around, "killing grass."

But what really made Allen infamous was the way his career ended. The Eagles released Allen early in the 1986 season, just before he was charged with the Labor Day rape of a woman on the beach in Margate, New Jersey. Allen eventually plead guilty—a plea he later said he regretted—and served 33 months in prison in New Jersey. He was later reinstated by the NFL and tried to mount a comeback, but only managed a season with Orlando's franchise in the World League.

Allen appeared in just 16 games for the Eagles, all as a rookie.

---

it proved temporary; a year later, he sold the team to Norman Braman, who would keep it in Philadelphia.

Tose's Phoenix flirtation made for a really interesting final week of the 1984 season, as the Eagles prepared for what would become a 26–10 loss at Atlanta.

"I'm glad I'm not suiting up Sunday," Jaworski, sidelined by a broken fibula, told reporters. "With all this going on, it's a major distraction. It's a major, major happening."

Montgomery told reporters he found out about the proposed move while listening to the radio.

"You don't know what to expect," he said. "Everyone is in a daze. We don't know what's going on. You don't know how to react to something like this."

"Right now, it's all speculation. You can't believe it until you hear it from the boss's mouth. But, as a player, you hate to see something like this happen. You hate to see something leave a city that's done so much for it."

Given the twists and turns of the week, the loss at Atlanta wasn't a shock, even if the Falcons hadn't won in more than two months previously. The Eagles found out Saturday night, the night before the game, that the team would not be moving, after all.

"This was definitely not a good performance on our part," said Marion Campbell, after his team lost four fumbles.

The Tose era ended in March with the sale of the team to Braman, a Miami car dealer with Philly roots. Braman

BUDDY RYAN

AFTER BUDDY RYAN became a stunningly successful defensive coordinator in the NFL (and eventually a memorable, if less successful head coach), it was easy to trace his coaching style to his roots as a master sergeant in the Korean War. Ryan built a fierce, almost tribal bond with the men serving directly under him. Like a good sergeant, he was definitely an enlisted man, at home in the trenches, not in the officers' club.

In Ron Jaworski's book, *The Games That Changed the Game*, he recalled a scene that occurred just before Ryan came to Philadelphia, at the end of Chicago's Super Bowl victory over the Patriots:

Just moments after the final gun sounded at Super Bowl XX, I saw something I'd never seen before on a football field," Jaworski wrote. "As expected, a group of Bears lifted [Mike] Ditka onto their shoulders and carried their head coach off on a victory ride. But just a few feet away, several members of the defense did the same thing for Ryan. That was unheard of: carrying off an assistant coach. But that's how much Buddy's players loved and respected him. They also understood this would be a farewell tribute. Within hours, Buddy Ryan became the new head coach of the Philadelphia Eagles.

I was curious to find out what inspired that kind of devotion, and I didn't have to wait long once Buddy arrived in Philly. From the start, he embraced the defensive players, while keeping his distance from us guys on offense. One of my teammates, six-time Pro Bowl cornerback Eric Allen, explained to me why the defensive players became so loyal to their new coach. In the past, the offense had always been the 'glamour' side of the ball, but Buddy made the Eagles' defense the star unit.

Ryan might not have been the winningest Eagles coach ever, going 43-35-1 and never winning in the postseason, but he absolutely was the most outspoken.

Eagles fans disliked their patrician, penny-pinching owner, Norman Braman, so they delighted at the way Ryan tweaked Braman, calling him "the guy in France." (Braman had a lot of contract holdouts, and he always seemed to be vacationing in the South of France when training camp opened, making communication with the media difficult in the pre-wireless era.)

True to his reputation, Ryan built a ferocious Eagles defense, but aside from installing Randall Cunningham at quarterback, he had very little offensive vision. He was particularly unsuccessful at building an offensive line to protect Cunningham.

The game that might best exemplify the Ryan era occurred on November 24, 1989, when the host Cowboys alleged that Ryan had put a bounty out on kicker Luis Zendejas and quarterback Troy

Buddy Ryan made a name for himself as the hard-nosed defensive coordinator of the Super Bowl champion Chicago Bears, and he brought that toughness along with him to Philadelphia. *Andrew D. Bernstein/Getty Images*

Aikman. Zendejas took a fierce hit from linebacker Jessie Small on a kickoff.

"I have absolutely no respect for the way they played the game," Cowboys coach Jimmy Johnson fumed afterward.

"I got a call Friday from one of my friends [on the Eagles], and he said, 'They're coming after you.' I didn't make much of it, then the [unnamed assistant] coach told me before the game, 'They're going to come after you,'" Zendejas said. "That just tells you what Buddy Ryan is. They can deny it, all their players and coaches, because they all came up to me after the game and said, 'We weren't in this. You know how Buddy is. You know how Buddy is. He'll pay somebody to do this and that.'"

Ryan's polarizing but entertaining tenure ended after a wild-card loss to the Redskins following the 1990 season. It was easy to see why management was frustrated, having been constantly mocked by a coach who built a contending team but couldn't win a playoff game.

Of course, Ryan's ever-loyal soldiers didn't see it that way.

GAMEDAY

PHILADELPHIA
EAGLES

Head Coach
BUDDY RYAN

**TODAY'S
LINEUPS**

Bears vs. Eagles September 14, 1986 Soldier Field **$2.00**

MVP Books Collection

"I think it's the most ridiculous thing I ever heard," said linebacker Seth Joyner. ". . . It's like all the positives about the team are just gone out the window right now. It's just going to be a totally different attitude. When you start changing things, you change offenses, you change defenses, we're confident and comfortable with what we're doing as far as the way the defense is run. You put in something else that we have to learn, and the confidence level is down. Guys don't want to have to put up with those things. I'm just really lost for words right now, I don't know what to say about this whole thing. I don't know what's going to happen."

Tight end Keith Jackson delivered a neat bit of foreshadowing. After the 1991 season, he would become part of a free-agent migration.

"I think everything is crazy right now; everybody is going crazy around here; the players are going crazy. . . . Now that Buddy's gone I don't want any ties to this team anymore. I don't want to be here anymore. . . . I think a lot of other players will say it too," Jackson said. "We don't want to be around here anymore."

Ryan would return as defensive coordinator in Houston, where he got back in the spotlight by punching offensive coordinator Kevin Gilbride, then he served two troubled seasons as the head coach of the Arizona Cardinals, going 8-8 and 4-12 before retiring to his Kentucky horse farm.

Veteran coach Wade Phillips, a Ryan assistant with the Eagles, once talked about why so many people who worked with Ryan didn't appreciate his plainspoken style.

"Buddy says a lot of things. He's said things that have hurt me and my family," Phillips said. "I don't think he means to do that, but that's part of the problem he's had in his career. . . . He's just so sure he's right on everything, and he isn't always right."

A year after rumors swirled that he would move the Eagles to Phoenix, owner Leonard Tose sold the team to Norman Braman. *George Gojkovich/Getty Images*

initially was hailed as a savior, given what the fan base had just endured, but he would eventually become the most reviled owner in franchise history. This was also the year Reggie White arrived from the USFL, and Wilbert Montgomery departed via a trade to Detroit.

On the field, Campbell stirred hope by getting the team to 6-5 after a 1-4 start; the offense benefited from Quick in his too-short prime, as he tallied 73 catches for 1,247 yards and 11 touchdowns. But four successive losses vanquished playoff hopes once again, as well as Campbell, who was fired with a game left to play. Assistant Fred Bruney led the team to a season-ending 37–35 victory at Minnesota; the final record was 7-9.

BUDDY BALL

As the Eagles searched for a new coach, Braman read a *New York Times* article about Buddy Ryan, the brash, unconventional defensive coordinator for the Chicago Bears, who were about to win Super Bowl XX. Apparently, Braman was untroubled by the fact that Ryan and Bears head coach Mike Ditka were virtually at war—Ryan challenged Ditka to a fight during the Bears' only loss of the season, against the Dolphins—or maybe the *Times* didn't get around to mentioning that.

At any rate, the new owner was intrigued, and on January 29, 1986, Ryan began one of the most significant coaching tenures in Eagles history.

If you told Eagles fans today they could pull a coach out of the time machine from any Eagles era and put him in charge again, Ryan would be the hands-down winner. This despite the fact that Ryan's five-year run included an 0-3 playoff record.

Ryan would not have become hugely popular in a lot of cities. He was given to rash pronouncements, sarcasm, and boasting; his manner with everyone, most especially Braman, was exactly the opposite of diplomatic. So Philadelphia loved him.

It helped that under Buddy Ryan's leadership, Randall Cunningham became the team's thrill-a-minute quarterback, and that his voracious, attacking defense, led by Reggie White, terrorized the league.

Ryan spent his first year revamping the roster, with all the upheaval producing a 5-10-1 record. But Cunningham began the process of taking the reins from Jaworski, and White made the Pro Bowl.

"That summer in training camp, I couldn't help but notice how much emphasis was put on forcing defensive turnovers—then having those guys score off them," Jaworski wrote in his book, *The Games That Changed the Game*. "He wanted his defense to become the offense. Buddy's defenses in Philadelphia were always aggressive, trying to punch the ball out, gambling on turnovers. I think this mindset was both Buddy's strength and his ultimate failing."

Later in the same chapter of his book, Jaworski wrote: "Buddy Ryan and I were hardly the best of friends. He didn't always treat me with respect. I thought his behavior was often unprofessional, and I still don't think he has a clue about offensive football. But I know a genius when I see one."

Team president Harry Gamble and owner Norm Braman watch a game from the sidelines. Braman brought the incomparable Buddy Ryan to Philadelphia, but the two never had an easy relationship. *Al Messerschmidt/ Getty Images*

MVP Books Collection

The next year might have produced a playoff berth except for an NFL players' strike that intruded after the second week. Teams fielded rosters of replacement players and played on. Ryan, a players' coach, did not embrace the replacement concept, and the Birds fielded a terrible team that lost all three games it played by a combined score of 92–35.

In some cities, the replacement players were considered a colorful novelty, a bunch of refreshing, unspoiled dream-chasers. That was not the view in union-friendly Philadelphia, where union workers picketed games, actively discouraging fans from attending contests played by nonunion players. That also was not the view of Ryan, who built credibility among the fan base and among his players by being openly antagonistic toward the replacements.

"He was just not for it, and he wore it on his sleeve—it was not something he tried to hide," recalled wide receiver Mike Quick, then one of the team's biggest stars. "That

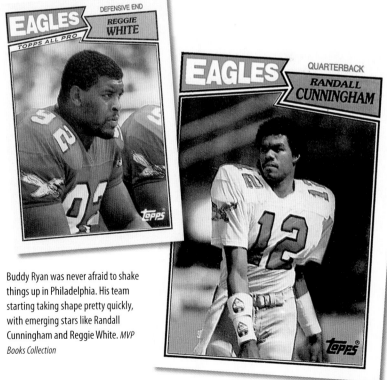

Buddy Ryan was never afraid to shake things up in Philadelphia. His team starting taking shape pretty quickly, with emerging stars like Randall Cunningham and Reggie White. *MVP Books Collection*

The players' strike in 1987 took its toll on everyone, and Randall Cunningham showed his fatigue on the picket lines. *Bill Ingraham/AP Images*

In the *Daily News*, Tim Kawakami suggested Ryan might have jeopardized his job by making his pro-player sentiments so clear.

"They emerged from the failed strike united, strong, and crediting Buddy Ryan, but now face the distinct possibility that Ryan has lost the confidence of owner Norman Braman through the very actions that earned their respect," Kawakami wrote. "So, many players suggested both privately and publicly yesterday that the team must turn around its 1-4 record, beginning Sunday against the Dallas Cowboys, or all the togetherness that was forged through the strike could dissipate if Braman decides he has had enough of Ryan.

"'We feel we've got an obligation toward the coach,' said defensive end Reggie White, one of the stalwart union supporters on the team. 'We know if we come out losing a lot, Buddy might be gone.'

"With an opportunity to defuse the situation and deny that he was angry at Ryan, Braman told an Eagles spokesman yesterday that he would not comment on the subject."

Ryan felt he had a score to settle with the Cowboys, who had blown out the Birds' replacement players, several Dallas regulars having crossed the picket line and played. When the complete teams met a few weeks later at the Vet, Ryan's team held a 30–20 lead late in the fourth quarter. The Eagles got the ball needing only to kneel down three times to run out the clock. Cunningham knelt twice. On third down, he started to kneel, then, following Ryan's orders, fired the ball downfield to Quick. Dallas corner Everson Walls took a pass interference penalty, and the Eagles got the ball at the Dallas 1. On the next play, Keith Byars ran for a touchdown.

"Buddy hated the Cowboys, and especially Tom Landry. And Tom never understood Buddy," linebacker Garry Cobb, who played for both men, recalled in the book *Game Changers*.

The "real" players went 7-5 that year, despite the interruption, and White won the award for NFL Defensive Player of the Year. At his final news conference of the 7-8 season, Ryan made his opinion of the replacement players very clear. He attempted to present director of player personnel Joe Woolley and assistant to the team president George Azar with oversized, plastic "scab rings" in mock appreciation of their help building the 0-3 replacement or "scab" team. He first attempted to call Azar to the podium, but Azar had left the room, so Ryan summoned Woolley.

endeared Buddy to his players. They loved the fact that Buddy would stick up for us."

After the replacements played their final game, an October 18 loss at Green Bay, Eagles owner Norman Braman addressed the ersatz Eagles. He apologized for the way they were treated by fans, the media, and Braman's coaches.

The day after that game, the Eagles became one of only three NFL teams to release its replacement players en masse, with no exceptions. Ryan said he and team president Harry Gamble made the decision on the plane ride home from Wisconsin.

Tough decision?

"Well, it was a short flight. And we had dinner," Ryan replied.

A five-time Pro Bowl selection with the Eagles, Mike Quick's career was cut short by serious patellar tendinitis. *Ali A. Jorge/NFL/Getty Images*

"We went to a lot of expense, the coaching staff and the trainers and the equipment people all went together, put a lot of money into it," Ryan said, "and bought Joe and George a couple of scab rings for all they did for us to get that scab personnel."

Some members of the media, going along with the joke, asked for Woolley to make a few remarks.

"Joe can't say anything. His [butt] is on the line. He'd rather have his job than talk. But we do appreciate everything you and George did for us—especially since one game might have been the difference," said Ryan, even though the way the tiebreakers fell, the Eagles actually would have needed to win two of their replacement games to garner a playoff berth.

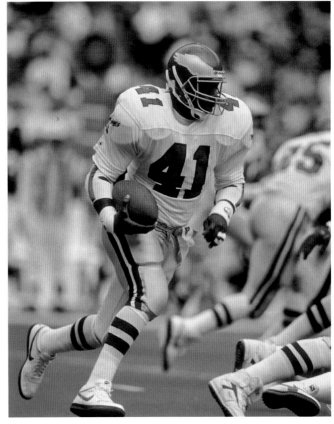

Keith Byars was the total package. He could run the ball, he could block, and he had great hands. He even threw well, passing for four touchdowns in 1990, all on the same trick play that defenses never seemed to figure out. *Joe Patronite/Allsport/Getty Images*

REGGIE WHITE

EAGLES FANS might argue that their franchise hasn't benefited all that much from good fortune over the years, but there have been some notable exceptions. The biggest exception, physically and in every other way, might have been Reggie White.

In 1984, the Birds selected White, then a rookie with the Memphis Showboats of the USFL, in a supplemental draft. At the time the Eagles had no idea how long the USFL would last, or when they might actually get to see White play in Philadelphia. Only one year later, with the USFL on its deathbed, the Showboats agreed to let the Birds buy out White's contract for $1.38 million. The Eagles had just acquired the man whom many would come to call the greatest player ever to wear a Kelly green and white uniform, certainly the greatest defensive end.

White managed 13 sacks in 13 games as a rookie, then 18 in 1986, turned loose in new head coach Buddy Ryan's attacking defense. It's hard to say what sort of single-season record White might have produced in 1987, had the season not been shortened four games by the NFL players' strike. White rampaged to 21 sacks in a dozen games.

Painfully to Eagles fans, as the years go by, White often seems to be recalled by the nation at large at least as much as a Green Bay Packer as an Eagle. That's because he played in two Super Bowls and won one in Green Bay, after leaving Philadelphia amid acrimony in 1993 (hard to leave any other way, really, if you're a great player still functioning at a high level). The Ryan-era teams, as entertaining and occasionally awe-inspiring as they were, never won a postseason game, and the two subsequent years White played in Philly under Rich Kotite also fell well short of the ultimate prize (though Kotite did manage a wild-card win).

White's departure began a migration of 12 veteran players, all disgruntled with owner Norman Braman's fiscal policies.

"I didn't give up on the Eagles. It seemed as though they gave up on me," White told the audience when he received the Wanamaker Athletic Award on March 25, 1993.

As great as White's legend is, it would be even greater if the Eagles had managed to grab

MVP Books Collection

"The Minister of Defense" was among the greatest defensive players the game has ever seen. *Ronald C. Modra/Sports Imagery/Getty Images*

the postseason spotlight a few times when Reggie was terrorizing opposing tackles with the unmatched power and quickness of his under-30 years. The Green Bay White was amazingly productive, but by the time he made it to the Super Bowl he was 35 years old. White, who racked up 124 sacks in 121 games with the Eagles—more than a sack a game—managed 68.5 in 96 games with the Packers. He retired for a year after his second Super Bowl, then played a final season in 2000 for the Carolina Panthers. He appeared in 13 Pro Bowls over the course of his Hall of Fame career.

White is well remembered in Philadelphia for his community work as an Evangelical minister, which is what earned him the nickname "the Minister of Defense." But his beliefs generated controversy after a March 1998 speech to the Wisconsin state legislature, in which he professed a theology that many people found offensive, attributing cultural "gifts" from God to various groups (Asians had a gift for creativity that allowed them to "turn a television into

Focus on Sport/Getty Images

Reggie White seemed unstoppable at times, tallying more sacks than games played in his Eagles career.

a watch," whites knew "how to tap into money," and blacks had a gift for "celebration"). Just for good measure, White declared homosexuality one of the biggest sins.

After saying such things, many people might never have been taken seriously or loved by the public again. But as wrongheaded as White may have been that day, most people seemed to understand that his heart was not poisoned by hatred. By the time of his sudden death from sarcoidosis on the day after Christmas in 2004, White had taken a break from the ministry and was said to be studying the Torah.

White's death at 43 shocked the NFL world and, of course, the Eagles, who were getting ready to play a Monday Night Football game in St. Louis.

Buddy Ryan called White "the best defensive lineman who ever played the game," noting that "he was 305 pounds and ran a 4.6 40, and you just don't see people like that. And I coached a lot of great ones."

Andy Reid, a Green Bay assistant during White's time there, was only slightly less lavish with his praise, terming No. 92 "the greatest defensive end ever to play the game," and summing up his impact with three simple words: "He changed games."

Bernstein Associates/Getty Images

Channel 10 sports anchor Al Meltzer told Ryan most people thought he didn't care about the replacement games.

"We busted our [butts] trying to coach those dumb jerks, but they couldn't play football," Ryan replied. "We didn't have one guy that hung on in the league anywhere. That tells you something about them."

Graciously, Woolley went along with the joke.

"I was 0-3; he was 7-5," Woolley said. "I've never been a head coach in the league before."

THE FOG BOWL

In 1988, Ryan really started to bring it all together. The 10-6 Eagles won the NFC East, with six victories in their final seven games. Cunningham passed for 3,808 yards and ran for 624, tops on the team.

But Buddy Ryan–coached Eagles teams are remembered for their maddening habit of promising greatness and stumbling horribly in the postseason, and this was the year it all began, with a puzzling loss to the Bears on New Year's Eve.

The return to the playoffs captured imaginations; fans loved it when the Eagles flew to Chicago and Ryan had the bus drivers circle Soldier Field, honking their horns.

The game itself, known to Eagles fans as the "Fog Bowl," was less fun. Just before halftime, players started noticing what they thought must be smoke from some sort of tailgating mishap outside Soldier Field. Very quickly, the mist thickened. It was fog coming in off frigid Lake Michigan on a warm December day, and it settled itself around the old concrete porticos like a worn comforter spread across a battered sofa.

"There was a point out there that visibility was no more than 10 yards at the most," said Bears head coach Mike Ditka, whose team led 17–9 when visibility worsened. The Bears might have grounded the Birds' high-powered attack anyway, but the fact that the Eagles were able to push Ditka's vaunted defense (built by Ryan, a few years earlier) down the field repeatedly, gaining 430 yards, lent credence to the idea that Chicago had a little meteorological assistance down near the end zone, where precision is a little more important. The teams scored a field goal apiece in the second half, and the Bears advanced with a 20–12 victory.

"I think the game should have been suspended," Eagles owner Norman Braman said afterward. Braman angrily

With his players barely visible in the background, coach Buddy Ryan patrols the sideline during the "Fog Bowl." *NFL Photos/AP Images*

prowled the sideline in the third quarter, getting a first-hand view of the conditions players faced.

At the time, players were more reluctant to pin the loss on something as ephemeral as fog.

"We had opportunities; we could have won," said Eagles all-pro defensive end Reggie White. "The fog was not a factor. I'm not going to blame it on the fog."

Ryan noted that football is not baseball, where weather routinely forces postponements, and pointed out his team's missed opportunities. The Eagles had a pair of touchdowns called back when the skies were still clear, both on penalties incurred by running back Anthony Toney. Tight end Keith Jackson dropped a touchdown pass after a fumble recovery.

Referee Jim Tunney, who communicated with the league office about what to do, contended afterward that he could see both goal posts for almost the entire game, a statement no other participant made.

"The broadcasters for CBS-TV were baffled, sending a messenger to the sidelines to relay what was going on," the next day's *Philadelphia Inquirer* said. "The stadium announcer often mistook completions for dropped passes."

Cunningham huddles the offense during the "Fog Bowl," played in Chicago in 1988.
Al Messerschmidt/ Getty Images

Fans left their seats to watch concourse TVs, which offered only a slightly less scrambled view. CBS announcer Verne Lundquist openly questioned the decision to continue, and frequently stopped giving play-by-play with an explanation along the lines of "he just disappeared."

"I guess that's the difference between announcers and referees. We have such great eyesight that enables us to do our jobs," Tunney said, under intense questioning about his remarkable end-to-end view. Tunney, who suspended the play clock, said there was never a time when he couldn't see at least 50 yards. Of course, no one asked him to throw a ball to a receiver, or to try to catch a pass or a punt.

All in all, not a great ending for the first Eagles postseason game in seven years.

RANDALL CUNNINGHAM

SPORTS ILLUSTRATED once declared Randall Cunningham "the Ultimate Weapon," but that was more a declaration of potential than fact.

Cunningham was 6-foot-4, 215, and most of his height seemed to be legs. He was the author of some of the most memorable moments in Eagles history. Unfortunately, they were moments—games or plays—not an era, or a series of championships, which is what he seemed to have the ability to produce, but never did.

Cunningham was drafted from UNLV in the second round of the 1985 draft, but he became the Eagles' starting quarterback for good in 1987, when Buddy Ryan was the defensive-minded head coach.

Linebacker Garry Cobb, now a Philadelphia broadcast personality, was a Cunningham teammate back then.

"It was Buddy who saw the greatness in him, but probably didn't develop it the way he could have, because Buddy was a defensive coach. He didn't really have respect for the offensive side of the ball. Like he used to say, 'All we need is five fat guys and we have an offensive line.' Randall was always running for his life. What [Ryan] didn't do was put him in a system."

Popular wisdom holds that Cunningham's development was stalled when quarterbacks coach Doug Scovil died of a heart attack in the team's workout room in 1989. Cunningham has acknowledged that he took his gifts for granted and didn't study or work the way he should have. But he did make three Pro Bowls as an Eagle, and he set the career rushing record for a quarterback that still stands today: 4,928 yards on 775 carries (although current Eagles QB Michael Vick ended the 2010 season less than 300 yards shy of that mark).

Cobb said that instead of being taught to use his talents within the context of an offense, "the fact that he had the ability to scramble and create things became the offense, and unfortunately against a good team, you can't do that."

Cunningham never won a playoff game until 1992, by which time Ryan had been replaced by Rich Kotite. A 1991 knee injury had taken away much of Cunningham's elusiveness, though he still had a great arm.

No. 12's signature play came in a Monday night game on October 10, 1988, against the Giants. The host Eagles had the ball at the Giants' 4 in the second quarter when Cunningham took the snap and was flushed out of the pocket, rolling to his right. Giants linebacker Carl Banks was waiting, and he unloaded, driving Cunningham backward. Somehow, Cunningham stayed on his feet, touched down lightly with one hand, regained his balance, and whipped a touchdown pass to tight end Jimmie Giles. The Eagles won, then continued on to capture their first NFC East title since

There are a handful of dual-threat quarterbacks in today's NFL, but when Randall Cunningham came into the league, he was one of a kind. *George Gojkovich/Getty Images*

1980. The play was chosen the greatest in Eagles history in the book *Game Changers: The 50 Greatest Plays in Eagles History.*

"I tried to run right through him," Banks said afterward. "I hit him, but he backed out of it. . . . I saw him catch himself and stay up. It was a great effort on his part. The average guy would have gone down. That's the kind of play that makes him different. That's what makes him Randall Cunningham."

"It amazes me; I amaze myself," Cunningham said afterward. "God's given me talent to throw and run with the ball, but things like that just aren't supposed to happen."

Cunningham, a punter at UNLV, also booted the ball 91 yards when called upon to do so by the Eagles, in a December 3, 1989, cameo appearance, with regular punter John Teltschik injured and replacement Max Runager struggling.

MVP Books Collection

Cunningham's ability to run the ball as a quarterback is well known to all. *Al Messerschmidt/ Getty Images*

Early in the 1993 season, Cunningham suffered another season-ending injury—this time a broken leg—and his Eagles career began to fade. By 1995, new offensive coordinator Jon Gruden was implementing a West Coast offense, and Gruden saw Rodney Peete as a better fit. The Eagles made it to the second round of the playoffs behind Peete. Cunningham got permission to leave the team briefly, to attend the birth of his first child. Then he elected to stay an extra day and missed the last practice. This became a big deal when Peete was injured and Cunningham had to play, demonstrating no grasp of the game plan whatsoever in a 30–11 loss that ended the team's season and his Eagles career.

Incredibly, no team signed the 33-year-old Cunningham for the 1996 season. He finally signed in Minnesota the next year, to back up Brad Johnson. When Johnson got hurt in 1998, Cunningham was given the controls. Sensing this was his last chance to show what he could have been, and given weapons like rookie Randy Moss that he never had in Philadelphia, Cunningham authored an astonishing season: 34 touchdowns, 10 interceptions, and a 106 passer rating for a 15-1 team that came within a missed field goal of going to the Super Bowl. He later played a backup role for the Cowboys and the Ravens before retiring following the 2001 season.

His ability as a punter, on the other hand, is a better kept secret. *NFL Photos/AP Images*

Keith Jackson won the Rookie of the Year Award for his performance in 1988, capped off by his 7 catches for 142 yards —but one costly dropped touchdown— in the Eagles'"Fog Bowl" loss to the Bears. Mike Powell/Getty Images

THE DISAPPOINTMENT CONTINUES

The 1989 season brought an 11-5 record and the first home playoff game at the Vet since 1981. Early on, September 17, the team signed Cunningham to a five-year, $15 million contract, making him the NFL's highest-paid QB at the time. Later that same day, Cunningham showed his appreciation with a 34-for-46, 447-yard, five-touchdown performance at RFK Stadium, leading the Eagles to a 42–37 victory over the host Redskins. Cunningham was

21-for-27 for 267 yards and four touchdowns in the second half alone, as he led the Birds back from a 20-point hole. He later called it the best game he ever played.

On December 3, Cunningham was pressed into punting duty; regular punter John Teltschik was injured, and the guy signed to replace him, Max Runager, was not doing well. With the ball on the Birds' 3, the score tied at 17, Cunningham, a standout punter and QB at UNLV, took the snap and blasted the ball. It sailed over returner

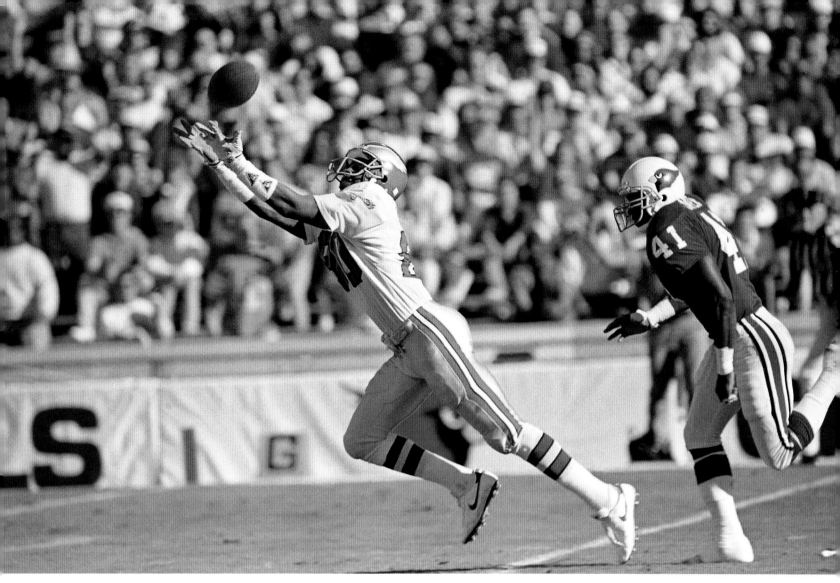

After leading the team with 11 touchdown catches in 1989, Cris Carter was surprisingly released by Buddy Ryan, who refused to put up with his abuse of drugs and alcohol. Carter would eventually get his act together and have a successful career with the Minnesota Vikings. Rob Schumacher/AP Images

Dave Meggett's head and stopped rolling 91 yards later. Next play, the Giants fumbled the ball away, and three plays after that, the Eagles scored the game-winning touchdown.

Ryan's defense led the league in takeaways that year with 56 and set a franchise record with 62 sacks. But the Rams won the wild-card game, 21–7, jumping to an early lead and exploiting the Eagles' lack of a deep threat, with Quick unavailable after season-ending knee surgery.

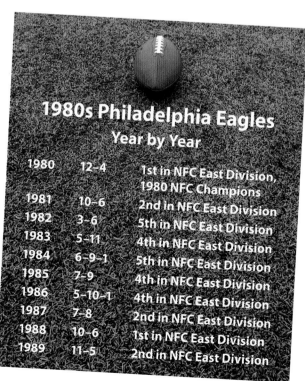

1980s Philadelphia Eagles
Year by Year

Year	Record	Finish
1980	12–4	1st in NFC East Division, 1980 NFC Champions
1981	10–6	2nd in NFC East Division
1982	3–6	5th in NFC East Division
1983	5–11	4th in NFC East Division
1984	6–9–1	5th in NFC East Division
1985	7–9	4th in NFC East Division
1986	5–10–1	4th in NFC East Division
1987	7–8	2nd in NFC East Division
1988	10–6	1st in NFC East Division
1989	11–5	2nd in NFC East Division

7 CHANGE IN THE AIR
The 1990s

MVP Books Collection

The 1990s started with great expectations for the Eagles. Randall Cunningham and Reggie White were in their primes; Keith Byars caught 81 passes in the 1990 season and the Birds went 10-6. Cunningham had one of the great years in franchise history, throwing for 3,466 yards and 30 touchdowns and running for 942 yards on 118 carries—an outstanding average of 8 yards per carry.

The Eagles added a seminal chapter to Ryan-era lore with what came to be known as "the body bag game." Eight Redskins were injured in their 28–14 loss to the Eagles on November 12, including quarterbacks Jeff Rutledge and Stan Humphries.

"It seemed like every time I turned around, somebody else was getting carried off. It was frustrating," Washington defensive end Charles Mann said afterward.

But somehow, as always seemed to happen, Ryan did not get the last word. The Redskins' subsequent 20-6 wild-card playoff victory never acquired a catchy nickname or its own Wikipedia entry, but it brought an abrupt end to the Ryan era. Against the backdrop of an 0-3 playoff record, the feisty coach failed in his bid to get his expiring contract renewed.

Ryan clearly was outcoached by Joe Gibbs, at one point seeming to panic and sending in backup Jim McMahon to replace Cunningham for three downs. McMahon was well past his magical Super Bowl Shuffle days as a Chicago Bear, and Cunningham was about to win both the Bert Bell Award and the Pro Football Writers' season MVP vote. It was especially puzzling when Ryan conceded after the game that the offense's biggest shortcoming was pass blocking. "It's hard to win when you don't block anyone," Ryan said.

"I think . . . Buddy made it to the playoffs for the third consecutive time, and he was willing to try anything to win the game," Cunningham said the day after elimination

One of the strangest things Buddy Ryan is remembered for is his perplexing decision to pull Randall Cunningham for a washed-up Jim McMahon in the midst of a 20–6 playoff defeat to the Redskins. *Mike Powell/Getty Images*

as the Eagles emptied their lockers and packed their belongings. "And whether people say it was the panic button or not, something happened yesterday."

"A few people said, 'If Randall can't do it because of the [pass] protection or whatever, how can Jim do it? He's not as mobile,'" Cunningham said. "It's kind of insulting, when I think about it."

When Cunningham spoke, players had already seen an *Inquirer* story written right after the game in which Norman Braman was quoted as saying: "Seven points behind and he embarrasses Randall before a national television audience."

When the ax fell on January 8, Ryan was his usual defiant self.

"I've been fired before, but usually it's for losing," Ryan joked. He later would raise horses, and he named one of them Fired For Winning.

"I think it's a winning philosophy," Ryan continued. "I think the program speaks for itself. . . . Everybody's trying to make a big deal out of putting McMahon in, well, that's bull. I was trying to win the game. Somebody said it was an emotional decision. That's bull. It was something I tried to do to win. That's the only way I know how to play the game, to try to win."

In the *Daily News*, Rich Hofmann pointed out that a franchise with seven winning seasons in the previous 24 years had just fired a coach who'd authored three winning seasons in a row. It was a lot like the more recent controversy over Andy Reid's tenure, except Reid, unlike Ryan, hasn't gone to great lengths to antagonize his owner. And Reid does win playoff games, just not Super Bowls.

That was the part of the Ryan firing that made many fans uneasy—was Braman really firing Ryan and promoting offensive coordinator Rich Kotite because he thought Kotite could unlock the secret to postseason success? Or was it because Braman was tired of being publicly mocked by a man who worked for him?

"I think you can win in the NFL without being a 'bad boy,'" Braman said at the news conference announcing the change. Braman said the hiring of Kotite would bring "discipline and precision on both sides of the ball that [GM] Harry Gamble and I think are going to make a difference."

"Mr. Braman wants us to have a clean image. He wants us to be a classy organization like the 49ers," Cunningham earnestly explained at the 1991 Maxwell Club banquet. "And I'm sure he'll build that type of team. With Richie as

Rich Kotite inherited a contender when he was promoted to the head coaching position, and he did manage to accomplish what Buddy Ryan never did: he won a playoff game after the 1992 season. *Donna Bagby/AP Images*

Jeff Kemp started two games for the birds in 1991, one of five quarterbacks to play for the team that year. *Rick Stewart/Allsport/Getty Images*

our coach, Richie will allow us to be ourselves, but at the same time, we'll be disciplined. We'll be the team that we need to be to win games."

In 1992, an *Inquirer* story about Braman said: "Freed of the awkwardness caused by Ryan's poor relationship with the team's management, Braman is reveling in the easy rapport he has found among himself, team president Harry Gamble, and coach Rich Kotite."

The reveling was short-lived.

Kotite was a former NFL tight end and Muhammad Ali sparring partner who had run the Jets' offense before coming to the Eagles. Unlike many new coaches, Kotite inherited the makings of a strong contender. But Cunningham went down on opening day against Green Bay with a season-ending knee injury, dooming what might have been the best of the Cunningham-White teams to another 10-6 record, which amazingly was not even good enough to qualify for the playoffs. McMahon, Jeff Kemp, Brad Goebel, and Pat Ryan played QB for the Birds after Cunningham went down.

Bud Carson's defense wasted a year for the ages. The Eagles led the league in fewest yards allowed overall, fewest passing yards, and fewest rushing yards, only the fifth time that had been done.

The highlight of the season, since there were no playoffs, might have been the so-called House of Pain game at Houston. On December 2, the Eagles traveled to the Astrodome, which had gained that nickname—"The House of Pain"—because of the Oilers' awesome run-and-shoot offense, helmed by Warren Moon. The Birds won 13–6 on national TV.

"In the 'House of Pain' game, we wanted to intimidate," linebacker Seth Joyner later recalled for the Eagles' website. "The Oilers were a finesse team, especially their offense, and we knew if we played a very physical game, the game would be ours to win. That was a tough game; both defenses came to play that night."

THE DAWN OF FREE AGENCY

In 1992 Cunningham was back, but Pro Bowl defensive tackle Jerome Brown was gone, killed when his Corvette turned over on a wet road in Florida June 25. Despite the tragedy, the Birds regrouped to go 11-5. Their defense was tremendous. They got a great year from underrated linebacker Seth Joyner, a fierce leader who would retire as the

JEROME BROWN

To be called the best by Buddy Ryan is no small bit of praise, but Jerome Brown was an extraordinary presence on the Eagles' defensive line. *Jonathan Daniel/Getty Images*

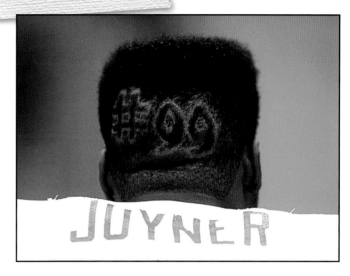

The entire team mourned the loss of Jerome Brown, and Seth Joyner even paid tribute on the back of his head. *Jeff Hixon/Allsport/Getty Images*

REGGIE WHITE WAS ABOUT TO SPEAK at a Veterans Stadium rally held by evangelist Billy Graham, on June 25, 1992, when he learned of the death earlier that afternoon of his friend and teammate, Jerome Brown.

White, weeping, went onstage and eulogized "one of the greatest men I ever knew in my life."

Buddy Ryan, deposed that offseason as the Eagles' coach, learned of Brown's death watching TV in Los Angeles. Ryan called Brown "the best defensive lineman in the league," an understandable bit of overstatement during a time when the league and the Eagles also had White.

Brown might have been the best defensive tackle to ever wear an Eagles uniform; he certainly was one of the most memorable personalities. But he died at age 27 in a senseless, careless tragedy that also claimed the life of his 12-year-old nephew, Gus Brown.

Coming off what he felt was his best NFL season—Brown recorded 150 tackles and nine sacks while making the Pro Bowl in 1991—the Eagles' 1987 first-round pick was killed when his black '91 Corvette left the road, bounced off a palm tree, and flipped over in his hometown of Brooksville, Florida.

Brown apparently stomped on the gas as he was leaving Register Chevrolet, where he was friends with many of the workers. He lost control only a few hundred yards up Wade Avenue from the dealership. His friends from the body shop were the first people on the scene.

Brown had been more than a football player in Brooksville; he had been a unifying force in the community, someone who never lost touch with his roots. The loss of his extralarge personality and talent reverberated across the NFL.

At Brown's funeral, former Miami Hurricanes teammate Michael Irvin said: "Football players are easily replaced. But I'll tell you what, man, when you get a true friend, they're not easily replaced at all. Because true friends are blessings from heaven. You don't find true friends on the streets every day. You can find a ballplayer on the street any day. Not a true friend. Not a Jerome Brown. The guy was a blessing to so many people."

Brown became the sixth Eagle to have his number retired when White presented Brown's No. 99 jersey to Brown's parents before the Birds defeated the Saints, 15–3, on September 6, 1992, at the Vet.

ERIC ALLEN

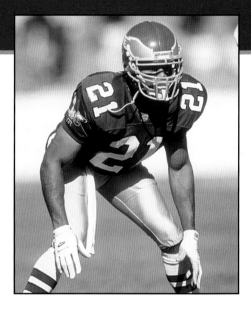

Eric Allen was a key cog in Buddy Ryan's defense, a ball-hawking defensive back with a great knack for reading quarterbacks and a nose for the end zone. *Stephen Dunn/Getty Images*

ERIC ALLEN made five Pro Bowls in his seven Eagles seasons and was a key component of the Birds' 1991 defense, one of the best in NFL history. When he left in free agency after the 1994 season, Allen was tied for the franchise lead in interceptions, with 34, and held the record for interceptions returned for a touchdown, with five.

Four of Allen's interceptions for TDs came in the 1993 season, including a 94-yarder against the Jets that made the NFL Films video *The 100 Greatest Touchdowns of All Time*. It was a key play in a 35–30 victory at the Meadowlands that was dampened by the loss of quarterback Randall Cunningham to a broken fibula.

Allen didn't think about scoring when he first picked off Boomer Esaison's pass.

"I'm thinking, 'Just get out of bounds,'" Allen said afterward. "'A lot of things have been going bad for us all day. Just get out of bounds before you fumble the ball.'"

Then he changed his mind.

"As I looked downfield after I intercepted the pass, I saw some of the Jets almost walking off the field," Allen said. "I said, 'Hey, someone has to make the play today. We've been playing awful all day. Something good has to go along with this. We can't just lose the game like this.'"

On the Birds' sideline, head coach Rich Kotite was amazed.

"It was the greatest interception return I have ever seen under the circumstances," Kotite said.

"It was the damnedest thing I've ever seen," said safety Wes Hopkins.

"I read Boomer's eyes on the play," Allen said. "He threw the pass, but the receiver wasn't able to get to his position where he wanted to be. So I caught the ball. Then I just tried to stay alive. I was like a wolf in a chicken barn. It's like the guy's coming to get you, you've got the chickens, and you're just trying to get out of there. Guys were yelling, 'Come this way, come this way.' All kinds of guys were getting blocks.

"After I got downfield, two guys were coming after me with the angle. I heard [corner] Ben [Smith] behind me saying, 'Pitch the ball, pitch the ball.' I tried to slow down so Ben could come up. He came up and made the block [on Jets tight end Johnny Mitchell] that allowed me to get by the last guy."

After he crossed the goal line, Allen ran over to the runway behind the end zone, where Cunningham stood on crutches, and gave the quarterback the ball.

A year and change later, Allen was the last of the greats from Buddy Ryan and Bud Carson's defenses to depart. Like Reggie White, Clyde Simmons, Seth Joyner, and Wes Hopkins before him, he did so with acrimony, decrying the front office's penny-pinching ways, even though the roundly disliked Norman Braman had sold the team to Jeffrey Lurie by then.

"It's very surprising, but that's the kind of relationship players had with the Eagles," Allen said after signing with the Saints. "I knew I wasn't going to be an Eagle early in the offseason. The whole environment around there has to change. It's so negative, so pessimistic. It just wasn't right and I knew the best thing for me would be to go elsewhere. Sometimes, you just have to make a change.

"Instead of hearing what I and others have had to say and doing something about it, changing their approach and some of the people involved in the bad feelings, it seems like they think it's no big deal, you know? Most teams, I would think, would stop for a second and say, 'Wait a minute, something's very wrong here.' It's like they think anyone can wear the jersey number and get in there and play at a high level. That's why it was important to me to find a team and people who were different. The Saints, like a lot of other teams, do business differently.

"I wish Ray Rhodes all the best, I really do, because I think he's a good man who deserves better than he might get in Philly. I hope they let him run the show, but I don't think that's going to happen. It's a shame."

Allen's anger had been building since the previous preseason, when the new regime unsuccessfully courted free agent Deion Sanders, instead of reaching a long-term accord with Allen.

"I understand it's a business, but to bring people in and treat them better than those who've been here, and just throw money at them, like, 'Here, it's yours' . . . It was the ultimate disrespect," Allen said. "For them to go chasing Deion Sanders around when they had important people at home to take care of . . . What was that? And it's happened over and over and over and over.

"People wonder why we always seemed incomplete. That's why. We never could get over that final hurdle, because we never felt the people upstairs were committed to win the way you have to be today. It just gets to you. It's just best for me to go elsewhere and be in the right place, where the people upstairs are committed, really committed to win."

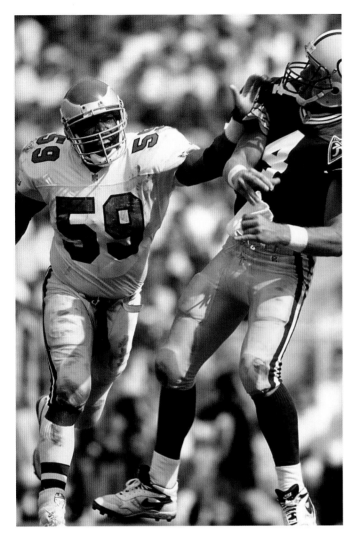

Seth Joyner was a great fit in an Eagles' defense that thrived on creating turnovers. For his career, he recorded 52 sacks, 24 interceptions, and 26 forced fumbles. *Jonathan Daniel/ Allsport/Getty Images*

The fearsome Reggie White puts a vicious hit on the Redskins' Mark Rypien. White's free agency departure after the 1992 season was a major blow to the Eagles' defense. *John Iacono/Sports Illustrated/Getty Images*

MVP Books Collection

only player in NFL history with at least 20 interceptions and 50 sacks.

Former Eagles corner Eric Allen summed up Joyner in the book *Game Changers: The 50 Greatest Plays in Eagles History.* "Seth had a great feel for the game like a middle linebacker, but was very athletic, like an outside linebacker, and had the ability to rush the passer, like a defensive end," Allen said. "He was flat-out nasty on the football field."

At the end of the 1992 season, Kotite did something Ryan never managed, winning a wild-card playoff game, 36–20, at New Orleans. But the next postseason round brought a familiar return to futility—a crushing 34–10 loss at Dallas.

More discouraging than the loss was the aftermath. Free agency was new and Reggie White clearly seemed inclined to take advantage of it, White sounding off as the players cleaned out their lockers. His complaint would quickly become the conventional wisdom about Braman's ownership.

"I don't think they are as committed as the Cowboys or the Redskins," White said when asked about the Eagles' priorities. "They haven't shown it. Now I'm not trying to attack the organization in any kind of way, but you asked the question and my honest opinion is no. You should be making your players feel comfortable."

White would leave for Green Bay, for $17 million over four years, and the team Ryan assembled would slowly dissolve into mediocrity over the next two seasons.

"It's been really trying and tiresome, and in some ways maybe I left Philadelphia with some hard feelings. But there are some good friends there I'm going to miss. Now I've got to let go of all that," White said.

White's departure was a sign to other players that hard times were coming.

"Instead of adding outstanding players, we were subtracting them," Allen said in *Game Changers*. "I would have loved to have played my whole career in Philly, but there were so many issues we dropped the ball on as a franchise. I mean, how do you let Reggie White leave? I don't care how much money he wants, the guy is the best player in the National Football League. And you just let him leave? No way anybody can say they're a better team without a Reggie White. I looked around and thought, 'This is just not the team I envisioned.'"

Allen would leave in free agency for the Saints after the 1994 season.

The 1993 Eagles beat White and the Packers in Week 2, 20–17, and started off 4-0, but Cunningham went down for the season again, this time with a broken fibula. A six-game losing streak led to an 8-8 record and another year out of the playoffs.

That was Braman's last year in charge. Jeffrey Lurie paid $185 million for the Eagles in the offseason, which was a record price for a pro sports franchise at the time.

"I'd like my signature mark to be winning championships," Lurie said. Of course, that's a mark Lurie has yet to make, but he has overseen the building of the first stadium ever controlled by the Eagles and the state-of-the-art NovaCare practice facility, as well as the most extended period of winning in the history of the franchise.

Lurie initially expressed faith in Kotite, which turned out to be misplaced. The 1994 Eagles started out 7-2, with Kotite challenging Lurie's stated intention to evaluate the coach after the season, adding that he would do his own evaluation of whether he wanted to stay or go. Then they lost their last seven games, an excruciating flameout that, if nothing else, settled the Kotite question. He was

In 1994, Jeffrey Lurie paid a then-record $185 million to purchase the Eagles from Norman Braman. *Al Messerschmidt/Getty Images*

dismissed two days after the season ended, his 37-29 overall record notwithstanding.

"I think the direction of the ball club over the last half of the season has been disturbing," Lurie said. "I don't think we played to our potential. I don't think we exhibited the ability to take it to the next level. I think, in fact, we dropped a level. Let's face reality—that's not a pleasant situation to be in—0-7. Believe me, I was very unhappy about it, disturbed. And I felt a change was necessary."

Kotite would be hired right away to take over the Jets— there was speculation he had the Jets deal in his back pocket when he made his "evaluation" statement—but he would win just four games in two seasons, and the Jets finished with the worst record in the league both years. After that, Kotite would never coach again.

For his part, Lurie embarked on a long and confusing head coach search, at one point seeming close to bringing

Eric Allen returns an interception against the 49ers in 1994, which would be Allen's last year as an Eagle, continuing the frustrating trend of free agency departures by their star players.
George Rose/Getty Images

MVP Books Collection

The first coach hired by new owner Jeffrey Lurie, Ray Rhodes showed tremendous promise in his first two seasons at the helm for the Eagles. Unfortunately, things quickly took a turn for the worse. *Rogers Photo Archive/Getty Images*

Dick Vermeil out of the broadcast booth. They parted acrimoniously, with Lurie unwilling to meet Vermeil's requirements for salary and control of the football operation. Lurie called Vermeil's requests "outrageous," but the former coach won the PR battle with fans, who still considered him a Philly icon. That held true even after he subsequently returned to coaching with the Rams and won a Super Bowl there.

In retrospect, it's probably fair to point out that, after firing Buddy Ryan, Braman had other options available to him, namely, Ryan's defensive coordinator, 32-year-old Jeff Fisher, who was the NFL's longest-tenured head coach when he was dismissed by the Titans in February 2011. Braman chose Kotite. If he had gone the other way, would Fisher now be embarking on his third decade as the Eagles' coach?

NOT QUITE THE COLOSSUS OF RHODES

Lurie eventually settled on former San Francisco and Green Bay assistant Ray Rhodes, the Eagles' first African American head coach, a man with five Super Bowl rings as an assistant.

"He epitomizes the word 'winner,'" Lurie said. "Football in the 1990s is about recruiting, talent evaluation, player respect, integrity, discipline."

Rhodes, a former NFL wideout and cornerback, was a tremendous evaluator of defensive talent; in his four years in charge, the Eagles acquired the backbone of the defense that would get the subsequent Andy Reid era off to a successful start, with Troy Vincent, Hugh Douglas, Jeremiah Trotter, and Brian Dawkins.

Rhodes had been a scrapper as a player, and he had that grittiness Philadelphia prizes. When his first team went 10-6 and blew out Detroit in a wild-card game, 58–37, the new coach became wildly popular with the fans. He was Buddy Ryan without the need to antagonize.

"This has been a great experience for our entire team, as far as getting to this point. I want the fans of Philadelphia to know that within the next year or so, we'll get to the top of this thing," Rhodes said after the season ended in a 30–11 divisional playoff loss at Dallas. "Give me a couple of years and I can get this thing done. I know I can."

That finale was Cunningham's last game as an Eagle, though he hadn't expected to play at all. He had missed the week of practice while attending to the birth of his son in Las Vegas, and he compounded that problem by forgetting to take his playbook with him. But when Rodney Peete suffered a concussion, Cunningham had to play. It didn't go well. If any doubt had lingered that the Eagles wanted to move on, Cunningham removed it.

Rhodes's second season started out 7-2, and a legend seemed to be in the making.

Then it all blew up. The 1996 season went sour down the stretch, ending 10-6, capped by a dismal 14–0 loss to the 49ers in the playoffs. Rhodes's final two seasons plunged steadily downhill, to shocking depths.

"This year my expectations were a whole lot higher," Rhodes said after the wild-card loss at San Francisco. "We didn't reach them."

But Lurie remained convinced Rhodes was on the right track. "We're getting there. There's no question in everybody's mind that we're getting there," he said after the loss to the 49ers.

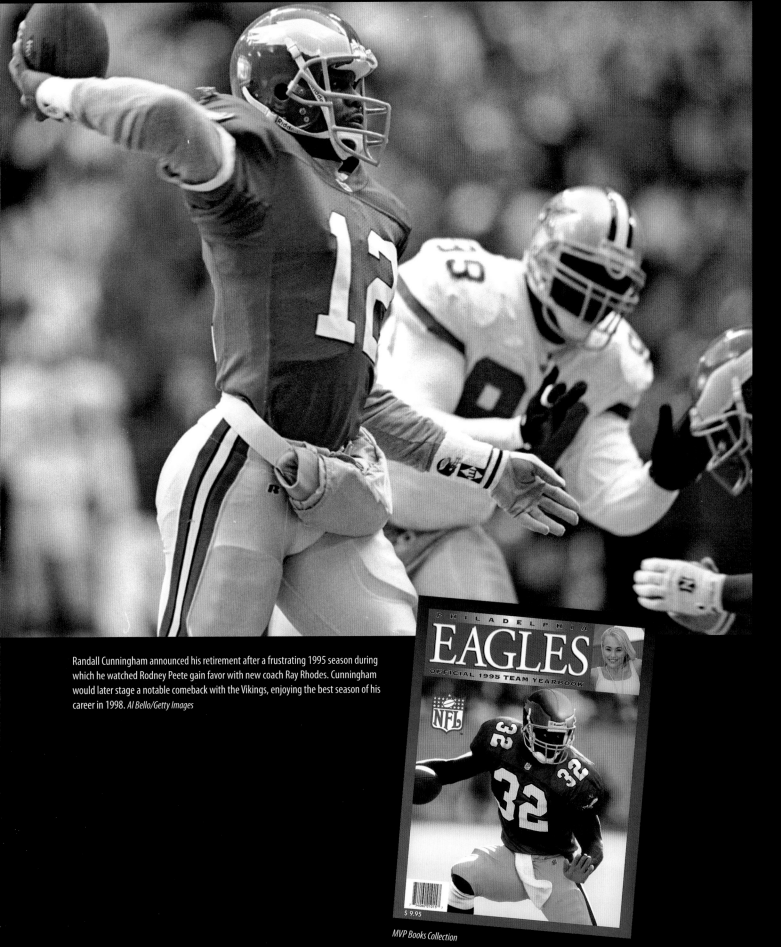

Randall Cunningham announced his retirement after a frustrating 1995 season during which he watched Rodney Peete gain favor with new coach Ray Rhodes. Cunningham would later stage a notable comeback with the Vikings, enjoying the best season of his career in 1998. *Al Bello/Getty Images*

PHILADELPHIA
EAGLES
OFFICIAL 1995 TEAM YEARBOOK

NFL

32

$ 9.95

MVP Books Collection

Eagles fans know a great player when they see one, and Brian Dawkins was always a fan favorite. He finished his Eagles career having started 182 of 183 possible games, recording 898 tackles, 34 interceptions, and 21 sacks along the way. *George Gojkovich/Getty Images*

MVP Books Collection

In the 1997 preseason, when hope still reigned, Rhodes was asked whether he thought about getting an extension on his contract, which was to expire in 1999.

"You'll never hear me talk about 1999. That's bull. Nineteen ninety-nine? The way I pursue the game and do things, I might not be living in 1999. Ray Bob ain't promised the earth in 1999. . . . It ain't like I live a stress-

free life," Rhodes said. "If I don't have at least a case of those antacids I take every day, it's hard. You don't put off something that you can do today 'til tomorrow. Ain't putting nothing off. I want to win now. The players know that."

Maybe they knew it, but when all was said and done, it was apparent that Rhodes had given his players too much

Hugh Douglas (left, *Rick Stewart/Allsport/Getty Images*) and Troy Vincent (right, *Al Bello/Allsport/Getty Images*) were two of the great young defensive players Ray Rhodes acquired during his brief run as Eagles head coach. Douglas trails only Reggie White and Clyde Simmons on the Eagles all-time sacks list.

A staple for years in the basement of Veterans Stadium, "Eagles Court" was disbanded shortly after the team moved to Lincoln Financial Field in 2003. *Dan Loh/AP Images*

credit, too much slack. As a player who'd clung to the fringes of the roster, Rhodes had given everything he had, every day. One of his flaws as a coach was that he assumed everyone was like that, that each of his players despised failure as much as he did and would do anything to avoid it. Like a lot of "players' coaches," he gave the players too much respect.

One of the most memorable pratfalls in Eagles history happened in the third game of 1997, at Dallas, early in what would become a 6-9-1 season, the worst since 1986. The Eagles, who would go 0-7-1 on the road, lined up for a 21-yard field goal try with four seconds remaining, trailing, 21–20. But the holder, Tommy Hutton, bobbled a perfect snap. Kicker Chris Boniol stutter-stepped, then prepared to kick the ball flatfooted, but Hutton didn't see Boniol stop and instead stood up to run. He rolled left and actually had a receiver open in the end zone, but right about the time that became apparent, Hutton fumbled the ball away, untouched. Game over.

"It's nobody's fault but mine," Hutton said afterward.

The Cowboys certainly were appreciative.

"That holder better check his locker," Deion Sanders advised. "He may have a suitcase in there with a lot of money."

A fluke play, yes, but mistakes and a lack of discipline came to characterize Rhodes's tenure. People around the team came to feel the coach was coming unglued, and his day-after news conferences dissolved into profane lamentations. Once, with the cameras rolling, Rhodes compared a loss to watching intruders sodomize your family.

EAGLES COURT

Crowds at Veterans Stadium grew anxious and impatient as the losses piled up. During a Monday Night Football game against the 49ers, a 24–12 loss on November 10, 1997, crowd behavior hit a new low. Police reported that there were about 60 fights in the stands that night, and someone even fired a flare gun into some luckily empty seats across the way—a prelude to catastrophe, if there ever was one. Judge Seamus McCaffery, a veteran of the Philadelphia Police Department and of the Vietnam War, had seen enough. Embarrassed by the fans' unruly behavior, McCaffery was the driving force behind an ad hoc courtroom in the basement of Veteran's Stadium that came to be known simply as "Eagles Court."

If you were going to handpick someone to preside over a court adjudicating brawling and drunken misbehavior

RICKY WATTERS

NOBODY EVER GOT OFF to a worse start with Eagles fans than Ricky Watters. Probably, no one ever will.

Remarkably, though, by the time his three-year Philadelphia tenure was over, he had recovered a large measure of popularity. He remained controversial, but Watters did have his supporters, quite a few of them, which says something about the city (something different from what you often hear about the Philly faithful) and something about Watters, who proved to be tougher and classier than he had seemed to be the afternoon of his disastrous debut.

It was September 3, 1995, at the Vet, Ray Rhodes's first game as the Eagles' head coach, against previously hapless Tampa Bay. Locally, there was not great excitement about the dawning of a new era; the local TV broadcast of the game was blacked out because not enough tickets sold in time. But fans who weren't there to see what happened heard about it soon enough.

Watters fumbled twice, losing 1 of them while gaining just 37 yards on 17 carries in a 21–6 loss. But that wasn't the worst part. Randall Cunningham targeted him twice over the middle with passes, and both times, with a defender closing fast and the ball hanging, Watters failed to extend to catch the ball. The slang term for this gutless practice: "Alligator arms." But Watters soon ensured his afternoon would be remembered in a different argot, as memorable and enduring locally as Allen Iverson's rant about "practice."

Asked about the receptions that weren't, Watters explained his thinking. "I'm not gonna jump up there and get knocked out," he said. "For who? For what?"

More than 15 years later, the words "For who? For what?" need no context. Even the most casual Eagles fan knows what you're talking about.

Watters went on to complain about fans making noise—basically, booing—while the offense was trying to call signals. "I don't care about the crowd," Watters said.

There was more. During the game, when he was replaced by Charlie Garner in the third quarter, Watters became visibly upset and held an animated sideline phone conversation with coaches in the booth.

Philadelphia Inquirer columnist Bill Lyon immediately understood the enormity of Watters's gaffe. How could a guy who grew up on the fringes of Eagles territory, Harrisburg, Pennsylvania, have such a faulty understanding of the requirements to play here?

"It was as though someone had written on a blackboard all the things a professional athlete shouldn't do, and all the things he shouldn't say," Lyon wrote. "And then Rick Watters defiantly stood up and did them and said them—every last regrettable, stupid, self-absorbed one of them.

Despite his "For who? For what?" statements, Ricky Watters earned the respect and adoration of Eagles fans when he helped lead the team to the playoffs in 1995 and 1996. *Focus on Sport/Getty Images*

"It was the most graceless, clueless, classless debut by a Philadelphia athlete in memory."

But shortly after "For who? For what?," Watters said something else. Though it received much less attention, it proved to be prescient over time: "There's another day," he said. "I'm gonna make a whole lot of plays here. I made a whole lot of plays where I was at before [San Francisco]. I've always made plays."

Rodney Peete, Ty Detmer, and Bobby Hoying took turns playing QB for the Eagles after Randall Cunningham left the team. The lack of a star QB was one of the primary problems for head coach Ray Rhodes.

After Irving Fryar's 1997 campaign, the Eagles wouldn't see another 1,000-yard receiver until a guy named Terrell Owens came along in 2004. *Rick Stewart/Allsport/Getty Images*

ANDY REID

Eagles fans clamored for a big-name head coach to fill the vacancy left by Ray Rhodes. They got Reid instead, and he's led the Eagles to one of the most successful stretches in franchise history. *H. Rumph Jr/AP Images*

ANDY REID WAS THINKING about a medical career as his senior year at BYU approached; Reid's mother, Elizabeth, had been a pioneering radiologist.

Then head coach LaVell Edwards asked the big guard from Los Angeles if he'd considered coaching.

"I hadn't, at the time, but it sounded pretty good," recalled Reid, who then embarked on that journey, as a BYU grad assistant in 1982, the season after he graduated.

Growing up, Reid said, he didn't think beyond his playing career; he aspired to play in the NFL. But in the final game of his second year at Glendale (California) Junior College, Reid wrecked a knee, and Stanford subsequently withdrew a scholarship offer. Reid ended up at BYU, playing for Edwards, which turned out to be a good break—particularly, Reid said, after he realized he was going to be no more than a "pretty average" college guard.

More than 20 years later, Edwards was Reid's guest for the Eagles' Super Bowl XXXIX appearance.

"He treated you as a human being," Reid recalled that week. "It didn't matter if you were first team or third team, or if you were a walk-on, he treated you the same way. On the sideline, he represented the university very well. He didn't have any highs and lows, he kind of kept things consistent."

This is exactly how Reid's Eagles players and coaches have described and continue to describe him, as Reid works quietly and steadily toward his unprecedented thirteenth season in charge.

Brad Childress, Reid's offensive coordinator in that Super Bowl, later the Vikings head coach, once said that working with Reid "is not a peaks and valleys type of thing. Whether you have a big win or you get your doors blown off, he's the same, because you've got to come back, and you've got to keep those guys that you're coaching for 16, 19 weeks, realizing that the next one's the most important one. I think he puts that out there. Not that it doesn't hurt when you lose, but you've got to continue to move."

at Eagles games, you'd choose Seamus McCaffery every time. With his shaved skull and clenched jaw, McCaffery always looked like he could step down from the bench and crack a few heads if need arose. And in a stand-and-deliver city like Philadelphia, everyone knew he was more than just tough-*looking*.

Eagles Court lasted until the team moved from the Vet to Lincoln Financial Field, in 2003. (Technically, it was still around in 2003, but more cameras, a different seating setup, and more security guards made its presence moot, as McCaffery acknowledged before disbanding it. He went on to become a justice of the Pennsylvania Supreme Court.) The fact that it didn't last long hardly matters. Much like the snowballs thrown at Santa, the courtroom in the stadium has become a symbol of Eagles fans' unique behavior.

What Reid does best is set a tone, people who work closely with him have said.

"What Coach Reid does is unbelievable," Eagles offensive line coach (now defensive coordinator) Juan Castillo once said. "He gives the backup players and the coaches a lot of confidence. You can't help but work your butt off for him, because he trusts you. He believes in you. You know what? That doesn't happen all the time."

Reid is far and away the franchise's winningest coach, 128-82-1 in 12 seasons, which also is the best winning percentage in Eagles history. When Tennessee parted ways with Jeff Fisher last winter, Reid became the NFL's longest-tenured coach. Reid is one of only four coaches in NFL history to lead a team to more than 100 wins in a decade, along with Bill Belichick, Tom Landry, and Don Shula.

It would be nice to be able to say Reid is revered in Philadelphia, but that isn't really the case. The coach has his admirers. Their number tends to increase during the second half of each season, when it becomes apparent that Reid is producing another playoff-worthy team (nine postseason berths in 12 years, only two losing seasons, one being his first season). Then the bandwagon gets less crowded again at the end of every year when the Eagles fail to win the Super Bowl. Far, far less crowded.

To many fans, Reid is a mustache and a monotone, a man who doesn't let them see under his mask. During an 0-2 start in 2003, with fans in an uproar, Reid was asked what needed to change. "That's for me to know," Reid replied, and the entire fan base hit the ceiling.

In an odd way, such circumstances showcase one of Reid's strengths: he really doesn't care what anyone thinks. He'll follow his convictions. This is the guy who stunned the NFL in February of 2011 by turning his defense over to his offensive line coach. But Eagles fans want their coach to care what they think. They want to embrace him, and they want him to embrace them, with passion. Reid's stolidity exasperates more here than it might in some other cities.

Fans got a rare sense of connection with their coach at his most difficult moment. Two of Reid's sons were arrested on drug charges

Eagles fans are known for being critical of their team's head coaches, and Andy Reid has been no stranger to that criticism over the years. *Rusty Kennedy/AP Images*

on January 30, 2007. Reid took a leave to deal with the crisis; the fans, who could be cruel about things like Reid's weight or his time management in games, voiced little but support.

There were a lot of rumors about Reid stepping aside in the wake of his family troubles, but once he felt he had dealt with the situation, he went back to basically living out of his office. In 2009, his contract was extended through 2013.

Reid's decision to bring Michael Vick back into the NFL in 2009, as Donovan McNabb's time with the Eagles was winding down, might have ensured his team of contender status for several more years.

FRUSTRATION ABOUNDS

Among other things, Rhodes couldn't come up with a quarterback, burning through Rodney Peete, Ty Detmer, and Bobby Hoying, all of whom showed flashes of brilliance but couldn't sustain success behind an offensive line that hadn't been strong and stable since the days of Dick Vermeil. Hoying was a particular disappointment; he looked like a franchise QB in the making in 1997, but

he turned skittish and unreliable in 1998, and the team around him dissolved into chaos. Running back Ricky Watters, the focal point of the offense, left as a free agent after the 1997 season.

Another key departure after 1997 was offensive coordinator Jon Gruden, often Watters's foil in feuds over the direction of the offense, who left to become the head coach of the Raiders. Rhodes, like Buddy Ryan, was a defensive specialist who delegated a lot of authority to his offensive coordinator. When Rhodes hired inexperienced Dana Bible to replace Gruden, solely on the recommendation of Rhodes's friend and then–Stanford coach Ty Willingham, Rhodes was doomed. Seven games into the '98 season, with the Eagles 1-6, Rhodes took play-calling duties away from Bible and gave them to Bill Musgrave, a just-retired backup quarterback who had been hired earlier in the season as an offensive assistant.

"It's already driven me beyond that," Rhodes said, when asked if the situation had him at the end of his rope.

"Gruden was a sergeant," wideout Irving Fryar said. "A drill sergeant. You have to have discipline on a team to win games. We've had a lot of games where we hadn't had enough discipline."

The Eagles would finish 3-13 in 1998, the most losses in the history of the franchise. Observers started counting down the days to Rhodes's departure pretty quickly after the Eagles were blown out of their opener, 38–0, by the Seahawks. That began a streak of five straight losses.

With two games left in the season, Rhodes calmly acknowledged in a conversation with beat writers covering the team that he would be fired when the final game was done.

"I do feel that, hey, I've had an opportunity here, we didn't get it done and there's nothing for me to . . . complain about. I didn't get it done, so . . . move on. It's time to move on," he said.

Someone familiar with the front office's thinking recalled that management quickly came to the conclusion that, especially on offense, this wasn't a case of needing time to gel or gain experience. It was just that the talent and the coaching direction were seriously lacking. The players figured that out at about the same time.

Someone asked Fryar to compare the 1998 Eagles to the 1990 Patriots team he played on that went 1-15.

"This is worse than that," Fryar said. "In some games, we haven't been competing. We were in every game [in 1990]. We put up a fight. We were playing; having fun."

Fryar could see that the road back to the playoffs wasn't going to be quick or easy.

"Maybe it's not fixable this year," he said. "Maybe it's not fixable next year."

"This year was a total embarrassment to me," Lurie said. "The way the team played in the middle of the season, you just wanted to turn off the TV or walk out."

Lurie went on to say, "I don't think we got the best of Ray Rhodes the last few months. We lost so many games the last year and a half, it probably has an effect on you. It's just a question of being human. As you continue to lose, you just kind of get beaten down."

Part of the lesson the owner took from this debacle was that he hadn't paid enough attention to structuring his organization, had been too fixated on the personality of the head coach. Even though Lurie's next coach, Andy Reid, would eventually assume control over personnel, team president Joe Banner and the three GMs of the Reid era—Tom Modrak, Tom Heckert, and Howie Roseman—have played much stronger roles than anyone in the front office did during Rhodes's tenure.

THE TIES THAT BIND(ER)

The hiring of Andy Reid on January 11, 1999, to replace Ray Rhodes was not greeted as an epochal moment. Philadelphia's historically prickly sports media had been badly burned in the Rhodes venture, wildly misled by his early success. This big, chubby quarterbacks coach from Green Bay was relatively unknown. Nobody was in the mood to get gushy right away.

"With his lineman's bull-neck bulk crammed into a dark blue suit, the new head coach of the Philadelphia Eagles looked like an oversized sofa with the stuffing popping out," *Inquirer* columnist Bill Lyon wrote from the introductory news conference. He continued,

> The kindest thing to say is that Andy Reid seems like a reach. The Iggles have taken quite a risk by settling on a successor to Ray Rhodes two weeks to the day after they sacked him, by hiring an unknown while choosing not to wait to interview some glamour names with sexy résumés who are still untouchable because their teams are in the playoffs.
>
> But everyone has to start somewhere, and the plain truth is, no one knows whether the Iggles have snatched themselves a genius-in-waiting or an overmatched rookie. Of course, this being Philadelphia, where prejudging people is as popular as witch-burning was in Salem, a lot of minds already have been made up.
>
> We lead the league in jumping to conclusions,

and sure enough, the early wisdom is that a quarterbacks coach from Green Bay was not what the Iggles needed. The fans and the fan-inflamers wanted someone with experience, someone proven. Give us Parcells, they moaned. Give us Seifert or give us Shanahan. And if not them, then give us Chris Palmer or Brian Billick or Gary Kubiak. We want a who's who and you give us who's he.

Much speculation had been fixed on then-Steelers defensive coordinator Jim Haslett, who had history with Tom Modrak, the Eagles personnel czar at the time. Mike Holmgren, mentor to Rhodes and Reid, also was briefly at large before signing with Seattle. And there was Dom Capers, who had just been fired as head coach by the Carolina Panthers, who had been an expansion start-up success story.

Modrak definitely wanted his pal Haslett, stories at the time said, but Jeffrey Lurie and team president Joe Banner were quite taken by Reid. There had been a lot of seat-of-the-pants, reactive decision making from Kotite and Rhodes, Lurie and Banner's first two head coaches. They found themselves completely charmed at the level of detail Reid was able to bring to his interview, including the now-famous binders in which Reid had collected all kinds of data on how Holmgren ran things at Green Bay and how Reid would want to do things if he became a head coach.

"He had a book like this," Banner said at the time, holding his fingers about three inches apart, "and it had every procedure and every minute of practice and his philosophy. And he had another, smaller book with his own thoughts and answers and all of the questions. Very thorough. Very thorough."

Banner recalled years later that they discussed assistant coaches, and Reid ran down his list of, say, the top five defensive line coaches in the NFL and their backgrounds, strengths, and weaknesses.

On the day of Reid's hiring it was clear that Lurie, at least, was impressed.

"Today, the turnaround begins," the owner intoned. "We needed somebody who is confident they can take something that's been on a downhill slide the last year and a half and not only reverse that, but have a real focused plan on how to succeed in a big way. Not just talk, but a detailed, detailed plan."

H. Rumph Jr/AP Images

Then mayor of Philadelphia, Governor Ed Rendell was an adamant supporter of draft prospect Ricky Williams, the running back from the University of Texas, pictured here with Eagles' director of team security Butch Buchanico during a visit to Philadelphia.

Chris Gardner/AP Images

It was quite a task, that turnaround. Even those who lived through it tend to forget the details now, but Reid, a few months shy of his forty-first birthday, inherited a 3-13 team that was playing and practicing in a dump of a stadium whose artificial surface was the NFL's most notorious for causing crippling injuries. That all factored into the hiring reaction: yeah, they hired some guy who was only a QB coach, but really, who wanted to come here? Haslett, in fact, left his interview with the Eagles to interview in Seattle, where he waxed enthusiastic over the Seahawks' practice facility and stadium plans, and indicated the Eagles were not his first choice.

Also, after the Kotite and Rhodes debacles, Lurie and Banner had a reputation as meddlers, dilettantes who didn't know what they were doing. They would shed much of that reputation during the Reid years, but in 1999, it poisoned a well or two with potential coaching candidates. At least one potential hiree was openly skeptical and antagonistic. Reid probably gained points just by not judging Lurie and Banner on the basis of what he'd heard.

"The thing I told Jeff Lurie was, this is not a quick-fix situation," Reid said when he was introduced. "I'm not here to quick-fix the Philadelphia Eagles. I'm here to supply them with a tremendous, solid organization that is going to win football games. That doesn't happen overnight. In Green Bay, we built a program, and we ended up in the Super Bowl."

The franchise's prime asset, other than more stable and solid ownership than it had enjoyed in quite some time, was the second overall pick in the 1999 draft. This quickly became the region's focus after Reid assembled his staff. And Philadelphia being Philadelphia, it didn't take long for a consensus to emerge.

Texas running back Ricky Williams was the Heisman Trophy winner and a former Phillies draft pick. For a fan base more familiar with the slug-it-out game that had long characterized the NFC East than the West Coast attack Reid touted, a franchise running back was a prize not to be spurned. To some, the fact that there were five highly touted quarterbacks in the 1999 draft only made the case for drafting a running back stronger: So many QBs were flops, clearly all five of those guys weren't going to become stars, and what if you took the wrong one? It could set your rebuilding project back half a decade. A running back was a lower risk pick, with success at that position easier to predict.

But this being Philadelphia, the debate did not remain lofty and philosophical. As it became clear Reid was setting his sights on a franchise QB, Williams supporters became strident. Philadelphia Mayor Ed Rendell, who retained his slot as an analyst on Comcast SportsNet's *Postgame Live* show even after being elected governor and moving to Harrisburg, whipped up the indignation, as did WIP Radio talk-show host Angelo Cataldi. Ultimately, Cataldi chartered a bus he filled with fans to drive up to the site of the draft in Manhattan and boo the Birds' pick.

City Councilman Frank Rizzo, son of the late Philly mayor of the same name, even sponsored a resolution exhorting the Eagles to draft Williams. (In the resolution, Lurie's name was misspelled "Lurey.") It failed. "One of the dumber resolutions before us," an anonymous council member told the *Daily News*.

Draft day dawned, and the Browns took Kentucky quarterback Tim Couch first overall. They had worked out a contract in advance, so that was no surprise. The Eagles then took Donovan McNabb, the quarterback from Syracuse, and the boos rained down in a big way. Obviously, the fans who booed had no idea what they were starting. In the national sporting ledger, this act has gone down right beside the much-referenced 1968 pelting of Santa with snowballs as evidence of the depravity of the Philadelphia fan base.

In fact, the Eagles made the correct call on McNabb. Of the five hot QB prospects of 1999, all taken in the first 12 picks, McNabb would turn out to be the most successful by far. He was also more of a building block than Ricky Williams proved to be, after the Saints traded their entire draft to take him fifth overall. In the new millennium, it turned out, running backs would become much more interchangeable—certainly not insignificant, but not that hard to come up with, either. Franchise QBs, on the other hand, would remain solid gold.

And the yowling of the self-described "dirty 30" got the city's relationship with McNabb, ultimately the franchise's all-time leading passer, started off on exactly the wrong foot.

In the *Daily News*, columnist Bill Conlin glumly recounted what he told a fan from another city who asked him about the spectacle: "I tell the Steelers fan—and many who come after him—that booing Donovan McNabb after his selection was not an aberration. Their

The Eagles' new QB shows off his new shirt and tries to ignore the chorus of boos raining down from the reaches of Radio City Music Hall. McNabb and Andy Reid would surprise their share of Eagles fans in the coming seasons. *Ezra O. Shaw /Allsport/Getty Images*

DONOVAN McNABB

From draft day drama to Rush Limbaugh to the Terrell Owens saga, it wasn't always an easy run for Donovan McNabb in Philadelphia. All this considered, though, McNabb was one of the greatest Eagles of all time—and he holds almost every Eagles' passing record as proof. *Jeff Haynes/AFP/Getty Images*

THE JUDGMENT OF HISTORY takes a while. As this book was being written at the end of the 2010 season, it was impossible to assess the Eagles legacy of Donovan McNabb. You would have to say McNabb's stock seemed to be at an ebb for such an important figure in the history of the franchise.

In 2010, the Eagles said good-bye to No. 5, after a strong 11-season run as their starting quarterback, a run that included six Pro Bowl berths. He left at age 33, with virtually every franchise passing record—yards, completions, attempts, and touchdowns—and he won nine playoff games (losing seven). But McNabb's departure to the Washington Redskins was not widely lamented. There was a certain amount of trepidation over sending him to an NFC East rival, but it proved to be unfounded. (McNabb had only minimal success with the 'Skins in 2010, and he clashed with both offensive coordinator Kyle Shanahan and his dad, head coach Mike Shanahan. He was ultimately benched toward the end of the season, in favor of the much maligned Rex Grossman.) The fact is, after watching the Birds chase a return to the Super Bowl for the second half of a decade that initially held such incredible promise, many people were ready to see something new in Philadelphia.

The first post-McNabb season, the only Donovan-less Eagles season of the twenty-first century so far, produced a profound lack of nostalgia and regret, mostly because Michael Vick's unexpected reemergence as a Pro Bowl QB gave the Birds a better performance at that position than they'd seen since McNabb's Super Bowl year of 2004. This almost never happens when an established QB leaves, but it seemed to be just McNabb's luck. He entered to an infamous chorus of boos at the 1999 draft and exited to find his old team performing better without him.

Everything that happened in between was a fascinating era of euphoric highs and crushing lows.

When he announced the trade on the evening of Easter Sunday in 2010, Eagles coach Andy Reid called McNabb "the greatest quarterback ever to play for the Philadelphia Eagles, to this point."

Asked what he thought his legacy would be, McNabb said he hoped to be remembered as "a guy who provided excitement, who gave them a chance to win every time he stepped out on the field, one that they had trust [in], knowing that I would do the right things, and most importantly, one that won ballgames."

Philadelphia responds to personalities, and it seems fair to infer that Philly never quite "got" McNabb, and vice versa, starting with the draft day debacle. McNabb is a restrained, careful person, a family man always cognizant of his status as a role model for young African Americans, particularly quarterbacks. He can come off sounding bureaucratic and boring, because everything he says runs through that filter.

Early on, it seemed his demeanor and approach—slightly goofy at times, seeing leadership as a matter of reducing pressure and breaking tension, instead of motivating—was a good fit for the spot he occupied at the epicenter of Philadelphia sports. But as McNabb aged, his approach never changed; he never seemed to fully grasp the reins and say the things a mature leader needs to say. Maybe more crucial to the way he was perceived, McNabb continued to hold fans at arm's length. Theirs was never a passionate romance.

Tracing McNabb's trajectory, things seemed to move ever upward from his rookie season to the Super Bowl. He had his critics in those days, but it seemed clear he was an elite QB, by far the best of the heralded 1999 draft group, and a solid, responsible leader. He could dazzle with his arms or his legs; he seemed to be a less flaky Randall Cunningham, with better coaching.

Then came the searing, puzzling Super Bowl XXXIX loss and two subsequent years marred by injury. He snatched his career out of a downward spiral near the end of the 2008 season, leading an improbable run to the NFC title game, but for the fourth time in five attempts, the McNabb-led Birds did not advance beyond that point.

For a segment of the fan base, toward the end of McNabb's Eagles days, nothing short of a Lombardi Trophy would have really moved the needle; it was impossible to assert that he had played well if the team lost. They didn't want to hear it.

Eagles fans reached a similar level of disillusionment with Cunningham, and with Ron Jaworski before that. Jaworski is a local pillar now, a fond memory of the 1970s and early 1980s Eagles. Cunningham doesn't appear on the local radar that much, but when he does, nostalgia trumps the pain of disappointment. In time, it will likely be that way for McNabb as well.

In Donovan McNabb, the Eagles had found their quarterback of the future. Nobody knew quite how that future would unfold, but McNabb was ready and willing to lead the Eagles into the twenty-first century. *Drew Hallowell/Getty Images*

As the 1990s came to an end, Andy Reid looked forward to a new decade of Eagles football. The years to come would be filled with success and heartbreak, with rarely a dull moment in Philadelphia. *Al Messerschmidt/Getty Images*

assumptions are correct: What those 'Let's Make A Deal' rejects were communicating on ESPN reflects the heart and soul of a city that is sports-dead in a spiritual sense. I told him the barbarians are not only at the gates, they have broken through and taken over.

"He was incredulous when I told him that Ed Rendell, the Jim Rome of American mayors, went on WIP-AM, gave out the Eagles' private number and exhorted fans to saturate the offices with 'Draft Ricky Williams' demands. During the peak hour of the phone blitz, harried Eagles phone persons fielded 150 calls. Many of them obscene."

At the time, McNabb declared the boos didn't bother him, that he didn't care what anyone said or wrote. As the years went by, there was ample reason to believe that wasn't quite the case. McNabb and his parents, Sam and Wilma, referenced the booing many times, long after most of the fan base had accepted the idea that Reid made the right choice. Donovan never dropped his wary, arm's-distance relationship with the fans and the media. Even during his best times—the four successive trips the Birds made to the NFC title game—McNabb never seemed to completely feel at home.

Eagles Nation was skeptical about McNabb, skeptical about the new coach, and in no mood for a long-term rebuilding project. Reid brought in veteran backup QB Doug Pederson to mentor McNabb and shield him from the syndrome that seems to affect rookie QBs pressed into starting too early for bad teams. People had little patience for this maneuver either, particularly since Pederson brought minimal ability and no flash to the table.

A fan's sign brought for what turned out to be a Halloween loss to the Giants at the Vet read: "No Offense We're All Pedered Out."

"Boos are like blitzes," Pederson joked in the days leading up to that game. "You know you're going to get them, so you'd better be prepared for them."

Other signs early that season, during an 0-4 start, from a fan base that had no reason to believe Reid and McNabb were going to make things better, included the following:

Worst Organization in Sports.

We Want a Refund.

Embarrassed to Be a Fan.

The fans' disposition improved a bit after McNabb took over as the starter on November 14, leading the team to a 35–28 home win over Washington. The Eagles also won their final two games of the season, over the Patriots and the Rams. It didn't seem like a big deal at the time, but Reid later touted these two wins as a key to building a winning foundation.

1990s Philadelphia Eagles Year by Year		
1990	10–6	2nd in NFC East Division
1991	10–6	3rd in NFC East Division
1992	11–5	2nd in NFC East Division
1993	8–8	3rd in NFC East Division
1994	7–9	4th in NFC East Division
1995	10–6	2nd in NFC East Division
1996	10–6	1st in NFC East Division
1997	6–9–1	3rd in NFC East Division
1998	3–13	5th in NFC East Division
1999	5–11	5th in NFC East Division

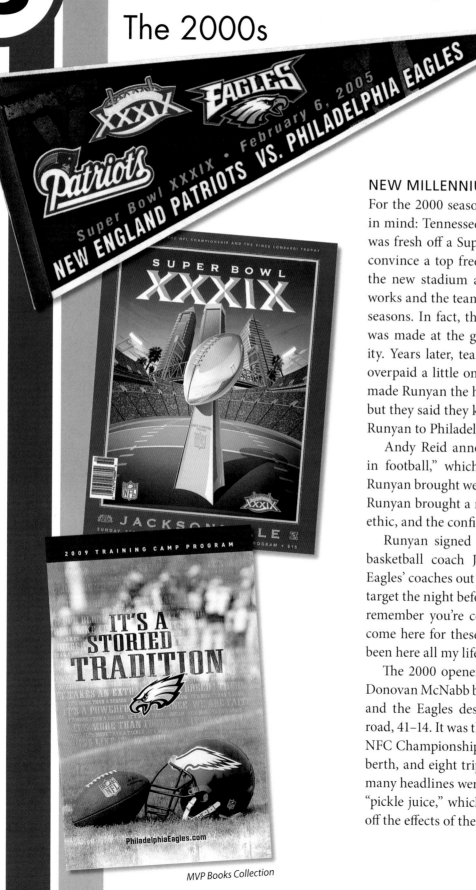

8 THE SOUR TASTE OF SUCCESS
The 2000s

MVP Books Collection

NEW MILLENNIUM, NEW IMAGE

For the 2000 season, Reid had a prime free-agent target in mind: Tennessee Titans right tackle Jon Runyan, who was fresh off a Super Bowl appearance. It wasn't easy to convince a top free agent to come to the Birds in 2000; the new stadium and practice facility were still in the works and the team had gone 8-24 over the previous two seasons. In fact, the announcement of Runyan's signing was made at the groundbreaking for the practice facility. Years later, team executives privately admitted they overpaid a little on a six-year, $30.5 million deal, which made Runyan the highest-paid NFL lineman at the time, but they said they knew it was what they had to do to get Runyan to Philadelphia.

Andy Reid announced him as "the best right tackle in football," which was debatable, but the intangibles Runyan brought were not. To a young O-line and offense, Runyan brought a nasty, physical edge, a relentless work ethic, and the confidence that comes with winning.

Runyan signed despite the advice of crusty Temple basketball coach John Chaney, who encountered the Eagles' coaches out to dinner with their prized free-agent target the night before the signing. "I want you to try and remember you're coming here for these coaches. Don't come here for these fans. Because I hate these fans. I've been here all my life, and I hate them all," Chaney said.

The 2000 opener had the feel of a big moment, with Donovan McNabb beginning his first season as the starter and the Eagles destroying the Dallas Cowboys on the road, 41–14. It was the start of a decade that would see five NFC Championship Game appearances, one Super Bowl berth, and eight trips to the postseason. After the game, many headlines were devoted to the restorative powers of "pickle juice," which supposedly helped the Eagles stave off the effects of the Texas heat, but McNabb and a stellar

Jon Runyan was the first high-profile free-agent pickup for the Birds in the twenty-first century. Andy Reid knew he needed a top-shelf left tackle to protect his new quarterback, Donovan McNabb. *Drew Hallowell/Getty Images*

The powerful Duce Staley carries the ball during a 2003 game against the Atlanta Falcons. *Jamie Squire/Getty Images*

defense assembled by coordinator Jim Johnson were the team's real magic elixir.

McNabb passed for 3,365 yards that season and ran for 629, leading the Birds to an 11-5 record and a wild-card playoff berth, despite losing his prime weapon, running back Duce Staley, to a Lisfranc injury. McNabb made plays with his legs, but only when his passing options broke down; center Bubba Miller referred to this as "controlled chaos."

It was an intoxicating season, filled with promise. A 21–3 win over Tampa Bay in the wild-card game was followed by a 20–10 thumping by the Super Bowl–bound Giants, but the Eagles had accomplished more than most supporters expected.

"I think we're very close," McNabb said after the play-off loss. "We're all young. We're going to get better."

Owner Jeffrey Lurie said: "I think we've got the pieces here to contend for the big game in the next few years."

But amid all the promise, the seeds of future frustrations were also planted. The loss to the Giants happened

because the Eagles didn't have enough skilled weapons to complement McNabb. In the *Daily News*, columnist Rich Hofmann cautioned: "But as long as the Eagles don't have the outside receiving weapons to make teams pay for concentrating so much of their attention on McNabb—as long as they don't have the blitz-busters who really make the West Coast offense go—the Eagles are always going to be vulnerable to days like this. And it was good that yesterday just reinforced the notion. Now, there is no way the Eagles can ignore it, or kid themselves that they can just get by."

The effervescent Freddie Mitchell points down the field in celebration of an Eagles first down. *George Gojkovich/Getty Images*

ANDY ASCENDS

The 2001 draft represented Reid flexing his muscles, insisting on taking control over personnel. General manager Tom Modrak, who had been hired away from the Steelers in 1998 to make those decisions, was dismissed as Reid got a six-year contract extension. Modrak might have been doomed from the time his Pittsburgh buddy Jim Haslett interviewed for the head coaching job that Reid got after the 1998 season; Lurie and Banner were said to have been surprised and disappointed by Haslett's pessimism about the organization and its plans, a view they came to feel was colored by Modrak.

Reid went out to UCLA to interview Freddie Mitchell and came home convinced he had made a deep connection with the flamboyant wideout, and that Mitchell would be a strong asset, on and off the field. Instead, he turned out to be a flaky, eccentric distraction, given to improvising on pass patterns and avoiding off-the-field work.

The year before, Reid opted in the second round for another wideout, supermodel-skinny Todd Pinkston, taken way too high for a receiver who was easy to manhandle off the line. Those were the Birds' only significant moves at the wide receiver position until they acquired Terrell Owens before the 2004 season. Not coincidentally, they then went to the Super Bowl for only the second time in franchise history.

Reid had a theory about wideouts that he had carried with him from Green Bay. The coach felt losing Sterling Sharpe to a career-ending neck injury in 1994 spurred Brett Favre's development into a Super Bowl winner.

"When I was in Green Bay, before Sterling got hurt, Brett always was looking for him," Reid said in 2002. "We might have a play called for the tight end and bam, Brett's right back to Sterling. When Sterling left, we were all very sad. But in the big picture, it made Brett spread the ball around. It made him a better quarterback."

It's unclear whether Reid ever grasped that Mitchell, James Thrash, and Pinkston were not equivalent to Robert Brooks, Antonio Freeman, and Andre Rison, or that Favre managing to win a Super Bowl with unspectacular wideouts was not necessarily a template for Super Bowl success.

The 2001 season saw more progress—an 11-5 record that included the Birds' first NFC East title since 1988 and a berth in the NFC Championship Game for the first time since the 2000 season. The Eagles won 8 of their last 10,

Yet, they did ignore it, essentially. And it was probably the biggest factor that stopped a championship-worthy defense and what sure seemed to be a championship-worthy quarterback a game short of the Super Bowl the next two years.

The only skilled offensive player of note whom the Birds added for 2001 was brash first-round rookie wideout Freddie Mitchell, who will forever go down as one of Reid's most grievous miscalculations.

JIM JOHNSON

Known for his creative blitz packages as one of the best defensive minds in the game, Jim Johnson was the perfect complement to Andy Reid. *Drew Hallowell /Getty Images*

JIM JOHNSON was the Eagles' defensive coordinator for Andy Reid's first 10 seasons as Eagles coach, and Johnson's defense was the guts of the contending team Reid built around quarterback Donovan McNabb.

Johnson, who died of metastatic melanoma at the onset of the team's 2009 training camp, was the master of the unorthodox blitz. One time, when a number of regulars were sidelined by injury, someone asked corner Sheldon Brown if being shorthanded would change Johnson's approach. Brown said no, it wouldn't, that Johnson would diagram a blitz for the cheerleaders, if they were all he had to work with.

But Johnson was more than a technician; he was loud, passionate, and demanding, a man who inspired fierce loyalty.

"I can remember my first year here [2002], he sat down and took the time to talk to my parents," Brown said after Johnson passed away, on July 28, 2009. "Many people don't do that; I can't think of how many other coaches have done that, since I've been here."

Reid liked to recall Johnson's Indianapolis Colts defense thoroughly embarrassing the high-flying Packers offense Reid helped run for Mike Holmgren in 1997. The drubbing left an impression that caused Reid to seek out Johnson at an ensuing Pro Bowl, and to call Johnson first when he was putting together a staff for the Eagles in 1999. Team president Joe Banner said he and owner Jeffrey Lurie, having gone through a similar experience in an Eagles-Colts game, quickly endorsed the choice.

Johnson, 68 when he died, coached as long as he could, taking in 2009 postdraft minicamp action while riding a motorized scooter. The scooter had showed up abruptly in the final weeks of the 2008 season, as the Birds drove toward the NFC Championship Game at Arizona. The Eagles said an MRI taken after Johnson coached the January 11 playoff victory over the Giants from the press box, because of back pain, raised concerns that were confirmed after the loss at Arizona a week later. But in his remarks to reporters a few hours after Johnson passed away, Reid seemed to indicate that insiders knew or at least suspected the extent of Johnson's problem before the end of the season.

"There's very few of us who knew the extent of Jim's illness at that time. That's the way Jim wanted it," successor Sean McDermott said. "I look back to pictures that were in the media, or just thoughts that I remember, of Jim, in the [hotel] lobby of the NFC Championship Game with friends and family, and you think back, and you think to yourself, just like anyone would, 'Did he know? And I wish he would have told me.' But I just recall in the locker room after the game . . . I remember sitting next to Jim, both of us kind of having our heads in our hands and wishing it would have gone

differently, obviously. There is nothing that I would want more than for Jim to be able to call one more game right now. So you think back to those moments."

"The whole Andy Reid regime here that's taken place, wouldn't have been possible without Jim," Reid said that evening, when the lighted sign outside Lincoln Financial Field beamed the words "Jim Johnson, 1941–2009" down to passing motorists on I-95.

"He really represented everything this city is all about, with his toughness and grit," Reid said. "That's the way he fought this cancer."

"It's been an amazing run with Jim. He's been a great friend and partner, and [it's] a tremendous testimony to the life he led, the outpouring of feelings from people," Banner said. "I think his legacy is the words from the people who knew him best, [along] with his family—the Steve Spagnuolos and John Harbaughs and Brian Dawkins and Troy Vincents, the guys that lived with him every day."

Middle linebacker Stewart Bradley said: "He definitely could get into you, but that was Jim—he was an equal-opportunity yeller. It wasn't like he played favorites; he got into everybody, if they made a mistake. That honesty made guys respect him."

Among Johnson's talents was finding ways to emphasize the strengths and disguise or downplay the weaknesses of his players.

"He was an absolute blessing to me, with the way he used me on the football field and allowed me to show my God-given ability," said Brian Dawkins, a seven-time Pro Bowl safety. "His confidence in me meant so much—he looked to create new defenses each week to utilize my talents."

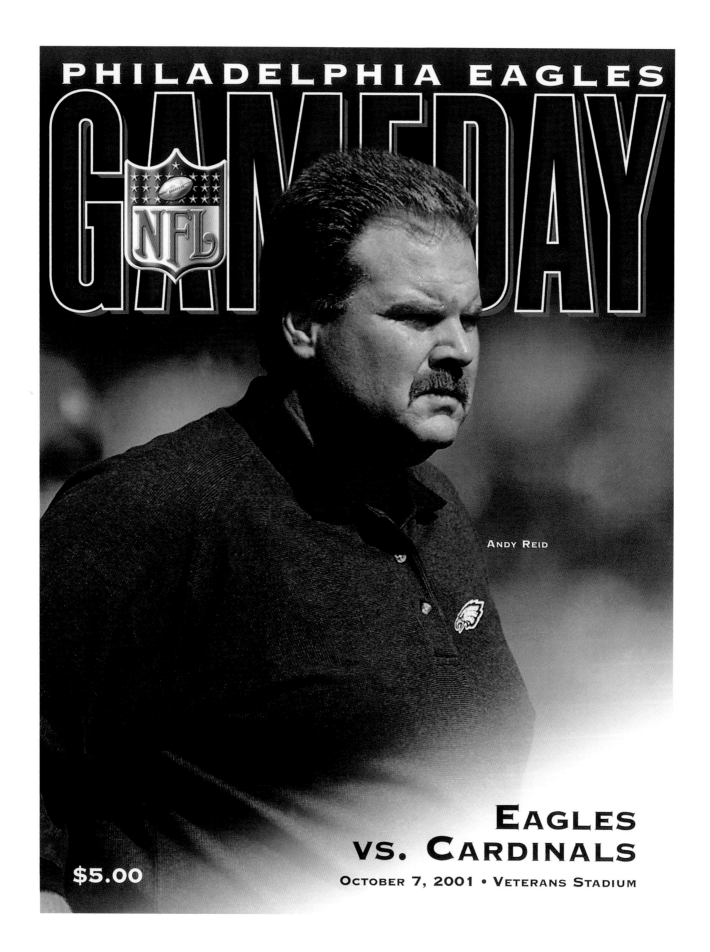

PHILADELPHIA EAGLES

GAMEDAY

ANDY REID

EAGLES
VS. CARDINALS

OCTOBER 7, 2001 • VETERANS STADIUM

$5.00

Todd Pinkston and James Thrash had some good moments with the Eagles, but most acknowledge they were not the weapons Donovan McNabb needed to take the team to the next level.

including a 24–21 win over the Giants on December 30 that clinched the division.

The Birds again vanquished the Bucs in a wild-card game. For the divisional round, they went to Chicago, the city where McNabb grew up. He led the way to a 33–19 victory that established him on the national stage as one of the league's top stars.

When the Eagles lost the NFC title game, 29–24 at St. Louis, McNabb left the visiting locker room to watch the Rams celebrate. He wanted to file the experience away, for future reference.

In 2002, Staley returned to top form after a year spent coming back from his foot injury, and the Eagles might

have had their best defense of the Reid–Jim Johnson (defensive coordinator) era, with one glaring omission. An ugly offseason salary spat with heart-and-soul middle linebacker Jeremiah Trotter led first to Trotter's being franchised, and then, when he took umbrage, to his outright release. It was an amazing turn of events for a 25-year-old, two-time Pro Bowl selection, and Trotter promptly signed with the division rival Washington Redskins.

The Trotter situation presaged several messy, dramatic departures. The Eagles felt their strong position among NFC contenders had a lot to do with the way they managed the salary cap. Part of that management was not overpaying for veterans who might be on the downside—not the

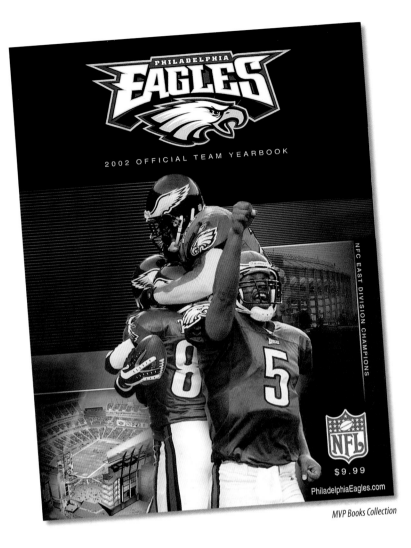

Linebacker Jeremiah Trotter recorded 361 tackles, nine sacks, five interceptions, and four forced fumbles from 1998–2001. *Doug Pensinger/Getty Images*

case with Trotter, but part of the equation when it came to letting Staley, corner Troy Vincent, defensive end Hugh Douglas, and other prominent veterans walk away over the next few years.

The 2002 Eagles went 12-4 in the thirty-first and final season at Veterans Stadium. They sent 10 players to the Pro Bowl. On November 17, McNabb authored one of the great efforts of his Eagles career: he suffered a broken fibula on the third play of a 38–14 victory over the Cards and kept playing; his ankle wasn't x-rayed until after the game, in which he threw four first-half touchdown passes and completed 20 of 25 passes overall, for 255 yards.

McNabb was sidelined for the remainder of the regular season. Things really changed when backup Koy Detmer went down the next week while leading the team to a stunning 38–17 Monday night win at San Francisco. Detmer, who was amazingly sharp in his first significant action in three years (18-for-26, 227 yards), dislocated his left elbow.

"It hurt going out, and it hurt the same going back in," Detmer said after the elbow was popped back into place. "The pain was unbelievable."

Also in pain was the fan base, which saw its promising season placed in the hands of third-string quarterback A. J. Feeley, a 2001 sixth-round draft choice from Oregon who had never even been a starter at the college level.

So what happened? Well, the Eagles won their next four games, of course, in no small part because of their dominant defense (which, for example, scored the only touchdown of a 10–3 win over the Rams). Even a regular-season-ending loss at the Giants couldn't separate the Eagles from the top playoff seed in the NFC, giving them a crucial bye week for McNabb to heal. McNabb returned for a 20–6 victory over the Falcons, and the Super Bowl stage seemed set.

CLOSING WITH A THUD

In an upset that profoundly scarred the fans' faith in both Reid and McNabb, the Tampa Bay Bucs—who had been no problem for the Birds in a 20–10 victory in October—pulled off a startling 27–10 upset in the NFC Championship Game.

The Eagles had beaten the Bucs four times in a row, and they led 7–0 two plays into this game. Somehow, everything went wrong from there. Reid abandoned the running game that had both fueled the earlier win against Tampa and handed his team an early lead in this game. McNabb's repaired fibula was fine, but under pressure, the rust from an eight-week layoff became apparent. And the Bucs exploited the one spot where the Eagles' defense wasn't top-notch, the middle linebacking tandem of 300-pound-plus Levon Kirkland and Barry Gardner.

The most memorable play of the day was a 71-yard pass from Tampa's Brad Johnson to Joe Jurevicius, a short toss over the middle on third down with the Eagles leading 7–3 in which Jurevicius ran away from Gardner and strong safety Blaine Bishop, who was hobbled by a groin injury. After that play, the game was never the same.

"At the end of the game, I'm looking across the field saying, 'They're wearing my hat,'" Troy Vincent said afterward, referring to the championship hats the Bucs wore. "You couldn't have a better stage set. . . . The fans were ready, the city was ready. The atmosphere was right. For us to lose this football game, this is a tough one to swallow."

SOMETHING OLD, SOMETHING NEW

For 2003, the Eagles had a new toy. The glittering Lincoln Financial Field was the Eagles' first exclusive home in the history of the franchise, but even in a new venue, the bad taste from the end of the previous season lingered. The Birds lost their first two home games by a combined score of 48–10, to the Bucs and the Patriots—the previous Super Bowl winner and the team that would win it that season.

Donovan McNabb grimaces with pain on November 17, 2002, the day he played through a broken ankle to lead the Eagles to a decisive victory over the Cardinals. *Chris Gardner/AP Images*

In fact, with several key injuries piling up early, an air of crisis descended. Larry O'Rourke of the Allentown *Morning Call* wrote that the team was "circling the Escalades" down at the NovaCare in advance of what became a 23–13 Week 3 victory at Buffalo. That day is better remembered for then–ESPN commentator Rush Limbaugh opining that one of the team's problems was really McNabb, whom he called overrated by some sort of white liberal media conspiracy.

"I don't think he's been that good from the get-go. I think what we've had here is a little social concern in the NFL," Limbaugh said. "I think the media has been very desirous that a black quarterback do well. They're interested in black coaches and black quarterbacks doing well; I think there's a little hope invested in McNabb, and he got a lot of credit for the performance of his team that he really didn't deserve."

Limbaugh would lose his analyst position over those remarks, and the Eagles would go on a nine-game winning streak after a 23–21 loss to the Cowboys October 12.

The catalyst came with a 14–10 victory against the Giants on October 19. It was one of the most surprising wins ever, an almost certain loss that shape-shifted into a victory in the time it took Brian Westbrook to scamper 84 yards down the left sideline. The Giants outgained the Eagles 339 to 134, held the Birds to 47 net passing yards, yet

THE LINC

Lincoln Financial Field before its first-ever game, on August 22, 2003. In the fall of 2010, the Eagles unveiled a plan to add wind turbines, solar panels, and a cogeneration plant at the Linc. Lurie hopes to take the stadium beyond self-sufficiency in the near future. *Mike Mergen/AP Images*

AS VETERANS STADIUM AGED, particularly in the late 1990s, it became a symbol of the Eagles' declining fortunes, their less-than-prominent status in the NFL hierarchy. Jon Gruden, after he fled the Birds' offensive coordinating job for head coaching roles in Oakland and Tampa Bay, loved to tell a story about cats chasing rats and falling through the Vet's basement ceiling, onto his desk.

But in 2001, the Eagles opened the NovaCare Complex—a $37 million, 108,000-square-foot, state-of-the-art practice facility, built on the site of a former naval hospital on the corner of Broad and Pattison, across the street from the Vet. And two years later, after many years of confusion and changed plans relating to relationships with the city, the state, and the Phillies of Major League Baseball, with whom the Eagles had shared the Vet, the Eagles opened the first home stadium under their control in the then-69-year history of the franchise, Lincoln Financial Field.

"The stadium goes so far beyond the Eagles," team president Joe Banner said as the $512 million, 67,532-seat stadium was preparing to open. "You leave something that will be a part of the fabric and the image of the city way beyond me or Jeff Lurie or Andy Reid or Donovan McNabb. A structure of that size and visibility, to the world

it kind of makes a statement about where you're from or what you're about. Those kind of details or subtleties matter. . . . I don't know that many people get to work on something that the effect of, the use of, and the visibility [of] goes way beyond their own lives. This building will be a part of the fabric and memories of this city, probably longer than I'll be alive."

Team chairman Jeffrey Lurie said: "You don't often have the opportunity to start a new era, or change the course or history of a franchise." Lurie called the Linc "the final legs of a foundation" for winning.

The Linc has more than three times the luxury suite seating the Vet had, plus more amenities and better sightlines. The team contributed $330 million to construction costs, atypical in an era when teams routinely expect municipalities to build stadiums for them.

The Eagles won the January 2005 NFC title game in their new palace, the franchise's most significant victory since the 1980 season. The Linc has hosted the Army-Navy Game, sold-out concerts by performers such as Bruce Springsteen, and currently is the homefield for Temple football.

found a way to lose the game. The culprit was Jeff Feagles, one of the best directional punters in NFL history, who failed to kick the ball out of bounds, thanks in part to a strong block attempt from that side by Sheldon Brown.

"We stole it," said linebacker Ike Reese, who threw a key block on the return.

Special-teams coordinator John Harbaugh quoted defensive coordinator Jim Johnson as saying Westbrook "looked like Seabiscuit" on the winning gallop. Someone asked Westbrook if he took that as a compliment.

"I don't know," Westbrook replied. "I ain't seen the movie."

Despite some injuries on the defensive side of the ball, the Eagles were rolling along quite nicely when they went to play the Redskins on December 27. They won their regular-season finale, 31–7, but the price was too high—Westbrook went down with a season-ending torn triceps during a 96-yard, 14-play touchdown drive in the first quarter. As if Eagles fans needed a reminder of the cruel and fickle fate of their team, the crucial blow was delivered by Jeremiah Trotter.

After McNabb, Westbrook was the Eagles' top weapon. Their 12-4 finish netted them their third NFC East title in a row and another first-round playoff bye, but they weren't the same team in the postseason. Eight players had landed on injured reserve.

A miracle got the Birds past the Packers in the first playoff game played at the Linc. They trailed by 14 points in the first quarter, and they had cut Green Bay's lead to 3 with just 1:12 left on the clock. They faced a seemingly impossible fourth down with 26 yards to go, from their own 26. Their season was over; it was hopeless.

"You never want to be in that position. Your chances are not in your favor," McNabb noted afterward, on a day when he set a playoff QB record by rushing for 107 yards on 11 carries, making up at least partly for the gap left by Westbrook.

His line gave him time and McNabb made the throw of his career, eyeball-high to Freddie Mitchell, down the middle of the field. You would think the Packers' task would be pretty simple in such a spot, but somehow, Mitchell found a seam in the coverage. He was hit by corner Bhawoh Jue, but held onto the ball, and the hit only served to propel Mitchell over the spot needed for the first down. He was given a friendly spot on the Green Bay 46 for a gain of 28 yards. The season was not yet dead.

Brian Westbrook adds to Eagles-Giants lore as he crosses the goal line following a game-winning 84-yard punt return at the Meadowlands on October 19, 2003. *Chris Gardner/AP Images*

"Any defense would love to be in a situation where it's fourth-and-26," Jue said. "We had it, man."

"I just tried to beat my man across from me and go deep, and I went deep," Mitchell said. "I didn't see the guy on top of me but Donovan McNabb read that and threw it to my back shoulder, and I saw it in the air and made a play."

Six plays later, David Akers was kicking a 37-yard field goal to tie the score at 17, and the game was headed to overtime.

On fourth down and 26 yards to go in the divisional playoff against Green Bay, Freddie Mitchell caught a bullet across the middle to help keep the Eagles' 2003 season alive. *Doug Pensinger/Getty Images*

On the first Packers snap of OT, Brett Favre hung a fat balloon of a pass that Brian Dawkins settled under like it was a punt. Dawkins ran the pick back to Green Bay's 24, setting the stage for Akers' 31-yard game-winning field goal, which sent the Eagles to the NFC Championship yet again.

There was a lot of talk about destiny and special feelings, but the endgame was sickeningly familiar. The Eagles, home favorites against the Carolina Panthers, lost all their magic on a bitter-cold afternoon.

They became the first team in either the AFC or the NFC to host the conference championship game two years in a row and lose both. They became the first team since the 1980–1982 Dallas Cowboys to make the conference championship game three years in a row and lose all three.

"Every year," Dawkins said, "the other team makes plays and we can't. That's the bottom line."

"They're all disappointing," Reid said, when asked to rank the awful string of title game failures. "You're asking me right now, [this] is the most disappointing. . . . I wanted this group to win a Super Bowl. I'm proud of them. They've overcome a lot of things."

But they didn't overcome the separated rib cartilage McNabb suffered with 4:22 left in the first half. Tripped by defensive end Mike Rucker of the Panthers, McNabb went to the ground, where Panthers linebacker Greg Favors drilled him in the ribs. The hit was legal. No whistle had blown. Reid said afterward when he complained to officials, they told him McNabb had been tripped by his own man.

McNabb couldn't throw or move well after that. He left the game at the start of the fourth quarter after going 10-for-22 for 100 yards and three interceptions, all to little-known Panthers cornerback Ricky Manning Jr. Manning terrorized Pinkston, who completely melted down and stopped competing for the ball long before Reid stopped dialing up plays designed to go in his direction.

The starting wideouts, Pinkston and James Thrash, combined for one catch for nine yards. Asked afterward if the team needed to upgrade its weapons, McNabb said, "That's not my call." It was a significant shift from a QB who previously had defended his low-star-power receiving group.

"Pinkston, he's not that strong," Manning said afterward. "He's pretty thin, I thought. And they really don't

David Akers is good for the game-winner to advance the Eagles to the NFC Championship Game. Akers, a lefty, set an NFL Record for most points in a decade, amassing 1,114 between 2000 and 2009. *Miles Kennedy/AP Images*

have too many moves off the line. . . . All week long, I was like, 'I can go get these guys.'"

Someone asked Ike Reese what it was like being the bridesmaid over and over. Reese said he considered the Super Bowl runner-up the bridesmaid. "We're the flower girl, or something," he said. "We just got to find a way to get over this hump. . . . It's going to be tough to come back and make it to a fourth title game."

Spoiler alert: Amazingly, they did just that. But let's not get ahead of ourselves.

THE UNHOLY TRINITY

FROM A DISTANCE, it doesn't seem like such an awful thing: three trips in a row to the NFC Championship Game. Hey, that's a successful season, any time you make the NFL's final four. Lots of teams that didn't make the playoffs at all from the 2001–2003 seasons would have taken that.

But the longest stretch of "almost" in Eagles history felt different from the inside. For the fans who lived through those successive disappointments, each adding a layer of frustration, the experience was downright Sisyphean. The well of angst bubbled so deep and hot that it spilled over in a toxic way after the Birds finally broke through the conference title-game ceiling in 2004, only to lose the Super Bowl to New England by three points.

But our subject here is the failed NFC title quests, and how they stacked up on the futility scale.

Let's take the easiest first. Nobody expected the Eagles to make it to the title game in 2001, and beating a St. Louis Rams team that had been dubbed "the Greatest Show on Turf" would have been a big upset. Sure, there were "what-ifs"—what if Troy Vincent hadn't had to leave the game in the second half after an injury worsened? What if Freddie Mitchell had been able to outfight Aeneas Williams for the jump ball Donovan McNabb threw up on what was starting to look like a last-gasp victory drive? But McNabb and the Eagles were young. Their time would come. They needed to play the game at home, healthy, then they would get the job done.

All those chips fell into place in the playoffs following the 2002 season, which made the championship game loss such a surprise.

The 27–10 loss to Tampa on January 19, 2003, has to be the worst of the group, for several reasons. Until then, the trajectory for Andy Reid and McNabb had been ever upward—a winning season in 2000, then a winning season with some playoff success, then a first-round playoff bye and homefield for the right to win a Super Bowl berth. There had been no steps backward.

Also, the whole thing just felt so right, going in. The Bucs were a familiar and not terribly scary foe. The title game was to be the final football contest at Veterans Stadium. Surely the Eagles would say good-bye in triumph.

But the Bucs learned a lot from their regular-season loss at the Vet, and they surprised the Eagles, throwing from a running formation, which kept pass-rushing ace Hugh Douglas on the bench.

"I kept telling [defensive coordinator Jim Johnson], 'Just put me in. I can handle it,'" Douglas recalled later.

Mistakes and missteps piled up, and before Eagles fans fully grasped what had happened, Ronde Barber had taken a McNabb interception for a touchdown to kill the final embers of hope. They were filing silently down the concrete ramps for the last time,

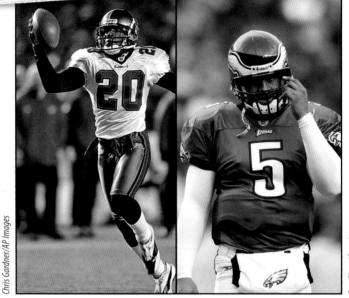

Chris Gardner/AP Images

Ezra Shaw/Getty Images

Donovan McNabb could only shake his head after Ronde Barber intercepted a pass in the NFC Championship Game following the 2003 season. Barber took the ball to the house, killing the Eagles' season as he crossed the goal line to put the game out of reach.

muffled marching feet the only sound audible in the evening chill.

There's a case to be made that the next year was worse, because the frustration heightened—It happened again! At home, in the new stadium!—but most people realized that the 2003 team wasn't going to win the Super Bowl against the New England Patriots, especially not without injured Brian Westbrook. Had they beaten Carolina to get to the Super Bowl, they also would have been without Donovan McNabb, who suffered a rib cartilage injury in the first half and left the game at the end of the third quarter. After the two previous losses, this one wasn't as much of a shock. Eagles fans had almost come to expect it.

Ultimately, the loss that closed the Vet was the most frustrating, especially since the Super Bowl opponent would not have been dynastic New England, but a creaky Raiders team.

"They're wearing our rings," Douglas, now a talk-radio host, said of the Bucs, near the end of the 2010 season, close to nine years later. Douglas still got emotional discussing the magnitude of the chance that got away.

"Even now, if Keyshawn [Johnson] or anybody from that team tried to rub it in on me about that, shove it in my face, we'd have a fight. Some things just aren't funny. Somebody called and left me a voicemail that night just laughing into the phone. It was a blocked number. If I'd found out who it was, my foot would have disappeared it would have gone so far up their [rear]."

THEY NEED A T.O., BABY

It was time for significant changes in the nucleus, which started with a handful of departing free agents, including Staley, Vincent, fellow corner Bobby Taylor, and stalwart linebacker Carlos Emmons. But the Eagles felt they had sufficient young talent on hand to plug those gaps. They were not looking at a rebuilding year, as became apparent when the team signed free-agent defensive end Jevon Kearse from Tennessee to an eight-year, $66 million contract. The news conference announcing the Kearse signing was held up because management was trying to pull off a double play and thought it had succeeded; the San Francisco 49ers had agreed to trade receiver Terrell Owens to the Eagles, but sent him to the Baltimore Ravens instead.

That wasn't the end of the Owens drama, though. It was barely the beginning. Owens and his agent, David Joseph, had worked out a contract with the Eagles, but not with the Ravens. The Ravens obtained Owens under the assumption that they didn't have to give him the new deal he sought because he was still under contract for three seasons. The whole ordeal started when Joseph didn't exercise an option clause that would have made Owens a free agent—the date for filing had been moved, which Joseph didn't realize, so the league, the 49ers, and the Ravens took the position that Owens had a valid contract that could be traded.

But Owens and the NFLPA disagreed. The case came to Philadelphia, to special master Stephen Burbank of the Penn School of Law. Going in, the Eagles had little hope that Owens would be sprung free.

"My feeling was that we needed to move on," Eagles president Joe Banner later recalled, "and this [proceeding] was going to finalize it."

But the NFLPA came up with an intriguing argument. The date for exercising Owens's option was different from the date in other NFL contracts, so maybe the changing of those dates should not have affected his date, since it was not mentioned in the revision.

Burbank never actually issued a ruling; he didn't have to. His serious consideration of the NFLPA's argument was enough to ignite talks of a settlement among the league, the Eagles, and the Ravens. The Ravens were essentially refunded the second-round pick they had sent to San Francisco in the trade, and the Eagles then gave a fifth-round draft pick and veteran defensive end Brandon

Known as "the Freak," Jevon Kearse was a key free-agent pickup for the Eagles in 2004. *Brian Bahr/Getty Images*

Whiting to the 49ers in exchange for Owens, one of the league's highest-profile stars.

"The most common word in our conversations was 'stunned,'" Banner said. "We were stunned."

McNabb was very enthusiastic. "I want a guy that wants the ball when it's time," the quarterback said. "I want a guy that will pump everybody up in the huddle,

Terrell Owens is flanked by Andy Reid and owner Jeffrey Lurie as they celebrate the newest addition to the Eagles' offense. *William Thomas Cain/AP Images*

on the sideline. . . . Guys can't say, 'Well, I'll wait for the next series,' or, 'If the ball comes to me, then I'll make a play.' I want somebody to say, 'I'm open. If you don't have anything, throw me the ball.'"

McNabb said getting Owens "kind of reminds me of when we signed Jon Runyan . . . adding an attitude and an aggressive approach."

Maybe it stood to reason that his new teammates would relish Owens's talents more than they would worry about his antics. After all, Owens had garnered more than 1,000 receiving yards each of the previous four seasons, while the Birds hadn't had a 1,000-yard receiver since Irving Fryar in 1997.

"I think my character has definitely been an issue as far as whether I'll fit in or how I will mesh with the coaches and my teammates," said Owens, who agreed to a seven-year contract that a source close to the situation said could be worth as much as $49 million with incentives, including signing and roster bonuses of $8 million

to $10 million in the first year. "We've talked. [Reid] has explained the structure. I'm very aware of that. I understand that. I think a lot of people get it misconstrued from my passion on the field vs. my personality off the field. . . . I think these guys have gotten to know me the last two or three years over in Hawaii [at the Pro Bowl, where the Eagles' coaching staff worked after each of its championship game failures]."

Later, Owens spoke of having "a clean rap sheet, so to speak . . . a fresh beginning for me."

Whether the Eagles would have made it to Super Bowl XXXIX without Owens or Kearse is an interesting philosophical debate. Kearse managed just 7.5 sacks. Owens had a much more dramatic impact, catching 77 passes for 1,200 yards and 14 touchdowns before suffering a broken fibula against Dallas on December 19. While Owens was out, the Birds won both their playoff games leading up to the Super Bowl, which might lead one to infer they could have gotten there without him.

But such an analysis ignores the situation the Eagles were in when they added Kearse and Owens, as well as the psychology of the locker room. After losing three NFC title games in a row, management needed to change the focus. Kearse and Owens did just that. Players looked forward to minicamps. Instead of a fed-up, jaded fan base, the Eagles welcomed record crowds to training camp at Lehigh University.

During the first minicamp, McNabb decreed "the start of something special. . . . A special year for us."

Asked then about the still-fresh third successive NFC title game failure, McNabb said: "You just have to turn the page. This is the time, obviously, to write a new chapter for the future."

Westbrook, the guy whose playoff absence probably doomed the 2003 team, almost seemed an afterthought to the public and media, amid T.O. mania. Westbrook said he didn't mind.

"I think [Owens's acquisition] takes a lot of pressure off everybody," Westbrook said after camp began in front of 6,240 people. "Takes pressure off me, Donovan, all the offensive players."

ROLLING SEVEN

Reid's teams had often started slow and finished strong, but the 2004 Eagles came out of the gate sprinting. They won their opener over the Giants at the Linc, by a score of 31–17. Owens caught three touchdown passes and McNabb looked sharper and more commanding than ever.

Not only did the Birds start out 7-0, but they won their first five by double digits. Westbrook suffered a rib injury the next week in an overtime win at Cleveland and missed the following week's victory over Baltimore, a game that really showed Owens's value.

In the fourth quarter, a Hollis Thomas fumble recovery stopped a Ravens drive and gave the Eagles the ball with a 9–3 lead. They drove downfield but seemed destined to settle for a fourth David Akers field goal, when McNabb hit Owens on a short pass over the middle, from the Ravens' 11 to the 5. One problem: it was third-and-10. Owens twisted out of a tackle by corner Gary Baxter and broke outside, outrunning linebacker Adalius Thomas to the pylon for the only Eagles touchdown of the day. Then he mocked Ravens linebacker Ray Lewis's celebratory dance, for good measure. Given the Eagles-Ravens tussle

over Owens's rights, this was not taken well.

But the next week, the Eagles had to go to Pittsburgh with a barely functional Westbrook. Perhaps a little too impressed with themselves for being the first team in franchise history to start 7-0, they went out and got pounded, 27–3. It would be the only loss of the season for the starters.

The next week the Eagles got right back down to business. They went to Dallas and set a record for a Cowboys opponent by scoring four second-quarter touchdowns en route to a 49–21 victory. The most spectacular score of the quarter was

MVP Books Collection

the last, set up when McNabb scrambled for an incredible 14.1 seconds, back and forth and back again, before finding Freddie Mitchell 60 yards downfield. It was one of the most astonishing plays in franchise history.

"I got away from the one guy and cut back," McNabb said. "By that time it was like a video game. The offensive line did an excellent job of blocking. . . . You're looking obviously to get the ball out of your hands. I saw Freddie had a lot of green in front of him."

This game started a string of four wins by more than 20 points apiece, which pretty much answered any lingering questions about the identity of the NFC's dominant team. Jeremiah Trotter, brought back from his unsatisfying exile in Washington, took over in the middle for Mark Simoneau and transformed the entire attitude of the team's defense.

The next two wins were close, low-scoring games: 17–14 over the Redskins and 12–7 at home in a rematch with Dallas. The season flashed before the Eagles' eyes in the Dallas game, when Owens was bent backward by safety Roy Williams and suffered an ankle injury that would require surgery to insert two screws, aimed at stabilizing a broken fibula and injured ligaments.

Tight end Chad Lewis sits in the end zone after a touchdown grab in the 2004 NFC Championship Game. *Joseph Labolito/NFL/Getty Images*

Dr. Mark Myerson, the Baltimore (of course!) specialist who did the surgery, said the normal healing time would be eight to ten weeks. Owens had seven weeks before Super Bowl XXXIX, which was scheduled for February 6 in Jacksonville, FL.

The Eagles had clinched the top seed in the NFC playoffs, so perhaps prodded by the Owens injury, Reid rested his starters for most of the losses to the Rams and Bengals—entirely understandable, but vexing to fans who feared the magic would be missing without Owens.

Somewhere in this interlude, the seeds of Owens's eventual estrangement were planted. When T.O. went down and the fan base started to panic, Reid and McNabb said the things people always say in such situations, that even though the injured player was irreplaceable, the team would soldier on and continue to win. Later it developed that Owens—as insecure as he was physically dominant—resented hearing the team say it could win the Super Bowl without him. He never revealed exactly what he thought the Eagles should have said.

THE FINAL STEP

Even without Owens, the Birds had no trouble in the divisional round of the playoffs, facing Randy Moss and the Minnesota Vikings and winning 27–14. Freddie "FredEx" Mitchell enjoyed his last big moment in the spotlight, catching five passes for 65 yards and a touchdown and scoring another TD when tight end L. J. Smith blooped a fumble in the air and Mitchell caught it.

"I just want to thank my hands for being so great," Mitchell told reporters afterward.

So the Birds were back in the NFC Championship Game for the fourth year in a row, third year in a row at home, this time against Michael Vick and the Atlanta Falcons. Defensive coordinator Jim Johnson had crafted a winning strategy against Vick in the 2002 playoffs, bringing his defensive ends upfield, asking them to contain Vick and turn him inside, instead of lunging at him and leaving big escape routes to the outside.

Johnson had the answers again. Vick ran for just 26 yards, completed just 11 of 24 passes, and was sacked four times. This time Johnson flip-flopped his two ends—Kearse and Derrick Burgess—moving Kearse from his regular left-end spot to the right side where he could use his speed to prevent Vick, who is left-handed, from rolling that way. Kearse and Burgess combined for three of the Eagles' four sacks.

Trotter notched eight tackles, one more than the number of first downs achieved by Atlanta's NFL-best running game.

"We didn't have any doubt in our minds that we were going to win the game today," Trotter said.

"I think we answered a lot of questions," McNabb said. "I think we answered a lot of critics."

"It was a great feeling," Reid said after his players took turns parading the George S. Halas Trophy around the Linc like it was the Stanley Cup. "Really, with about two minutes left, the place erupted. . . . The players felt it, and after that last touchdown, I think guys started getting caught up in that part. . . . I think it even makes it more worthwhile that we had to do it four times to get over the hump."

The last touchdown proved to be the final TD of tight end Chad Lewis's career. Lewis, a steady, sturdy target during McNabb's development years, suffered a Lisfranc tear in his foot while making the grab that set the final score with 3:21 left. Lewis later said he knew, even as he rolled around the end zone in celebration, that his season was over.

Owens remained determined that his fate would be different. Intense media interest followed every phase of his rehab, which he attacked like it was an undersized cornerback. The week before Super Bowl XXXIX, Myerson refused to clear Owens for the game, saying the ankle hadn't had time to heal.

Owens disagreed, and he had Eagles athletic trainer Rick Burkholder—who authored all those rehab sessions—on his side. "Obviously, I respect Dr. Myerson's position in not medically clearing me, but I know my body more than anybody," Owens said, after the Eagles arrived in Jacksonville for Super Bowl week. But before leaving Philly, Owens had taped Myerson's nonclearance letter in his locker, as motivation.

In Jacksonville, the Eagles clearly were the fans' choice, mostly because far more Philadelphians than New Englanders flocked to Florida to revel in the moment. No one wanted to miss what could be the crowning moment in franchise history.

CLOSER THAN EVER

The Eagles were seven-point underdogs in Super Bowl XXXIX to a Patriots team that was bidding for its third Lombardi Trophy in four years. Yet the Eagles dominated play in the first half; if McNabb had been a little sharper, they could have gained a commanding lead, instead of heading into the locker room tied 7–7. The Eagles turned the ball over twice in the first quarter.

The second half belonged to the Patriots, whose offensive adjustments really took the ball out of the Eagles' hands. Tom Brady guided New England to a 24–14 fourth-quarter lead. The Eagles cut the edge to three on a 30-yard touchdown pass from McNabb to wideout Greg Lewis, but they used up too much time on their scoring drive—3:52—starting from their 21. Only 1:48 remained when Lewis scored, and then the Birds failed to recover David Akers's attempt at an onside kick.

"Every time we got in a drive that had rhythm, we ended up scoring," Jon Runyan said. "All we needed at the end was one guy to make a play and one guy to miss a tackle."

Owens was the brightest spot for the Eagles, catching nine passes for 122 yards. Clearly, the Patriots, who had planned so well in areas such as using a 4-3 front instead of their usual 3-4, hadn't figured a healthy Owens into their calculations. But with McNabb getting picked off twice in Pats territory, three times overall, and Westbrook stymied (44 yards on 15 carries, with 22 of those yards on one "gimme" carry at the end of the first half), the Eagles just weren't quite good enough.

"We played a heckuva football team. We realize that," Reid said the next morning at the team hotel. "They ended up being the better football team last night. I was proud of the effort our guys gave."

They had little notion of the storm that would soon envelop them back home.

Greg Lewis makes a leaping touchdown catch in the Super Bowl against the New England Patriots. *Harry How/Getty Images*

McNabb celebrates after a first-quarter touchdown pass to tight end L. J. Smith. *Rusty Kennedy/AP Images*

Terrell Owens heroically returned from a broken ankle to shine in Super Bowl XXXIX. Unfortunately, it wasn't enough to push the Eagles to victory, and his relationship with the team went south very quickly. *Andy Lyons/Getty Images*

PUKEGATE

Losing a Super Bowl is hard. Losing a Super Bowl when your franchise has never won one, despite a heritage that goes all the way back to leather helmets, is really hard. Back in Philadelphia, all the bitterness and disappointment was channeled into the drive that took too long. Never mind that no team had ever come back to win a Super Bowl when trailing by 10 points in the fourth quarter. Never mind that, had the Eagles scored sooner, the Pats, whose offense dominated the Eagles defense in the second half, would only have had to punch out a first down or two to put the Eagles in the same situation they were in after Akers's onside kick.

The sparks kindled when center Hank Fraley—who had endured a worse game than McNabb—and Runyan appeared on a TV show and rehashed the loss. Asked about the plodding drive, Fraley earnestly explained that McNabb did everything he could to get the Eagles into the end zone, ignoring some sort of physical distress, "almost puking."

That was the magic word, "puking." Today, many Eagles fans will earnestly assert that their team lost the Super Bowl because McNabb puked. Never mind that no player ever actually said that happened, or saw that happen. "Puking" equates to "choking" and it felt much better to vent one's spleen over the quarterback being a choker than to have to admit the other team was better.

It didn't help that McNabb was in Hawaii for the Pro Bowl during all this. When he spoke, he only acknowledged getting tired.

"Yes, I was tired," he said. "But we scored on the drive, that's the main thing."

TERRELL OWENS

Streeter Lecka/Getty Images

David Drapkin/Getty Images

The many sides of Terrell Owens.

NO PHILADELPHIA ATHLETE HAS ever squandered so much goodwill as quickly as Terrell Owens did.

Nationally, Owens was already a controversial figure when he was traded to the Eagles in March 2004—controversial for denigrating his San Francisco quarterback, Jeff Garcia; for arguing on the sideline with his offensive coordinator, Greg Knapp; and for celebrating atop the Dallas Cowboys' midfield star, among other things.

The trade was a complicated mess, with the 49ers first trying to send him to the Ravens, in the midst of a dispute over whether documents were filed in time to make Owens a free agent. With such a contentious beginning, maybe Eagles fans should have been more wary. They weren't.

Through three straight unsuccessful trips to the NFC Championship Game, fans pleaded for more weapons, and finally, their prayers were answered. Owens was vain and brash? Never a problem in Philly as long as he could back it up. In fact, the more outrageous he acted, the more people ate it up, buying his No. 81 jersey, serenading him with a soccer-style "TeeOhh, TeeOhh, TeeOhh" song.

Record crowds flocked to training camp. Donovan McNabb, who had asked management for a difference-maker, immediately saw what Owens could mean for his career and his championship aspirations. Once the season started, everyone saw it.

"They've worked really hard at it, and you could see it getting better every day during training camp," Andy Reid said after McNabb hit Owens for three touchdowns in a season-opening win over the Giants. "I think it will continue on. I think you'll see it get even better as they continue to play together."

"This is what I've always expected," Owens said that day. "This is what I really lobbied to get here for. . . . That's the type of ability that [McNabb] has. That's the chemistry that we've kind of developed, the similar situations we've had in the Pro Bowl, with him scrambling and me coming across with him, just having that relationship with him."

Fans loved T.O.'s touchdown celebrations, speculating on what he might do next. A particular favorite followed his one hundredth career TD: with a hand towel draped over his arm like a waiter at an upscale restaurant, he hoisted the ball like a platter of food in celebration.

Owens caught 77 passes for 1,200 yards and 14 touchdowns in 14 games that season, before breaking his fibula against the Cowboys while being dragged down by one of Roy Williams's infamous horse-collar tackles. He threw himself into rehabbing the injury, including sleeping in a hyperbaric chamber, and he made it back for Super Bowl XXXIX. Most observers weren't surprised he played—he'd been saying he would, despite advice to the contrary from his surgeon—but they were surprised at how effective he was. Owens caught nine passes for 122 yards. On a day when many prominent Eagles didn't play up to expectations, T.O. exceeded them.

In the wake of the Super Bowl, T.O. mania hit record levels in Philly, but that was not his chief concern. Owens hired agent Drew Rosenhaus to try to get his contract reworked. When the Eagles declined to revisit the pact after just one year, Owens began making waves.

Owens quickly made it clear he would be just fine playing somewhere else if that was the only way he was going to get paid. Fans felt betrayed (though some took the attitude that whatever Owens said or did, his talent outweighed the trouble, and the Eagles should just do whatever it took to keep him happy, assuming that was actually possible).

"At the end of the day, I don't have to worry about what people think of me, whether they hate me or not," Owens told the Miami *Herald*. "People hated on Jesus. They threw stones at him and tried to kill him, so how can I complain or worry about what people think?"

Over the course of a summer and fall that looked a lot like a circus sideshow, Owens damaged and ultimately destroyed his relationship with McNabb, whom he apparently saw as a management surrogate. In the week leading up to their November 6 game at the Redskins, Reid suspended him for four games and eventually deactivated him for the remainder of the season. Owens would never play for the Birds again; in March 2006, he completed his dizzyingly quick descent from hero to villain by signing with the hated Cowboys.

The toxic reaction to this loss harmed McNabb's stature in Philadelphia forever and helped create cracks in the McNabb-Owens relationship that would blow apart the 2005 season, ultimately ensuring the Eagles wouldn't have to worry about losing any more Super Bowls for a while.

T.O. TURMOIL

The first hint of trouble came when Owens fired David Joseph, the agent who had missed the filing deadline in San Francisco, replacing him with the high-profile Drew Rosenhaus. This was a signal that Owens didn't like the contract forced on him at the time of the deal, when attitude questions made a top-drawer payday unlikely anywhere. For their part, the Eagles were not receptive to revising a seven-year contract after just a single season. But Owens had a bag of tricks he had employed successfully with the 49ers. He knew exactly which button to push to get the Eagles' attention. Owens told ESPN.com's Len Pasquerelli that he was not to blame for the Eagles' falling short, that T.O. "wasn't the guy who got tired in the Super Bowl."

Management still refused to redo the contract. Owens reported to training camp in camo fatigues and ignored reporters. He took more shots at McNabb.

Eventually Reid sent T.O. home, for blowing off an autograph session and for admonishing offensive coordinator Brad Childress not to speak to him until spoken to first. That really kicked off a media circus, with Owens doing sit-ups in his Moorestown, New Jersey, driveway for the TV cameras and appearing intermittently on ESPN to tearfully recount his perceived mistreatment. During one such appearance, Owens called McNabb a "hypocrite" because someone close to McNabb tried to set up a clear-the-air meeting, though McNabb had said no such meeting was needed.

McNabb clearly was surprised and unsettled to become Owens's target.

"As a child growing up, I dreamed of being an actor. And now I'm an actor in 'Days of Our Lives,'" McNabb said.

Eventually, everything got more or less patched up and the Eagles turned their attention to the season, but they soon learned all the different reasons why Super Bowl runners-up rarely get back the next year. Pinkston went down with an Achilles tear that ultimately would cut his career short. McNabb was limited by a sports

When Donovan McNabb struggled through injuries in 2006, Jeff Garcia filled in capably as his backup, leading the Eagles to a playoff win in the wild-card round. Garcia would come back to Philly for another short stint in 2009. *Hunter Martin/NFL/Getty Images*

hernia. There was a strange, bad karma affecting the whole scene: defensive end Jerome McDougle, the Eagles' first-round draft pick in 2003 and a projected starter in 2005, was shot in a robbery attempt the night before he was scheduled to fly to training camp, and missed the season while recovering.

The Birds started off 3-1, despite everything, but the early success was an illusion. A 33–10 loss at Dallas on October 9 kicked off a stretch of five losses in six games, the only victory coming on a late field-goal block run back for a touchdown against San Diego.

McNabb aggravated the sports hernia, ending his season, during a 21–20 loss to the Cowboys on November 14. By that time, Owens had been suspended for four games after granting an ESPN interview in which he again dissed McNabb. When a scripted public apology didn't

As much a threat to catch the ball as he was to run it, Brian Westbrook recorded a remarkable 90 receptions in the 2007 season. *Drew Hallowell/Getty Images*

go as planned—Owens omitted the part that dealt with McNabb, then left the whole thing sitting where reporters could see it—Reid deactivated him for the remainder of the season, an action upheld by an arbiter. Owens never played for the Eagles again.

The Birds limped to the close of a 6-10 season, the only losing season Reid has posted since his introductory year.

By the time the Eagles reconvened in 2006, Owens was a Dallas Cowboy. Philadelphia was a much calmer scene without him, but after a great 4-1 start, the team stumbled through the middle part of its season. The Eagles were 5-5 after a 31–13 loss to the Titans on November 13, but that wasn't even the worst news. Once again, they'd lost McNabb for the season, this time to an ACL tear. But Reid had learned something from 2005, other than how not to handle a diva wideout. One of the principal reasons for the 2005 team's awful finish was backup QB Mike McMahon, who just wasn't up to the task of replacing McNabb. For

2006, Reid brought in Jeff Garcia, a QB who could compare notes with McNabb on being abused by Owens.

Garcia lost his first start, at Indianapolis, but won his final five. It was a memorable run for a 36-year-old QB who had been discarded by the Browns and the Lions after each of the previous two seasons, sweeping the Eagles into the playoffs after many fans had abandoned hope. Garcia, a fiery leader, quickly became enormously popular in Philly—too much so for McNabb's mother, Wilma, who blogged that watching another QB take the team to the postseason was "bitter sweet." Mrs. McNabb was widely criticized, but her point was understandable to anyone who was familiar with the dynamics of Philadelphia sports. With Donovan suffering season-ending injuries two years in a row and turning 30, it was possible to wonder if his position might actually be up for grabs in the offseason. Or, as she put it, if there was a potential for "off season madness worse than last year's fiasco."

Andy Reid showed a great amount of confidence in Kevin Kolb when he spent a valuable 2007 draft pick on the young quarterback. Ultimately, the decision would spell the end of the Donvan McNabb era in Philadelphia. *Drew Hallowell/Getty Images*

But after a stirring first-round playoff win over the Giants, Garcia's limitations were exposed in a divisional-round loss at New Orleans. The Eagles would ultimately let Garcia move on to Tampa Bay in the offseason.

DONOVAN ON THE CLOCK

McNabb would still be the starter for 2007, but the clock was ticking. He learned that lesson while taking his family for ice cream on draft day; a cell phone call from a brother-in-law told McNabb the Eagles had traded their first-round pick, then used an early second-round selection on a quarterback, Kevin Kolb of Houston.

"I was shocked just like all the rest of the people were," McNabb said. "It was kind of shocking, to the point where you're wondering, 'Was that really our first pick, did we take a quarterback?' But it was nothing that bothered me to the point where I had to get on the phone and call

[Reid]. . . . My phone started vibrating, I got text messages from everybody—friends, teammates, people from other teams. I wasn't in front of the television, so I didn't have any answers."

Years later, it seems possible the Reid-McNabb relationship started to fray a little when Garcia took the Eagles to the playoffs, and maybe passed a tipping point when the organization made drafting McNabb's successor its top priority in 2007, despite a glaring shortage of offensive weapons.

"That was part of the 'shocking' deal, was that you'd think you would get somebody that would help you right now. It's nothing to do with Kevin Kolb," McNabb said.

This was also the year when Reid took a leave of absence to deal with the drug arrests of two of his sons. Everyone around the situation said the leave, undertaken before the draft, had no effect on the team, but what followed was an out-of-kilter 8-8 season, defined by narrow losses that should have been wins. The tone was set in the season opener, when the Eagles lost at Green Bay, 16–13, largely because they'd neglected to secure the services of an experienced punt returner. The Packers scored 10 of their 16 points directly off punts fumbled away by Greg Lewis and J. R. Reed.

The Birds wasted the greatest year of Brian Westbrook's career, one of the greatest all-around years any back has ever had. Westbrook ran the ball 278 times for 1,333 yards, and caught 90 passes for 771. His 2,104 total yards from scrimmage were a franchise record.

McNabb suffered an ankle sprain in a 17–7 victory over Miami on November 18 that brought the Eagles' record even at 5-5. The next week, A. J. Feeley summoned some of his 2002 magic by nearly ending the Patriots' unbeaten season in a 31–28 loss. But the Birds gained no traction from the near miss, losing the next two weeks to the Seahawks and the Giants. The loss to New York, at the Linc, marked McNabb's return to the lineup. When he didn't produce a spark, there was much speculation that 2007 would be his last season, that the Eagles would move ahead with Kolb in 2008. But McNabb rallied the Eagles for three season-ending victories, meaningless except that they provided a .500 record and maybe showed that McNabb still had some gas left in the tank. Management made it clear that the Birds would not be moving on just yet.

NEARLY MIRACULOUS

The 2008 draft brought something very precious and rare for the Reid-era Eagles—a game-breaking wideout and return man. California's DeSean Jackson, whose 168-pound frame and oversized attitude caused him to slip to the second round, was the Eagles' pick at number 49 overall.

The season started with a 38–3 thumping of the hapless Rams. Seven games later the Birds were 5-3 after a win at Seattle, and things were looking promising until a shootout loss to the Giants started an ugly skid. First the Birds went to Cincinnati and blundered through a 13–13 tie. McNabb threw three interceptions, compiled a 50.9 passer rating, then really got the fans excited when he acknowledged he'd had no idea games just ended in ties if no one scored in the 15-minute overtime. To his critics, this episode seemed to illustrate something about the aloof, disconnected air often projected by the franchise's all-time passing leader.

The next week, in Baltimore, McNabb threw two second-quarter picks and had gained only 59 passing yards by halftime. Reid benched McNabb for the second half in favor of Kolb, who fared no better in a dismal loss that left the Eagles 5-5-1. Again, the end of the McNabb era was heralded, as it had been the previous year, when the team sat at 5-8. Once again, the obits were premature. Four days later, on Thanksgiving, McNabb unfurled one of the best games of his career against visiting Arizona, going 27-for-39 for 260 yards, four touchdowns, and a 121.7 passer rating. Somehow, the Eagles were back on track.

They beat the Giants and Cleveland, but seemed dead yet again when the offense stalled in a 10–3 loss to Washington. The Eagles needed a final Sunday miracle to make the playoffs—they had to beat the Cowboys in a 4 p.m. game. All Dallas needed was a win to make the play-offs, while the Eagles needed the win as well as help in the early games: a loss by either the Vikings or the Bears, and a win from Oakland, a four-win team and a 13-point underdog at Tampa Bay.

Somehow, it happened. Houston beat the Bears, Oakland won, and the 8-6-1 Eagles controlled their destiny. Given the gift of life, they grabbed it for all it was worth, blowing away their most hated rivals, 44–6. It was the largest margin of victory ever in an Eagles-Cowboys game, sending the Birds on the road for a wild-card play-off game at Minnesota.

"I've been kind of revived, I guess," McNabb said, after breaking his own franchise record for passing yards in a season, set in 2004. He finished with 3,916, and his offense, despite its well-publicized inconsistencies, set a franchise points record with 416. "They've thrown me out, they ran over me, spit on me . . . but you know what . . . I just continue to prevail. . . . Since y'all talked about me not being in the playoffs the last four years, I'm in. It's sweet . . . but I've got a job to do [at Minnesota]."

The Eagles went to Minnesota and won a wild card round matchup, 26–14, Westbrook taking a screen pass 71 yards to break the game open. Then they went to the Meadowlands to face a defending Super Bowl champion Giants team that had earned a first-round bye. Remember, the Eagles entered the playoffs on the strength of a 9-6-1 record and a series of good breaks.

So what happened? The Birds won, of course, 23–11. They became the first team to beat New York twice in the same season at Giants Stadium. They were the first NFC

DeSEAN JACKSON

AS THE 2008 NFL draft approached, DeSean Jackson had two problems, his size and his reputation.

Jackson started to drift out of first-round projections when he weighed in at 168 pounds at the scouting combine. In the NFL, there are guys who weigh 168 pounds before they put the other foot on the scale. How was someone that insubstantial going to stand up to NFL-caliber hits?

Then there were the reports that Jackson didn't work hard, and speculation about the frustrations he and his family voiced at the University of California when the team failed to break through and became the upper-echelon program they had envisioned. Frail and plagued by a bad attitude? Not in the first round, not in this league.

And so it was that Jackson remained on the board when the Eagles made their second selection of the second round, the forty-ninth overall pick. Based on his performance thus far in his Eagles career, that would make him one of the greatest bargains in franchise history.

It was evident in training camp that Jackson had otherworldly speed, but nobody was knocking him around. When the season started, Jackson made even veteran cornerbacks look like the third-teamers he'd toasted on the field at Lehigh. And nobody questioned how hard Jackson worked; his fierce competitiveness became quickly apparent, and he was much too intent on proving himself to slack off.

Jackson's 912 receiving yards and 1,008 yards from scrimmage as a rookie were both team records—and he played all 16 games without being broken in half.

If 2008 was promising, 2009 was a revelation. Jackson became the first player in NFL history to make the Pro Bowl at two positions, returner and wide receiver. His eight touchdowns of 50 yards or more tied an NFL record held by Elroy "Crazy Legs" Hirsch and Devin Hester.

Jackson's specialty is the long strike. He is on a pace to compile historic yards-per-catch numbers. He has gotten banged around a bit, suffering a concussion in 2009 and another in 2010, but he has not been especially fragile so far. The attitude question got a little more complicated in 2010, when Jackson felt his contract should be reworked, given his extraordinary success. The team agreed,

DeSean Jackson spreads his wings to soar across the goal line for an Eagles touchdown.
Hunter Martin/Getty Images

but cited the expiring collective bargaining agreement and related rules restricting contract revisions in deferring an offer.

If Jackson is faulted for anything, it's for showboating, a common complaint about marquee receivers throughout the league. He literally threw away what would have been his first NFL touchdown on September 15, 2008, in Dallas. Jackson jettisoned the ball in celebration just before he crossed the goal line, instead of just *after*, as he'd planned. Oops. Two seasons later, he made that moment relevant again at the end of an amazing 91-yard TD run on a quick hitch in the fourth quarter of a tie game against Dallas. At the end of his run, Jackson paused before entering the end zone to execute a backward dive over the line. He drew a 15-yard penalty that could have been a huge problem for his team, though it turned out not to be.

"It was disrespectful," said Cowboys corner Mike Jenkins, the guy who wasn't able to cover Jackson on the play.

It was hard to say in the subsequent days whether Jackson got more attention for his end-zone dive or for his 210-yard receiving day, the third greatest in Eagles history. But as long as he was in the news for something, Jackson didn't seem to mind.

Asanta Samuel returns an interception for a touchdown against the Vikings in the playoffs following the 2008 season. *G. Newman Lowrance/Getty Images*

sixth seed to beat a top seed in 10 such matchups. McNabb put the cap on the proceedings with 2:59 left, when he was run out of bounds on the Giants' sideline. The quarterback found himself in front of a table that held the phone to the coaches in the press box. McNabb picked up the phone and pretended to converse. That meant a 15-yard penalty and an excellent photo that gained wide distribution.

The Eagles, however improbably, were headed for another NFC Championship Game, this one in Arizona where the Cardinals had won two playoff games in the same postseason for the first time in franchise history. After so many years of expecting the Super Bowl and not getting it, were Eagles fans about to get an unexpected title?

The answer, of course, was no. With a mature McNabb, Westbrook, and the explosive rookie Jackson, the offense was probably better than the units fielded by the Birds early in the decade. But when it mattered, the defense was not. The Eagles came back from an 18-point halftime deficit to take a 25–24 lead with 10:45 left, but Kurt Warner drove the Cards 72 yards in 14 plays and took back the lead for good.

"I want to apologize to the fans. We really thought this was it," said Dawkins, the seven-time Pro Bowl free safety, who turned out to be playing in his final Eagles game after 13 seasons in Philly. "We went out and gave what we could, but we came up short. I want to apologize to them."

Asked if the uncertainty over his future, as he headed for free agency, made the loss hurt more, Dawkins said: "It just hurts, period. When you burn your hand, I don't care how you burn it, it still hurts, and that's how I feel. No matter what the situation is here . . . as far as a contract goes, it still just hurts."

Donovan McNabb grabs a phone on the Eagles sideline after a long run in the 2008 divisional playoff game at the Meadowlands. *Bill Kostroun/AP Images*

GETTING YOUNGER

The ensuing offseason was about turning the page, with the Eagles not offering contracts to Tra Thomas or Jon Runyan, their bookend offensive tackles since 2000. Dawkins also departed, after a confusing dance with management, which wanted to bring him back but miscalculated the market. The best safety in Eagles history headed for Denver.

Another high-profile wideout, Missouri's Jeremy Maclin, arrived in the draft, as did LeSean McCoy, a flashy young running back from Pitt. McNabb was in an odd position: finally he had game-changing weapons, but they were all a generation younger than he was, gravitating more naturally to Kolb.

The 2009 Eagles were a team in transition, a situation they handled pretty well for quite a while. Revered defensive coordinator Jim Johnson lost his battle with cancer just as training camp was opening. Johnson coached the final few games of the 2008 season from the press box, riding a motorized scooter, officially because of a "back problem." During Super Bowl week, the team revealed the real situation. Johnson worked part-time through minicamps, then his health took a turn for the worse.

Johnson protégé Sean McDermott took over, without really having a chance to tailor the personnel to his tastes. Dawkins's departure left a gaping wound at the free safety position, and it never healed.

A team is usually lucky to secure one legitimate playmaker via the annual NFL draft, but in 2009 the Birds managed to find two very dangerous weapons in running back LeSean McCoy and receiver Jeremy Maclin. *Scott Boehm/Getty Images*

Drew Hallowell /Philadelphia Eagles/Getty Images

A stalwart member of the Eagles defense in the earlier part of the decade, Jeremiah Trotter returned to the Eagles for three seasons from 2004 to 2006, and once again in 2009 when the Birds lost linebacker Stewart Bradley to injury. *Hunter Martin/Getty Images*

Mitchell Layton/Getty Images

Matt Rourke/AP Images
Mixed emotions were the order of the day when McNabb was traded to the rival Redskins.

The strangest episode of the season came on August 13, when word leaked out during the preseason opener that the Birds were about to sign Michael Vick, just out of prison for running a dog-fighting ring. The signing had something to do with McNabb, who supported Vick's attempts to return to the NFL, and even more to do with Reid, who had gotten to know people who had gotten in trouble, and their relatives, during his visits to his sons at various facilities.

Before the signing, when Vick's future was first being talked about around the NFL, Reid was asked if he thought Vick deserved a second chance.

"Sure. I'm big on second chances at this phase in my life," Reid said.

Many fans welcomed Vick with open arms, but there was naturally a certain level of anxiety as well. One protester's sign bore the message "Hide your beagle, Vick's an Eagle," which eventually made its way onto T-shirts. Vick was extremely rusty and played a minimal role in the season, but perhaps most important, he maintained a relatively low profile off the field.

The Eagles were 11-4 as they headed into a Week 17 showdown with Dallas, having vanquished Dawkins and the Broncos the week before. The main knock on this Eagles team was that they played an easy schedule, not beating a single playoff-caliber team all season. That turned out to be a valid complaint. The Birds lost the season finale to the Cowboys, 24–0, particularly unfortunate in that they had to go back there the next week for a wild-card playoff game. The matchup was so one-sided, it was hard to see how they would turn it around in six days (the postseason meeting scheduled for Saturday). This time, the Cowboys won 34–14, looking dominant on both sides of the line of scrimmage.

The Eagles, who had undertaken quite a bit of change over the past few years, were headed for more. A season earlier, in the aftermath of the Arizona loss, President Joe Banner had referenced the old saying that the definition of insanity was doing the same thing over and over again and expecting different results. In the spring of 2010, it became clear that this sentiment would be applied to McNabb's 11-year tenure as the Eagles' quarterback, during which he'd done everything to make himself the best QB in franchise history—except win a championship.

TURNING THE PAGE

The Reid-Banner regime has never revealed much information on its decision-making process, so we don't know the details surrounding the decision to trade Donovan McNabb. We do know that when the Eagles' season ended, Reid seemed inclined to go forward with McNabb, who made his sixth Pro Bowl in 2009. But Reid did qualify his statements by making it clear that, at the time, he was speaking without considering possible contractual issues, and both McNabb and Kolb were heading into the final years of their deals. There was no way Kolb was going to sign an extension to remain a backup. There was no way management was going into the season with both QBs in contract years. The Eagles had to choose between the two, and they chose Kolb.

The decision was never announced, but it began to be inferred at the NFL meetings in Florida, when Reid allowed that he was fielding offers for all three quarterbacks. That statement was correctly read as an admission that the McNabb auction was officially under way.

On the evening of Easter Sunday, the Eagles called reporters to the NovaCare practice facility to announce that McNabb had been traded to Washington for a second-round pick in 2010 (the Birds took free safety Nate Allen) and a 2011 pick that could be either a third or a fourth (it turned out to be a fourth).

"Obviously, that was a tough decision to make, in trading Donovan. He's been such a great player here for 11 years, and set every record that you could set with this organization, and been a great example on and off the field in everything he's done. I have nothing but good things to say about Donovan. Unfortunately, things like this happen in the National Football League," Reid said.

Reid answered a lot of questions about his statements earlier in the offseason, when he maintained McNabb would be his starting quarterback.

"He was the starting quarterback," Reid said, "until he went elsewhere."

Two days later, at the Redskins' practice facility in Ashburn, Virginia, McNabb held up one of the most jarring-looking items in recent NFL history—a burgundy No. 5 jersey with his name on the back.

"I've always believed in finishing where you've started," McNabb said. "I think there is a lot to be said [for] that. Not a lot of quarterbacks in this league are able to do that nowadays. But it says a lot about the things you learn to accomplish throughout your years. Sometimes change is better. Sometimes you are forced into change."

FALSE START

The premise throughout the spring and through training camp was that Kolb was taking the reins. Players and coaches praised his maturity, his demeanor, and his accuracy. Vick was still around; one assumed it was because nobody had offered the Eagles anything for him. Bystanders marveled at his arm in training camp, just as they had done at practice in 2009. But this was Kolb's team. Vick was the veteran backup.

Then Kolb went down with a concussion in the second quarter of the season opener, his head slammed into the turf at the Linc as he was tackled from behind by Green Bay's Clay Matthews near the left sideline. Vick came off the bench and provided the offense a definite spark, but it wasn't quite enough to beat the Packers. After the game, Reid confirmed that, when healthy, Kevin Kolb was his starting quarterback.

The next week the Eagles went to Detroit. With Kolb still sidelined, Vick completed 21 of 34 passes for 284 yards and two touchdowns in a 35–32 win, withstanding six sacks and running seven times for 37 yards. The Birds' O-line was shaky at best, and a less mobile quarterback would have lost the game. Vick did not turn the ball over and finished with a passer rating of 108, after ringing up a 101.9 in his Week 1 relief effort. Only once before in his career had Vick put two such games together.

Afterward, Reid declared it was "not hard at all" to go back to Kolb, even though Vick had marshaled 52 points in six quarters as the number one guy and had led the team to five touchdowns in six trips to the red zone.

That was the public statement. But Reid began a series of conversations with Kolb over the next few days that ended with a Tuesday evening announcement: Michael Vick was being named the Eagles' starting quarterback. This was not going to be the learn-and-grow season everyone had envisioned, but something very different.

REDEMPTION AND DISAPPOINTMENT

For much of the year, Vick's redemption was the league's top story. Appearing on countless prime-time pre-game shows, he recounted his remorse for the activities that had

landed him in prison. He insisted he was a changed man and was determined to be a smarter, sounder quarterback than he had been with Atlanta. When the games started, Vick would back his words up on the field, dazzling the football world with a dual-threat skill set possessed by no one else in the league.

Monday Night Football had never seen anything quite like the Eagles' 59–28 victory at Washington on November 15, 2010. Vick did something no one had ever done, throwing for four touchdowns and running for two more, racking up 333 passing yards and 80 rushing yards as the Eagles romped to a 59–21 lead after three quarters.

"I could never have envisioned this," Vick said, when asked if this was what he saw happening when he began his comeback. "Signing here, I didn't even think I'd be starting as the quarterback this year."

Had Vick ever played better, at any level?

"I've had some great games in my day. I don't think I've had one quite like this," Vick said on the night the Eagles piled up a franchise record 592 net yards. They'd scored more points only once in their long history, when they tallied 64 against the Cincinnati Reds in 1934.

"It stings anytime you literally get your ass whipped," Redskins defensive tackle Albert Haynesworth said. "It was embarrassing. I couldn't wait for the game to be over. They played like they were racking up BCS points. They should be ranked No. 1 now."

That night was the 2010 Eagles' complete-game high-water mark, but more astounding in its own way was the 38–31 victory at the Giants on December 19, in which Vick led the visitors back from a 31–10 deficit with just eight minutes left.

"I've never been around anything like this in my life," Giants coach Tom Coughlin said. "It's about as empty as you get to feel in this business, right there."

"That was special," said a soggy Andy Reid, given the Gatorade bath by his players.

"I was jumpin' up and down, screamin', trying to

MICHAEL VICK

Chris McGrath/Getty Images

FROM FEDERAL PRISON to the NFL Pro Bowl in a year and a half is the kind of thing you see in movies, not in the real world. But that was Michael Vick's path exactly.

In 2007, Vick, a three-time Pro Bowl quarterback with the Falcons, was banned from the NFL for running a brutally inhumane dogfighting ring. He was reinstated to the league after serving 19 months at Leavenworth, then a couple more at a halfway house. The Eagles, known for their emphasis on character and avoiding off-field trouble, shocked everyone by signing him that August. Vick spent a year appearing mostly as a "Wildcat" gimmick, looking rusty and out of sync. It seemed likely the Eagles wanted to parlay him into a midround draft pick in the offseason.

That didn't happen. The Eagles later said they hadn't wanted to trade Vick, while other sources claimed nobody had offered anything. At any rate, Vick came back for 2010, supposedly as the mentor to new starter Kevin Kolb. That plan lasted until September 21, when Andy Reid made Vick the starter, and Vick turned the NFL on its ear.

Vick seemed unstoppable at first. He threw 11 touchdown passes and no interceptions in his first six games of the season. If he didn't see what he liked, he took off, with afterburners other QBs could only dream of—all to the tune of 341 yards on 44 carries in those games. But in his last seven games, including a wild-card playoff loss to the Packers, Vick threw 11 TDs and seven interceptions. He took too many hits and wasn't as effective as a runner, gaining 335 yards on his final 56 carries (although Vick did become the first Eagles quarterback to rush for nine touchdowns in a single season).

Though he wound up completing 62.6 percent of his passes and compiling a 100.2 passer rating, Vick became a vulnerable blitz target behind a wifty offensive line late in the year. It didn't help that his young receiving corps wasn't great at breaking off routes when rushers went in free, or that Vick didn't recognize and react as well as he might have.

"Obviously, we wish we could've [gone] farther, and I wish I could've taken some things back," Vick said, after throwing a late interception that blunted a last-minute comeback bid in the playoff loss. "But that's hindsight now; got to move on and got to figure out ways that I can get better."

Vick's emergence as the face of the Eagles was a tricky development for many fans. They marveled at his skills and approved of his straightforward leadership style. But a pretty significant group wondered if a man who repeatedly tortured and killed dogs over the course of several years could really become someone different just because he'd had to go to prison and declare bankruptcy.

It's been a long road of redemption for Eagles QB Michael Vick, whose 2010 season was as exciting as any single-season Eagles performance in recent memory.

Mike Ehrmann/Getty Images

What was truly in his heart was impossible to know. But Vick made a number of community appearances on behalf of the Humane Society, relaying to inner-city groups that dogfighting was wrong. It seemed clear that he was reaching an audience few NFL stars could relate to, people who sometimes knew a thing or two about prison and the hope of redemption.

Vick signed his franchise tender for the 2011 season, and hopes to reach a multi-year deal to stay with the Eagles long-term.

Michael Vick is the most potent run/ pass threat in the NFL today.

Drew Hallowell /Getty Images

Larry French/Getty Images

Brent Celek scored a 65-yard touchdown late in the fourth quarter of the latest "Miracle at the Meadowlands." This time, the Eagles came back to steal the victory by scoring 28 points in the final 7:28 of the game. *Hunter Martin/Philadelphia Eagles/Getty Images*

lose my voice," said Eagles tight end Brent Celek, who started the comeback with a 65-yard touchdown catch with 7:28 remaining, the longest of his career. "I've never been a part of anything like this game. When we came in the locker room, it was almost like you won the Super Bowl."

But the 2010 Eagles did not win the Super Bowl. In fact, they didn't win another game. The Birds were scheduled to host the Vikings the next weekend, in a game that was "flexed" from afternoon to Sunday night due to the Eagles' dominance of national TV ratings. The timing difference turned out to be crucial when an intense winter storm was forecast for Sunday night. League and team officials pondered the feasibility of trying to play with snow falling at a clip of one to two inches an hour and winds howling at around 40 mph—as well as the responsibility of inviting fans to drive to and from the

game in the teeth of all that. The game was postponed until Tuesday, but the Eagles clinched the NFC East title on Sunday anyway, when the Giants lost to the Packers. They might have played on Monday, but the league likely opted not to rock the boat with ESPN, who had grown accustomed to owning the airwaves for its Monday Night Football broadcasts.

Whether the delay figured into it or not, the Eagles, who hadn't suited up on a Tuesday since World War II, played their flattest, most inept game of the season in a 24–14 loss to the Vikings. Clearly, the Birds didn't think the going-nowhere Vikings were going to come in and play hard, and clearly, they were very wrong. Their shot at a playoff bye disappeared.

Locked into the NFC's third playoff seed, Reid elected to rest most of his starters in the finale, a 14–13 home loss to Dallas that set the Eagles' regular-season record

DeSean Jackson is almost as good at celebrating touchdowns as he is at scoring them—almost. *Drew Hallowell /Getty Images*

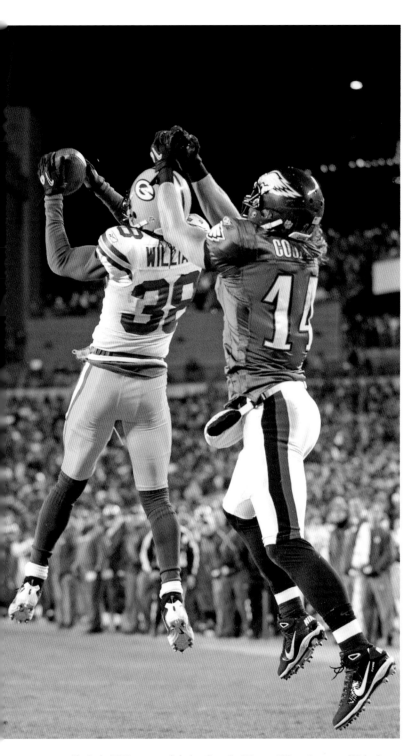

at 10-6. That meant a home date with the Packers, a wild-card playoff rematch of the season opener.

Unfortunately for the Eagles, it went very much like the season opener, minus the Kolb concussion. Green Bay was clearly the better team on both sides of the ball, and the Packers' blitzes and overall pass-rush pressure stifled Vick. The Eagles came back from a 14–0 deficit and had a shot to win it at the end, but Vick was intercepted in the end zone and Green Bay escaped with a 21–16 victory.

The fiftieth anniversary of the Birds' most recent NFL title would not produce another.

The abrupt end of the season produced casualties—Reid decided to part with defensive coordinator Sean McDermott, whose unit allowed a franchise-record 31 touchdown passes, along with defensive line coach Rory Segrest and linebackers coach Bill Shuey.

Then, after interviewing several candidates to replace McDermott, all with backgrounds in the defensive secondary, Reid left the NFL world scratching its head when he opted to make offensive line coach Juan Castillo his defensive coordinator. Reid explained that Castillo, renowned as a blocking technician, had often swapped theories with Jim Johnson, and had long aspired to coach defense.

It was an exceptionally bold move by a coach who probably needs to win a Super Bowl in the next two years to get another contract.

The Eagles' 2010 season ended when Green Bay's Tramon Williams intercepted Michael Vick's underthrown pass near the goal line late in the fourth quarter. Vick was attempting to connect with rookie receiver Riley Cooper for the game-winning touchdown. *Rob Tringali/ SportsChrome/Getty Images*

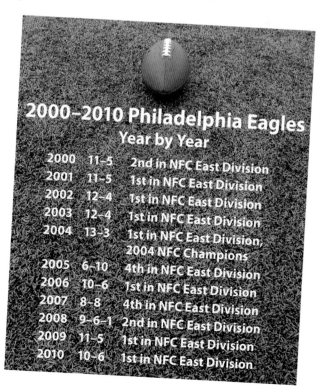

2000–2010 Philadelphia Eagles
Year by Year

Year	Record	Finish
2000	11–5	2nd in NFC East Division
2001	11–5	1st in NFC East Division
2002	12–4	1st in NFC East Division
2003	12–4	1st in NFC East Division
2004	13–3	1st in NFC East Division, 2004 NFC Champions
2005	6–10	4th in NFC East Division
2006	10–6	1st in NFC East Division
2007	8–8	4th in NFC East Division
2008	9–6–1	2nd in NFC East Division
2009	11–5	1st in NFC East Division
2010	10–6	1st in NFC East Division

APPENDIX

Philadelphia Eagles All-Time Record Book
(through the 2010 season)

INDIVIDUAL HONORS

PHILADELPHIA EAGLES HONOR ROLL

Name	Position	Years with Eagles	Induction Year
Chuck Bednarik*	C/LB	1949–1962	1980
Bert Bell*	Owner	1933–1940	1987
Bill Bergey	LB	1974–1980	1988
Bill Bradley	S	1969–1976	1993
Tom Brookshier*	DB	1956–1961	1989
Bob Brown*	OT	1964–1968	2004
Jerome Brown	DT	1987–1991	1996
Timmy Brown	RB	1960–1967	1990
Harold Carmichael	WR	1971–1983	1987
Randall Cunningham	QB	1985–1995	2009
Otho Davis	Trainer	1973–1995	1999
Jim Gallagher	Executive	1949–1995	1995
Bill Hewitt	WR	1936–1939, 1943	1987
Ron Jaworski	QB	1977–1986	1992
Sonny Jurgensen*	QB	1957–1963	1987
Ollie Matson*	RB	1964–1966	1987
Tommy McDonald*	WR	1957–1963	1988
Wilbert Montgomery	RB	1977–1984	1987
Early "Greasy" Neale*	Head Coach	1941–1950	1987
Pete Pihos*	WR	1947–1955	1987
Mike Quick	WR	1982–1990	1995
Pete Retzlaff	TE	1956–1966	1989
Jim Ringo*	C	1964–1967	1987
Jerry Sisemore	OT	1973–1984	1991
Norm Van Brocklin*	QB	1958–1960	1987
Steve Van Buren*	RB	1944–1951	1987
Dick Vermeil	Head Coach	1976–1982	1994
Stan Walters	OT	1975–1983	1991
Reggie White*	DE	1985–1992	2005
Al Wistert	OT	1943–1951	2009
Alex Wojciechowicz*	C	1946–1950	1987
1948 and 1949 NFL Championship Teams			1999

* Also a member of the Pro Football Hall of Fame

RETIRED NUMBERS

Name (Number)	Position	Years with Eagles
Chuck Bednarik (60)	C/LB	1949–1962
Tom Brookshier (40)	DB	1956–1961
Jerome Brown (99)	DT	1987–1991
Pete Retzlaff (44)	TE	1956–1966
Steve Van Buren (15)	RB	1944–1951
Reggie White (92)	DE	1985–1992
Al Wistert (70)	OT	1943–1951

FIRST-TEAM ALL-PRO SELECTIONS

Name	Position		Years
Reggie White	DE	6	1986–1991
Steve Van Buren	RB	5	1944, 1945, 1947–1949
Pete Pihos	WR	5	1949, 1952–1955
Chuck Bednarik	C/LB	5	1950–1954
Al Wistert	OT	4	1944–1947
Brian Dawkins	DB	4	2001, 2002, 20004, 2006
Bob Brown	OT	3	1965, 1966, 1968
Keith Jackson	TE	3	1988–1990
Bill Bradley	S	2	1971, 1972
Bill Bergey	LB	2	1974, 1975
Charlie Johnson	DT	2	1980, 1981
Mike Quick	WR	2	1983, 1985
Jerome Brown	DT	2	1990, 1991
Clyde Simmons	DE/DT	2	1991, 1992
Bill Hewitt	WR	1	1938
Vic Lindskog	C	1	1951
Norm Willey	DE	1	1954
Tom Brookshier	DB	1	1960
Norm Van Brocklin	QB	1	1960
Sonny Jurgensen	QB	1	1961
Maxie Baughan	LB	1	1964
Pete Retzlaff	TE	1	1965
Charle Young	TE	1	1973
Wes Hopkins	DB	1	1985
Eric Allen	DB	1	1989
Hugh Douglas	DE	1	2000
Jeremiah Trotter	LB	1	2000
David Akers	K	1	2001
Troy Vincent	DB	1	2002
Terrell Owens	WR	1	2004
Lito Sheppard	DB	1	2004
Shawn Andrews	G	1	2006
Brian Westbrook	RB	1	2007
Leonard Weaver	FB	1	2009

PRO BOWL SELECTIONS

Players with five or more Pro Bowl selections.

Name	Position		Years
Chuck Bednarik	C/LB	8	1950–1954, 1956, 1957, 1960
Reggie White	DE	7	1986–1992
Brian Dawkins	DB	7	1999, 2001, 2002, 2004–2006, 2008
Pete Pihos	WR	6	1950–1955
Donovan McNabb	QB	6	2000–2004, 2009
Tommy McDonald	WR	5	1958–1962
Pete Retzlaff	TE	5	1958, 1960, 1963–1965
Maxie Baughan	LB	5	1960, 1961, 1963–1965
Mike Quick	WR	5	1983–1987
Eric Allen	DB	5	1989, 1991–1994
Troy Vincent	DB	5	1999–2003
David Akers	K	5	2001, 2002, 2004, 2009, 2010

EAGLES 75TH SEASON ALL-TIME TEAM

As chosen by fans from a list of nominees selected by Merrill Reese (Eagles play-by-play announcer) and Ray Didinger (NFL Films Senior Producer)

HEAD COACH   Andy Reid

OFFENSE

QB	Donovan McNabb
RB	Steve Van Buren
FB	Keith Byars
WR	Harold Carmichael
LT	Tra Thomas
LG	Wade Key
C	Chuck Bednarik
RG	Shawn Andrews
RT	Jon Runyan
TE	Pete Pihos
WR	Tommy McDonald

DEFENSE

CB	Troy Vincent
DE	Reggie White
DT	Jerome Brown
DT	Charlie Johnson
DE	Clyde Simmons
CB	Eric Allen
OLB	Seth Joyner
MLB	Chuck Bednarik
OLB	Alex Wojciechowicz
SS	Andre Waters
FS	Brian Dawkins

SPECIAL TEAMS

K	David Akers
P	Sean Landeta
ST	Vince Papale
KR	Timmy Brown
PR	Brian Westbrook

INDIVIDUAL RECORDS

SERVICE

Most Seasons
14   Chuck Bednarik, 1949–1962
13   Harold Carmichael, 1971–1983
13   Brian Dawkins, 1996–2008
13   Frank (Bucko) Kilroy, 1943–1955
13   Vic Sears, 1941–1953
12   David Akers, 1999–2010
12   Jerry Sisemore, 1973–1984
12   Bobby Walston, 1951–1962

Most Regular Season Games Played
188   David Akers, 1999–2010
183   Brian Dawkins, 1996–2008
180   Harold Carmichael, 1971–1983
169   Chuck Bednarik, 1949–1962
166   Tra Thomas, 1998–2008

Most Consecutive Games Played
162   Harold Carmichael, 1972–1983
159   Randy Logan, 1973–1983
148   Bobby Walston, 1951–1962
144   Jon Runyan, 2000–2008
139   Ken Clarke, 1977–1987

OFFENSE

SCORING RECORDS

Most Points Scored
Career
1,323   David Akers, K, 1999–2010
881   Bobby Walston, WR/K, 1951–1962
475   Sam Baker, K, 1964–1969
474   Harold Carmichael, WR, 1971–1983
464   Steve Van Buren, RB, 1944–1951

Season
144   David Akers, K, 2008
143   David Akers, K, 2010
139   David Akers, K, 2009
133   David Akers, K, 2002
122   David Akers, K, 2004

Game
25   Bobby Walston, WR/K, at Redskins, 10/17/1954
24   Clarence Peaks, RB, vs. Chi. Cardinals, 11/16/1958
24   Tommy McDonald, WR, vs. Giants, 10/4/1959
24   Ben Hawkins, WR, vs. Steelers, 9/28/1969
24   Wilbert Montgomery, RB, at Redskins, 9/10/1978
24   Wilbert Montgomery, RB, vs. Redskins, 10/7/1979
24   Irving Fryar, WR, vs. Dolphins, 10/20/1996
24   Brian Westbrook, RB, vs. Cardinals, 11/27/2008

Touchdowns Scored
Career
79   Harold Carmichael, WR, 1971–1983
77   Steve Van Bruen, RB, 1944–1951
68   Brian Westbrook, RB, 2002–2009
67   Tommy McDonald, WR, 1957–1963
63   Pete Pihos, WR, 1947–1955

Season
18   Steve Van Buren, RB, 1945
14   Steve Van Buren, RB, 1947
14   Wilbert Montgomery, RB, 1979
14   Terrell Owens, WR, 2004
14   Brian Westbrook, RB, 2008

Game
4   Clarence Peaks, RB, vs. Chi. Cardinals, 11/16/1958
4   Tommy McDonald, WR, vs. Giants, 10/4/1959
4   Ben Hawkins, WR, vs. Steelers, 9/28/1969
4   Wilbert Montgomery, RB, at Redsksins, 9/10/1978
4   Wilbert Montgomery, RB, vs. Redsksins, 10/7/1979
4   Irving Fryar, WR, vs. Dolphins, 10/20/1996
4   Brian Westbrook, RB, vs. Cardinals, 11/27/2008

PASSING RECORDS

Quarterback Wins
Career
92   Donovan McNabb, 1999–2009
69   Ron Jaworski, 1977–1986
63   Randall Cunningham, 1985–1995
28   Norm Snead, 1964–1970
19   Bobby Thomason, 1952–1957
19   Norm Van Brocklin, 1958–1960

Season
13   Donovan McNabb, 2004
12   Ron Jaworski, 1980
12   Donovan McNabb, 2003
11   Ran Jaworski, 1979
11   Randall Cunningham, 1989
11   Donovan McNabb, 2000
11   Donovan McNabb, 2001

Pass Attempts
Career
4,746   Donovan McNabb, 1999–2009
3,918   Ron Jaworski, 1977–1986
3,632   Randall Cunningham 1985–1995
2,236   Norm Snead, 1964–1970
1,396   Tommy Thompson, 1941–1942, 1945–1950

Season
571   Donovan McNabb, 2008
569   Donovan McNabb, 2000
560   Randall Cunningham, 1988

| 532 | Randall Cunningham, 1989 |
| 493 | Donovan McNabb, 2001 |

Game

62	Randall Cunningham, at Bears, 10/2/1989
60	Davey O'Brien, at Redskins, 12/1/1940
58	Donovan McNabb, at Bengals, 11/12008
57	Sonny Jurgensen, vs. Giants, 9/23/1962
55	Three players tied at 55 attempts

Pass Completions

Career

2,801	Donovan McNabb, 1999–2009
2,088	Ron Jaworski, 1977–1986
1,874	Randall Cunningham, 1985–1995
1,154	Norm Snead, 1964–1970
723	Tommy Thompson, 1941–1942, 1945–1950

Season

345	Donovan McNabb, 2008
330	Donovan McNabb, 2000
301	Randall Cunningham, 1988
300	Donovan McNabb, 2004
291	Donovan McNabb, 2007

Game

35	Donovan McNabb, vs. Chargers, 10/23/2005
35	Donovan McNabb, at Chargers, 11/15/2009
34	Randall Cunningham, at Redskins, 9/17/1989
33	Three players tied with 33 completions

Completion Percentage

Career (min. 500 attempts)

59.0%	Donovan McNabb, 1999–2009 (2801–4746)
57.7%	Ty Detmer, 1996–1997 (372–645)
57.4%	Rodney Peete, 1995–1998 (434–756)
55.8%	Roman Gabriel, 1973–1977 (661–1,185)
55.7%	Randall Cunningham, 1985–1995 (1,874–3,362)

Season (min. 250 attempts)

64.0%	Donovan McNabb, 2004 (300–469)
62.6%	Michael Vick, 2010 (233–372)
61.5%	Donovan McNabb, 2007 (291–473)
60.7%	Randall Cunningham, 1992 (233–384)
60.4%	Donovan McNabb, 2008 (345–571)

Game (min. 20 attempts)

| 80.8% | Donovan McNabb, vs. Lions, 9/23/2007 (21–26) |

Passing Yards

Career

| 32,873 | Donovan McNabb, 1999–2009 |
| 26,963 | Ron Jaworski, 1977–1986 |

Edwin Mahan/NFL/Getty Images

22,877	Randall Cunningham, 1985–1995
15,672	Norm Snead, 1964–1970
10,240	Tommy Thompson, 1941–1942, 1945–1950

Season

3,916	Donovan McNabb, 2008
3,875	Donovan McNabb, 2004
3,808	Randall Cunningham, 1988
3,723	Sonny Jurgensen, 1961
3,553	Donovan McNabb, 2009

Game

464	Donovan McNabb, vs. Packers, 12/5/2004
450	Donovan McNabb, at Chargers, 11/15/2009
447	Randall Cunningham, at Redskins, 9/17/1989
437	Bobby Thomason, vs. Giants, 11/8/1953
436	Sonny Jurgensen, at Redskins, 10/29/1961

Longest Pass Plays from Scrimmage

99 yards (t)	Ron Jaworski to Mike Quick, vs. Falcons, 11/10/1985
95 yards (t)	Randall Cunningham to Fred Barnett, at Bills, 12/2/1990
93 yards	Randall Cunningham to Herschel Walker, at Giants, 9/4/1994
92 yards (t)	King Hill to Ben Hawkins, vs. Giants, 9/22/1968
91 yards (t)	3 tied for 91 yards, all resulting in touchdowns

Most Yards per Game
Career (min. 30 games)
222.1 Donovan McNabb, 1999–2009 (32,873–127)
208.9 Norm Van Brocklin, 1958–1960 (7,497–36)
189.9 Ron Jaworski, 1977–1986 (26,963–142)
187.5 Randall Cunningham, 1985–1995 (22,877–122)
184.4 Norm Snead, 1964–1970 (15,672–85)

Season (min. 10 games)
265.9 Sonny Jurgensen, 1961 (3,723–14)
264.7 Donovan McNabb, 2006 (2,647–10)
258.3 Donovan McNabb, 2004 (3,875–15)
253.8 Donovan McNabb, 2009 (3,553–14)
251.5 Michael Vick, 2009 (3,018–12)

Most Yards per Attempt
Career (min. 250 attempts)
8.7 Sonny Jurgensen, 1957–1963 (9,639–1,107)
8.1 Michael Vick, 2009–2010 (3,104–385)
7.5 Norm Van Brocklin, 1958–1960 (7,497–998)
7.4 Roy Zimmerman, 1943–1946 (3,219–435)
7.3 Tommy Thompson, 1941, 1942, 1945–1950 (10,240–1,396)
7.3 Bobby Thomason, 1952–1957 (8,124–1,113)

Season (min. 100 attempts)
8.9 Sonny Jurgensen, 1961 (3,723–416)
8.9 Sonny Jurgensen, 1962 (3,261–366)
8.7 Norm Van Brocklin, 1960 (2,471–284)
8.4 Tommy Thompson, 1947 (1,680–201)
8.4 Donovan McNabb, 2006 (2,647–316)

Touchdown Passes
Career
216 Donovan McNabb, 1999–2009
175 Ron Jaworski, 1977–1986
150 Randall Cunningham, 1985–1995
111 Norm Snead, 1964–1970
90 Tommy Thompson, 1941, 1942, 1945–1950

Season
32 Sonny Jurgensen, 1961
31 Donovan McNabb, 2004
30 Randall Cunningham, 1990
29 Norm Snead, 1967
27 Ron Jaworski, 1980

Game
7 Adrian Burk, at Redskins, 10/17/1954
5 5 players tied with 5 touchdowns each

Most Interceptions Thrown
Career
151 Ron Jaworski, 1977–1986
124 Norm Snead, 1964–1970
105 Randall Cunningham, 1985–1995
100 Tommy Thompson, 1941, 1942, 1945–1950
100 Donovan McNabb, 1999–2009

Season
26 Sonny Jurgensen, 1962
24 Sonny Jurgensen, 1961
24 Norm Snead, 1967
23 Adrian Burk, 1951
23 Norm Snead, 1969

Game
6 Bobby Thomason, vs. Chi. Cardinals, 10/21/1956
6 Pete Liske, vs. Cowboys, 9/26/1971

Fewest Interceptions per Attempt
Career Percentage (min. 250 attempts)
1.6% Bubby Brister, 1993–1994 (6–385)
1.6% Michael Vick, 2009–2010 (6–385)
2.1% Donovan McNabb, 1999–2009 (100–4,746)
2.9% Ty Detmer, 1996–1997 (19–645)
3.1% Roman Gabriel, 1973–1977 (37–1,185)

Season Percentage (min. 100 attempts)
1.1% Jeff Garcia, 2006 (2–188)
1.5% Donovan McNabb, 2007 (7–473)
1.6% Bubby Brister, 1993 (5–309)
1.6% Michael Vick, 2010 (6–372)
1.7% Joe Pisarcik, 1984 (3–176)

Quarterback Rating
Career (min. 500 attempts)
86.5 Donovan McNabb, 1999–2009
79.1 Sonny Jurgensen, 1957–1963
78.7 Randall Cunningham, 1985–1995
78.3 Ty Detmer, 1996–1997
75.7 Norm Van Brocklin, 1958–1960

Season (min. 250 attempts)
104.7 Donovan McNabb, 2004
100.2 Michael Vick, 2010
95.5 Donovan McNabb, 2006
92.9 Donovan McNabb, 2009
91.6 Randall Cunningham, 1990

RUSHING RECORDS

Attempts
Career
1,465 Wilbert Montgomery, 1977–1984
1,320 Steve Van Buren, 1944–1951
1,308 Brian Westbrook, 2002–2009

| 1,200 | Duce Staley, 1997–2003 |
| 975 | Ricky Watters, 1995–1997 |

Season
353	Ricky Watters, 1996
338	Wilbert Montgomery, 1979
337	Ricky Watters, 1995
325	Duce Staley, 1999
286	Wilbert Montgomery, 1981

Game
35	Steve Van Buren, vs. NY Bulldogs, 11/20/1949
35	Heath Sherman, vs. Redskins, 11/12/1990
35	Heath Sherman, at Buccaneers, 10/6/1991

Yards
Career
6,538	Wilbert Montgomery, 1977–1984
5,995	Brian Westbrook, 2002–2009
5,860	Steve Van Buren, 1944–1951
4,807	Duce Staley, 1997–2003
4,482	Randall Cunningham, 1985–1995

Season
1,512	Wilbert Montgomery, 1979
1,411	Ricky Watters, 1996
1,402	Wilbert Montgomery, 1981
1,333	Brian Westbrook, 2007
1,273	Ricky Watters, 1995
1,273	Duce Staley, 1999

Game
205	Steve Van Buren, vs. Steelers, 11/27/1949
201	Duce Staley, at Cowboys, 9/3/2000
197	Wilbert Montgomery, vs. Browns, 11/4/1979
190	Swede Hanson, vs. Cin. Reds, 11/6/1934
186	Timmy Brown, at Browns, 11/7/1965

Longest Run from Scrimmage
| 91 yards | Herschel Walker, at Falcons, 11/27/1994 |

Rushing Yards per Carry
Career (min. 400 carries)
6.62	Randall Cunningham, 1985–1995 (4,482–677)
5.67	Donovan McNabb, 1999–2009 (3,249–573)
4.58	Brian Westbrook, 2002–2009 (5,995–1308)
4.57	Charlie Garner, 1994–1998 (2,261–495)
4.53	Correll Buckhalter, 2001–2008 (2,155–476)

Season (min. 100 carries)
8.0	Randall Cunningham, 1990 (942–118)
6.8	Michael Vick, 2010 (676–100)
6.0	Randall Cunningham, 1989 (621–104)
5.8	Steve Van Buren, 1945 (832–143)
5.5	Swede Hanson, 1934 (805–146)

Doug Pensinger/AllSport/Getty images

Rushing Touchdowns
Career
69	Steve Van Buren, 1944–1951
45	Wilbert Montgomery, 1977–1984
37	Brian Westbrook, 2002–2009
32	Randall Cunningham, 1985–1995
31	Ricky Watters, 1995–1997

Season
15	Steve Van Buren, 1945
13	Steve Van Buren, 1947
13	Ricky Watters, 1996
11	Steve Van Buren, 1949
11	Tom Sullivan, 1974
11	Ricky Watters, 1995

Game
| 3 | Achieved 10 times, most recently by LeSean McCoy, at Lions, 9/19/2010 |

RECEIVING

Receptions
Career

589	Harold Carmichael, 1971–1983
452	Pete Retzlaff, 1956–1966
426	Brian Westbrook, 2002–2009
373	Pete Pihos, 1947–1955
371	Keith Byars, 1986–1992

Season

90	Brian Westbrook, 2007
88	Irving Fryar, 1996
86	Irving Fryar, 1997
81	Keith Jackson, 1988
81	Keith Byars, 1990

Game

14	Don Looney, at Redskins, 12/1/1940
14	Brian Westbrook, vs. Cowboys, 11/4/2007

Receiving Yards
Career

8,978	Harold Carmichael, 1971–1983
7,412	Pete Retzlaff, 1956–1966
6,464	Mike Quick, 1982–1990
5,619	Pete Pihos, 1947–1955
5,499	Tommy McDonald, 1957–1963

Season

1,409	Mike Quick, 1983
1,316	Irving Fryar, 1997
1,265	Ben Hawkins, 1967
1,247	Mike Quick, 1985
1,200	Terrell Owens, 2004

Game

237	Tommy McDonald, vs. Giants, 12/10/1961

Yards per Reception
Career (min. 100 receptions)

19.2	Tommy McDonald, 1957–1963 (5,499–287)
18.3	Ben Hawkins, 1966–1973 (4,764–261)
18.2	DeSean Jackson, 2008–2010 (3,135–172)
17.8	Mike Quick, 1982–1990 (6,464–363)
17.5	Kenny Jackson, 1984–1991 (2,139–122)

Season (min. 24 receptions)

23.1	Mike Quick, 1988 (508–22)
22.5	DeSean Jackson, 2010 (1,056–47)
22.4	Kenny Jackson, 1987 (471–21)
22.1	Jack Ferrante, 1945 (464–21)
21.4	Ben Hawkins, 1967 (1,265–59)

Game (min. 4 receptions)

52.5	DeSean Jackson, at Cowboys, 12/12/2010 (210–4)

Touchdown Receptions
Career

79	Harold Carmichael, 1971–1983
66	Tommy McDonald, 1957–1963
61	Pete Pihos, 1947–1955
61	Mike Quick, 1982–1990
47	Pete Retzlaff, 1956–1966

Season

14	Terrell Owens, 2004
13	Tommy McDonald, 1960
13	Tommy McDonald, 1961
13	Mike Quick, 1983
11	Achieved seven times

Game

4	Ben Hawkins, vs. Steelers, 9/28/1969
4	Irving Fryar, vs. Dolphins, 10/20/1996

SPECIAL TEAMS

KICKOFF RETURNS

Most Kickoff Returns
Career

169	Timmy Brown, 1960–1967
131	Brian Mitchell, 2000–2002
101	Al Nelson, 1965–1973
98	Allen Rossum, 1998–1999
88	Larry Marshall, 1974–1977

Season

54	Allen Rossum, 1999
53	Derrick Witherspoon, 1996
52	Quintin Demps, 2008
48	Herman Hunter, 1985
47	Duce Staley, 1997
47	Brian Mitchell, 2000

Game

8	Derrick Witherspoon, at Arz. Cardinals, 11/24/1996
8	Allen Rossum, vs. Ind. Colts, 11/21/1999
8	Quintin Demps, vs. Giants, 11/9/2008

Kickoff Return Yardage
Career

4,483	Timmy Brown, 1960–1967
3,311	Brian Mitchell, 2000–2002
2,625	Al Nelson, 1965–1973
2,427	Allen Rossum, 1998–1999
2,075	Larry Marshall, 1974–1977

Season

1,347	Allen Rossum, 1999
1,314	Quintin Demps, 2008

1,271   Derrick Witherspoon, 1996
1,162   Brian Mitchell, 2002
1,139   Duce Staley, 1997

Game
253   Derrick Witherspoon, at Arz. Cardinals, 11/24/1996
247   Timmy Brown, vs. Cowboys, 11/6/1966
222   Allen Rossum, vs. Redskins, 11/14/1999
220   Quentin Demps, vs. Giants, 11/9/2008
195   Duce Staley, vs. Bengals, 11/30/1997

Longest Return
105 yards (t)   Timmy Brown, vs. Browns, 9/17/1961
103 yards (t)   Russ Craft, vs. L. A. Rams, 10/7/1950
100 yards (t)   Dave Smulker, at Brooklyn Dodgers, 11/13/1938
100 yards (t)   Timmy Brown, vs. Stl. Cardinals, 9/22/1963
100 yards (t)   Quintin Demps, at Ravens, 11/23/2008

Yards per Kickoff Return
Career (min. 25 returns)
26.7   Steven Van Buren, 1944–1951 (2030–76)
26.6   Irv Cross, 1961–1969 (745–28)
26.5   Timmy Brown, 1960–1967 (4,483–169)
25.9   Al Nelson, 1965–1973 (2,626–101)
25.4   Wilbert Montgomery, 1977–1984 (814–32)

Season (min. 20 returns)
29.1   Al Nelson, 1972 (728–25)
28.6   Timmy Brown, 1963 (945–33)
28.1   Timmy Brown, 1966 (562–20)
27.9   Timmy Brown, 1961 (811–29)
27.7   Timmy Brown, 1962 (831–30)

Game (min. 3 returns)
59.0   Timmy Brown, vs. Cardinals, 9/22/1963 (177–3)

Kickoffs Returned for Touchdown
Career
5   Timmy Brown, 1960–1967
3   Steve Van Buren, 1944–1951
3   Derrick Witherspoon, 1995–1997
2   Brian Mitchell, 2000–2002

Season
2   Timmy Brown, 1966
2   Derrick Witherspoon, 1996

Game
2   Timmy Brown, vs. Cowboys, 11/6/1966

Punt Returns

Most Punt Returns
Career
148   Wally Henry, 1977–1982

Focus on Sport/Getty Images

117   John Sciarra, 1978–1983
117   Brian Mitchell, 2000–2002
111   Bill Bradley, 1969–1976
104   Larry Marshall, 1974–1977

Season
54   Wally Henry, 1981
53   Rod Harris, 1991
50   DeSean Jackson, 2008
46   Larry Marshall, 1977
46   Brian Mitchell, 2002

Game
9   Larry Marshall, vs. Buccaneers, 9/18/1977
8   Evan Cooper, vs. Chargers, 10/26/1986
8   Vai Sikahema, at Seahawks, 12/13/1992
8   DeSean Jackson, vs. Stl. Rams, 9/7/2008
7   Achieved 7 times

Punt Return Yardage

Career
1,369 Brian Mitchell, 2000–2002
1,231 Wally Henry, 1977–1982
1,112 DeSean Jackson, 2008–2010
1,086 Larry Marshall, 1974–1977
975 Bosh Pritchard, 1942–1951

Season
567 Brian Mitchell, 2002
503 Vai Sikahema, 1992
489 Larry Marshall, 1977
467 Brian Mitchell, 2001
441 DeSean Jackson, 2009

Game
140 Alvin Hammond, at Redskins, 10/6/1968
111 Vai Sikahema, at NY Giants, 11/2/1992
108 Reno Mahe, vs. Steelers, 12/5/2005
106 Ernie Steele, at Bears, 10/25/1942
106 DeSean Jackson, at Panthers, 9/13/2009

Longest Returns
87 yards (t) Vai Sikahema, at NY Giants, 11/22/1992
85 yards (t) DeSean Jackson, at Panthers, 9/13/2009
84 yards (t) Brian Westbrook, at NY Giants, 10/19/2003
81 yards (t) Tommy McDonald, vs. NY Giants, 10/4/1959
81 yards (t) Brian Westbrook, vs. 49ers, 12/21/2003

Yards per Punt Return

Career (min. 20 returns)
16.7 Ernie Steele, 1942–1948 (737–44)
13.9 Steve Van Buren, 1944–1951 (473–34)
12.9 Pat McHugh, 1947–1951 (402–31)
12.7 Brian Westbrook, 2002–2009 (498–39)
11.7 Brian Mitchell, 2000–2002 (1,369–117)

Season (min. 15 returns)
15.3 Steve Van Buren, 1944 (230–15)
15.3 Brian Westrbook, 2003 (306–20)
15.2 DeSean Jackson, 2009 (441–29)
13.4 Alvin Haymond, 1968 (201–15)
12.8 Reno Mahe, 2005 (269–21)

Game (min. 3 returns)
33.0 Brian Mitchell, at 49ers, 11/25/2002
28.3 Clyde Scott, at Steelers, 10/30/1949
28.0 Billy Wells, vs. NY Giants, 10/5/1958
28.0 Alvin Haymond, at Redskins, 10/6/1968
27.8 Vai Sikahema, at NY Giants, 11/22/1992

Punts Returned for Touchdown

Career
4 DeSean Jackson, 2008–2010
2 Steve Van Buren, 1944–1951
2 Brian Mitchell, 2000–2002
2 Brian Westbrook, 2002–2009

Season
2 Brian Westbrook, 2003
2 DeSean Jackson, 2009
   Accomplished 20 times (last: Roscoe Parrish, vs. Seattle, 9/7/2008)

KICKING

PAT Attempts

Career
447 David Akers, 1999–2010
383 Bobby Walston, 1951–1962
213 Sam Baker, 1964–1969
182 Tony Franklin, 1979–1983
166 Cliff Patton, 1946–1950

Season
50 Cliff Patton, 1948
48 Bobby Walston, 1953
48 Tony Franklin, 1980
48 Roger Ruzek, 1990
48 David Akers, 2006

PATs Made

Career
441 David Akers, 1999–2010
365 Bobby Walston, 1951–1962
205 Sam Baker, 1964–1969
172 Tony Franklin, 1979–1983
160 Cliff Patton, 1946–1950

Season
50 Cliff Patton, 1948
48 Tony Franklin, 1980
48 David Akers, 2006
47 David Akers, 2010
45 David Akers, 2008

PAT Percentage

Career (min. 50 attempts)
98.7% David Akers, 1999–2010 (441–447)
98.6% Gary Anderson, 1995–1996 (72–73)
98.3% Paul McFadden, 1984–1987 (117–119)
98.1% Luis Zendejas, 1988–1999 (53–54)
96.4% Cliff Patton, 1947–1950 (160–166)

Most Consecutive PATs Without a Miss

Career
173 David Akers, 2004–2009
153 David Akers, 2001–2004
84 Cliff Patton, 1947–1949

Field Goal Attempts

Career
357 David Akers, 2004–2009
157 Bobby Walston, 1951–1962
153 Sam Baker, 1964–1969

| 128 | Tony Franklin, 1979–1983 |
| 124 | Paul McFadden, 1984–1987 |

Season
40	David Akers, 2008
40	Tom Dempsey, 1973
38	David Akers, 2010
37	Paul McFadden, 1984
37	David Akers, 2009

Game
| 7 | Sam Baker, vs. Cowboys, 12/5/1965 |
| 7 | Tom Dempsey, at Houston Oilers, 11/121972 |

Field Goals Made
Career
294	David Akers, 1999–2010
91	Paul McFadden, 1984–1987
90	Sam Baker, 1964–1969
81	Roger Ruzek, 1989–1993
80	Bobby Walston, 1951–1962
80	Tony Franklin, 1979–1983

Season
33	David Akers, 2008
32	David Akers, 2009
32	David Akers, 2010
30	Paul McFadden, 1984
30	David Akers, 2002

Game
6	Tom Dempsey, at Houston Oilers, 11/2/1972
5	Gary Anderson, at Saints, 10/1/1995
5	Gary Anderson, vs. Ariz. Cardinals, 12/22/1996
5	David Akers, at Cowboys, 11/18/2001

Longest Field Goals Made
59 yards	Tony Franklin, at Cowboys, 11/12/1979
57 yards	David Akers, vs. Patriots, 9/14/2003
54 yards	Tom Dempsey, vs. Stl. Cardinals, 12/12/1971
53 yards	Accomplished 3 times

Field Goal Percentage
Career (min. 25 attempts)
84.0%	Eddie Murray, 1994 (21–25)
82.4%	David Akers, 1999–2010 (294–357)
79.7%	Gary Anderson, 1995–1996 (47–59)
75.0%	Roger Ruzek, 1989–1993 (81–108)
73.4%	Paul McFadden, 1984–1987 (91–124

Season (min. 10 attempts)
88.2%	David Akers, 2002 (30–34)
87.9%	David Akers, 2000 (29–33)
86.5%	David Akers, 2009 (32–37)
86.2%	Gary Anderson, 1996 (25–29)
84.8%	Roger Ruzek, 1991 (28–33)

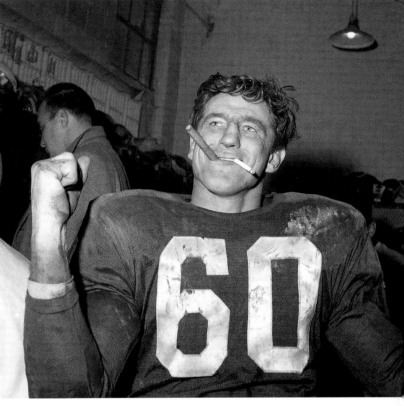

Herb Scharfman/Sports Imagery/Getty Images

PUNTING

Most Punts
Career
393	Adrian Burk, 1951–1956
376	Sean Landeta, 1999–2000, 2005
349	Tom Hutton, 1995–1998
345	John Teltschik, 1986–1989
332	Max Runager, 1979–1983, 1989

Season
108	John Teltschik 1986
107	Sean Landeta, 1999
104	Tom Hutton, 1998
98	John Teltschik, 1988
97	Sean Landeta, 2001

Game
| 15 | John Teltschik, at NY Giants, 12/6/1987 |
| 12 | Accomplished 4 times |

Total Yardage
Career
16,122	Adrian Burk, 1951–1956
16,092	Sean Landeta, 1999–2005
14,788	Tom Hutton, 1995–1998
13,828	John Teltschik, 1986–1989
13,448	Jeff Feagles, 1990–1993

Season

4,524	Sean Landeta, 1999
4,493	John Teltschik, 1986
4,339	Tom Hutton, 1998
4,221	Sean Landeta, 2001
3,958	John Teltschik, 1988

Longest Punts

91 yards	Randall Cunningham, at NY Giants, 12/3/1989
82 yards	Joe Muha, vs. NY Giants, 10/10/1948
80 yards	King Hill, vs. Packers, 11/11/1962
80 yards	Randall Cunningham, at Cowboys, 10/16/1994
77 yards	Jeff Feagles, at Cowboys, 9/15/1991

Yards per Punt
Career (min. 100 punts)

42.9	Joe Muha, 1946–1950 (7,688–179)
42.8	Sean Landeta, 1999–2005, 2008 (16,092–376)
42.8	Sav Rocca, 2007–2010 (12,249/229)
42.3	King Hill, 1961–1968 (10,765–254)
42.3	Tom Hutton, 1995–1999 (14,788–349)

Season (min. 40 punts)

47.2	Joe Muha, 1948 (2,694–57)
43.7	Sav Rocca, 2010 (3,195–73)
43.7	King Hill, 1961 (2,403–55)
43.6	Len Barnum, 1941 (1,788–41)
43.5	Sean Landeta, 2001 (4,221–97)

Punts Downed Inside 20-Yard Line (1976–2010)
Career

106	Jeff Feagles, 1990–1993
102	Sav Rocca, 2007–2010
96	Sean Landeta, 1999–2005
79	Dirk Johnson, 2003–2006
77	Tom Hutton, 1995–1998

Season

31	Jeff Feagles, 1993
29	Jeff Feagles, 1991
28	John Teltschik, 1988
28	Sav Rocca, 2010
27	Dirk Johnson, 2003

DEFENSE

INTERCEPTIONS

Most Interceptions
Career

34	Bill Bradley, 1969–1976
34	Eric Allen, 1988–1994
34	Brian Dawkins, 1996–2008
33	Herman Edwards, 1977–1985
30	Wes Hopkins, 1983–1993

Season

11	Bill Bradley, 1971
9	Ed Bawel, 1955
9	Don Burroughs, 1960
9	Bill Bradley, 1972
9	Asante Samuel, 2009

Game

4	Russ Craft, at Chi. Cardinals, 9/24/1950
3	Accomplished 9 Times

Interception Return Yardage
Career

536	Bill Bradley, 1969–1976
515	Brian Dawkins, 1996–2008
482	Eric Allen, 1988–1994
460	Lito Sheppard, 2002–2008
404	Ernie Steele, 1942–1948

Season

248	Bill Bradley, 1971
201	Eric Allen, 1993
182	Joe Scarpati, 1966
172	Lito Sheppard, 2004
168	Ed Bawel, 1955

Game

114 yards	Frank LeMaster, at Redskins, 12/21/1975
102 yards	Lito Sheppard, vs. Cowboys, 10/8/2006
101 yards	Lito Sheppard, at Cowboys, 11/15/2004

Longest Return

104 yards (t)	James Willis and Troy Vincent (lateral), at Cowboys, 11/3/1996

Most Interceptions Returned for Touchdown
Career

5	Eric Allen, 1988–1994
3	Joe Scarpati, 1964–1969
3	Sheldon Brown, 2002–2009
3	Lito Sheppard, 2002–2008
2	Accomplished by 10 players

Season

4	Eric Allen, 1993
2	Ed Bawell, 1955
2	Seth Joyner, 1992
2	Lito Sheppard, 2004

Game

2	Eric Allen, vs. Saints, 12/23/1993

SACKS (1982–2010)

Most Sacks
Career

124.0	Reggie White, 1985–1992
76.0	Clyde Simmons, 1986–1993
57.0	Trent Cole, 2005–2010
54.5	Hugh Douglas, 1998–2002, 2004
50.5	Greg Brown, 1982–1986

Season

21.0	Reggie White, 1987
19.0	Clyde Simmons, 1992
18.0	Reggie White, 1986
18.0	Reggie White, 1988
16.0	Greg Brown, 1984

Game

4.5	Clyde Simmons, at Cowboys, 9/15/1991
4.5	Hugh Douglas, at Chargers, 10/18/1998
4.0	Achieved 5 times

FUMBLE RETURNS

Most Fumble Returns for Touchdown
Career

3	Seth Joyner, 1986–1993
2	Achieved 7 times

Longest Fumble Return for a Touchdown

98 yards	Mike Patterson, at 49ers, 9/24/2006
96 yards	Joe Lavender, vs. Cowboys, 9/23/1974
96 yards	Joselio Hanson, vs. Cowboys, 12/28/2006

Bernstein Associates/Getty Images

TEAM RECORDS

League Championships (NFL)	3 (1948, 1949, 1960)
Conference Championships	2 (1980, 2004)
Division Titles	15 (1947, 1948, 1949, 1960, 1979, 1980, 1988, 1996, 2001, 2002, 2003, 2004, 2006, 2009, 2010)
Playoff Berths	23 (1947, 1948, 1949, 1960, 1978, 1979, 1980, 1981, 1988, 1989, 1990, 1993, 1995, 1996, 2000, 2001, 2002, 2003, 2004, 2006, 2008, 2009, 2010)
Winning Seasons	33
Most Wins, Regular Season	13 (2004)
Best Winning Percentage, Season	.917 (1949, 11–1)
Most Losses, Season	13 (1998)
Longest Winning Streak	9 games (10/19/2003–12/15/2003; 9/30/1960–12/4/1960)
Longest Home Winning Streak	13 games (12/14/1947–12/11/1949)
Longest Road Winning Streak	9 games (10/19/2003–10/24/2004; 11/12/2000–12/6/2001)
Longest Losing Streak	14 games (9/20/1936–9/21/1937)
Longest Home Losing Streak	8 games (9/20/1936–9/21/1937)
Longest Road Losing Streak	12 games (12/14/1997–10/3/1999; 10/15/1939–12/1/1940)
Most Consecutive Games Scoring Points	120 games (11/18/1962–10/3/1971)
Most Consecutive Games Scoring Touchdown	92 games (10/2/1977–10/16/1983)
Largest Deficit in a Comeback Victory	24 points (at Chi. Cardinals, 10/25/1959; at Redskins, 10/27/1946)

SCORING AND TOTAL OFFENSE

Most Points, Season	439 (2010)
Most Points, Game	64 (vs. Cin. Reds, 11/6/1934)
Most Points, Half	45 (first half, at Redskins, 11/15/2010)
Most Points, Quarter	31 (second quarter, vs. Lions, 12/30/1995
Largest Margin of Victory, Game	64 (64–0, vs. Cin. Reds, 11/6/1934)
Largest Margin of Defeat, Game	56 (0–56, vs. Giants, 10/15/1933)
Most Touchdowns, Season	50 (1948)
Most Touchdowns, Game	10 (vs. Cin. Reds, 11/6/1934)
Most PATs, Season	50 (1948)
Most Field Goals Made, Season	33 (2008)
Most Field Goals Made, Game	6 (at Houston Oilers, 11/12/1972)
Most Yards Total Offense, Season	6,230 (2010)
Most Yards Total Offense, Game	592 (at Redskins, 11/15/2010)
Fewest Yards Total Offense, Game	23 (at Lions,9/20/1935)
Most First Downs, Season	32 (1981)
Most First Downs, Game	34 (vs. Colts, 11/15/1981)

PASSING

Most Pass Attempts, Season	620 (2005)
Most Pass Attempts, Game	62 (at Bears, 10/2/1989)
Most Pass Completions, Season	362 (2008)
Most Pass Completions, Game	35 (at Chargers, 11/15/2009)
Most Yards Passing, Season	4,370 (2009)
Most Yards Passing, Game	486 (vs. NY Giants, 11/8/1953)
Fewest Pass Attempts, Game	3 (vs. Steelers, 12/1/1946)
Fewest Pass Completions, Game	0 (at Redskins, 10/18/1936)
Fewest Yards Passing, Game	0 (at Redskins, 10/18/1936)
Most Touchdown Passes, Season	34 (1990)
Most Interceptions Thrown, Season	36 (1936)

RUSHING

Most Rushing Attempts, Season	632 (1949)
Most Rushing Attempts, Game	64 (at Redskins, 12/2/1951)
Most Rushing Yards, Season	2,607 (1949)
Most Rushing Yards, Game	376 (vs. Redskins, 11/21/1948)
Fewest Rushing Yards, Game	-36 (at Bears, 11/191939)
Most Rushing Touchdowns, Season	25 (1949)
Most Rushing Touchdowns, Game	5 (accomplished 4 times)

SPECIAL TEAMS

Most Punts, Season	110 (1986)
Most Punts, Game	15 (at Giants, 12/6/1987)
Most Punting Yards, Season	4,547 (1986)
Fewest Punts, Game	0 (accomplished 4 times)
Most Punt Returns, Game	12 (at Browns, 12/3/1950)
Most Punt Return Yards, Game	148 (at Boston Yanks, 12/8/1946)
Most Kickoff Returns, Game	9 (at Giants, 11/26/1972 and 11/10/1946)
Most Kickoff Return Yards, Game	261 (vs. Cowboys, 11/6/1966)

DEFENSE

Fewest Points Allowed per Game, Season	7.7 (1934, 85 points/11 games)
Fewest Points Allowed, Season	85 (1934)
Fewest Points Allowed, Game	0 (accomplished 35 times)
Most Shutouts, Season	4 (1934, 1948)
Most Points Allowed, Season	377 (3010)
Most Points Allowed, Game	62 (at Giants, 11/26/1972)
Fewest Total Yards Allowed, Game	29 (vs. Brooklyn Dodgers, 12/3/1944)
Fewest Pass Completions Allowed, Game	0 (accomplished 5 times)
Fewest Passing Yards Allowed, Game	0 (accomplished 4 times)
Fewest Rushing Yards Allowed, Game	-33 (vs. Brooklyn Dodgers, 10/2/1943)
Fewest First Downs Allowed, Game	1 (accomplished 3 times)
Most Interceptions Made, Season	33 (1944)
Most Interceptions Made, Game	9 (at Steelers, 12/12/1965)
Most Opponents' Fumbles Recovered, Season	27 (1987)
Most Opponents' Fumbles Recovered, Game	6 (at Giants, 11/17/1968
Most Turnovers Forced, Game	12 (accomplished 2 times)
Most Sacks, Season	62 (1989)
Most Sacks, Game	11 (at Cowboys, 9/15/1991)

PENALTIES

Most Penalties, Season	138 (1994)
Most Penalties, Game	19 (vs. Houston Oilers, 10/2/1988
Fewest Penalties, Game	0 (several times, most recently vs. Cowboys, 12/28/2008)
Most Yards Penalized, Season	1,130 (2005)
Most Yards Penalized, Game	191 (at Seahawks, 12/13/1992

INDEX